PRAISE FOR
How Can I Forgive You?

"This book is a treasure—practical, illuminating, and wise. It's like a breath of fresh air that pulls forgiveness into a new and revealing light and provides clear steps to turn wounds into wisdom."

—JOAN BORYSENKO, PH.D., author of
Minding the Body, Mending the Mind

"If you are struggling with issues of betrayal—or the challenge of whether and how to forgive—here is the most helpful and surprising book you will ever find on the subject."

—HARRIET LERNER, PH.D., author of
The Dance of Anger

"A fresh and original approach to an ancient challenge. A clinically informed personal guide for the offender and the offended. *How Can I Forgive You?* should be read by us all."

—HARVILLE HENDRIX, PH.D., author of
Getting the Love You Want

"Finally a book has been written that teaches couples how to make genuine forgiveness a reality without rushing toward a superficial peace. This book can help couples construct a marriage that never existed before, one based on deep understanding and trust."

—JOHN GOTTMAN, PH.D., author of
The Relationship Cure

"This book is a treasure trove for anyone who has ever felt betrayed or hurt by a personal relationship. Dr. Spring cuts through all the clichés surrounding forgiveness and views it within a broad spectrum of common relationships—mother/daughter, father/son, student/teacher, husband/wife. She explores the intricate interplay of emotions in coming to terms with disillusion and provides informative and comforting guidelines for dealing with it. We owe her a debt of gratitude for this enlightened and penetrating view of a universal human dilemma."

—PEGGY PAPP, M.S.W., author of
Couples on the Fault Line

"*How Can I Forgive You?* is a very important book that enables violated individuals to start the healing process and at the same time maintain their self-esteem and dignity."

—AARON T. BECK, M.D., author of
Prisoners of Hate

"Dr. Spring puts forth fresh, provocative, practical, and useful ideas about how people can and should deal with hurts. She flies in the face of many of today's books that trumpet forgiveness for anything at any price. Agree or not—you will benefit from reading *How Can I Forgive You?*"

—EVERETT L. WORTHINGTON, JR., PH.D., author of
Forgiving and Reconciling,
and director, A Campaign for Forgiveness Research

"Clear, insightful writing . . . a thoughtful exposition on the nuanced role of forgiveness in relationships that goes beyond the average self-help book."

—*Publishers Weekly*

About the Authors

JANIS ABRAHMS SPRING, PH.D., is a nationally acclaimed expert on issues of trust, intimacy, and forgiveness. She is author of the best-selling *After the Affair: Healing the Pain and Rebuilding Trust When a Partner Has Been Unfaithful*. A Diplomate in Clinical Psychology and a recipient of the Connecticut Psychological Association's Award for Distinguished Contribution to the Practice of Psychology, Dr. Spring trains thousands of therapists each year and is known for the richness and originality of her clinical skills.

Dr. Spring received her B.A. from Brandeis University, magna cum laude, her Ph.D. in clinical psychology from the University of Connecticut, and her post-graduate training from Aaron Beck, M.D., at the Center for Cognitive Therapy at the University of Pennsylvania. She has served as a clinical supervisor in the Department of Psychology at Yale University and often appears as a guest expert in the national media. In private practice for close to three decades, Dr. Spring resides in Westport, Connecticut, and can be reached at www.janisabrahmsspring.com. She and her husband, Michael Spring, have four sons.

MICHAEL SPRING is a publisher of the Frommer's Travel Guides at John Wiley. He has a B.A. from Haverford College and an M.A. in English literature from Columbia University.

For my friend,
Audrey.

How
Love you—
Andrea

Can I
Forgive
You?

The Courage to Forgive,
the Freedom Not To

JANIS ABRAHMS SPRING, PH.D.,
WITH MICHAEL SPRING

Perennial Currents
An Imprint of HarperCollins*Publishers*

With love, to our growing family—
Aaron, Max, Evan, Declan, Robin, baby Caleb, and Pop

A hardcover edition of this book was published in 2004 by HarperCollins Publishers.

HOW CAN I FORGIVE YOU? Copyright © 2004 by Janis Abrahms Spring. All rights reserved. Printed in the United States of America. No part of this book may be used or reproduced in any manner whatsoever without written permission except in the case of brief quotations embodied in critical articles and reviews. For information address HarperCollins Publishers Inc., 10 East 53rd Street, New York, NY 10022.

HarperCollins books may be purchased for educational, business, or sales promotional use. For information please write: Special Markets Department, HarperCollins Publishers Inc., 10 East 53rd Street, New York, NY 10022.

First Perennial Currents edition published 2005.

Designed by Nancy Singer Olaguera

The Library of Congress has catalogued the hardcover edition as follows:

Spring, Janis Abrahms.
   How can I forgive you? : the courage to forgive, the freedom not to/Janis Abrahms Spring.—1st ed.
      p. cm.
   Includes bibliographical references and index.
   ISBN 0-06-000930-6 (alk paper)
      1. Forgiveness. I. Title.

BF637.F67S67   2004
179'.9—dc21

                                                          2003050932

ISBN 0-06-000931-4 (pbk.)

05 06 07 08 09 ❖/RRD 10 9 8 7 6 5 4 3 2 1

Contents

Acknowledgments

Any book on forgiveness should begin at home. I ask our children and family—Max, Aaron, Evan, Declan, Robin, Caleb, and Dad—to please forgive Michael and me for being so grossly preoccupied and unavailable these last two years as we threw ourselves into this book project. We intend to work hard to earn your forgiveness by showing you how much we love you in the years ahead.

Is there any activity more intimate than writing a book with your life partner? Michael, I forgive you, once again, for taking what I often believed to be an excellent (no, perfect) passage from my manuscript, and asking me to ask myself your four signature questions: "Is this interesting? Is it important? Does it follow? Is there a way of saying it with one word—one syllable—rather than two?" I forgive you for (almost) always being right, as annoying as that is. It has been a wonderful collaboration, filled with intimate battles over transitions and ways to bring abstract psychological concepts down to earth.

To Gail Winston, my remarkable editor at HarperCollins, thank you for your sensitive editing and good nature. To Jo-Lynne Worley, my agent, thank you for your enthusiastic support and thoughtful feedback. I'm touched that both of you voluntarily subjected yourself to one of my six-hour courses on trust and forgiveness, and appreciate your genuine interest in me and my work. My thanks as well to Christine Walsh for your patient, reliable assistance at Harper-Collins.

Rabbi Israel Stein of Congregation Rodeph Sholom in Bridge-port, Connecticut, thank you for repeatedly meeting with Michael and me and offering us your profound wisdom and sweet encouragement. I hunted hard for a rabbi who would shake me out of my indifference, help me bind my wounds, and inspire me to live more consciously. I found that person in you. You're a gifted, original thinker and a warm, dear friend. Forgive me for quoting you so often throughout this book.

Reverend Gary Wilburn of The First Presbyterian Church of New Canaan, Connecticut, thank you for making yourself available to me, even though I was a total stranger to you. You generously welcomed me into your office and shared your provocative and humane thoughts about forgiveness. Your congregation is fortunate to have a spiritual leader who cares so deeply about their suffering, and looks for profound spiritual answers to interpersonal grievances.

Sometimes inspiration comes from unlikely sources. Michael and I would agree that the two houses we rented to complete this book provided a setting for our most productive, creative, happy moments. We want to thank Mary and Dan Maffia for letting us use their amazing house on the Cape; and Emily and Albert Foss-brenner of Yardley, Pennsylvania, for their writer's cottage, which we occupied over Thanksgiving, and then, for going way beyond the cause, and insisting that we feast with them in their home for the holiday.

There have been many mentors whose ideas have shaped my thinking for this book. Dr. Jeffrey Young, Director of the Cognitive Therapy Centers of New York and Connecticut and a faculty member in the Department of Psychiatry at Columbia University, has been central. Thank you for permitting me to adapt your schema therapy model to the process of forgiveness, and for your friendship.

Of course, there would be no book without my patients. I'm indebted to you for allowing me to witness and participate in your bold search for an emotionally authentic response to your intimate wounds. You brought to life for me the wisdom of psychotherapist Jeanne Safer, who wrote, "Sometimes what people really need is permission not to forgive, to feel what they feel." Your struggle to find a resolution that's healthy and human—one that doesn't require you to forgive an unrepentant offender—inspired me to suggest a radical alternative—Acceptance. You taught me that your decision not to forgive "need not foreclose resolution; it may be the step that makes it possible."[1]

You also taught me that sometimes what the hurt party really needs is permission *to* forgive—to reframe forgiveness as an act of courage, not desperation or self-denial.

Finally, I want to thank the forgiveness experts who have laid the groundwork. It has been said that those who tend to be more open-minded tend to be more forgiving. I hope that those whose ideas I've challenged will be open-minded and forgive me, and continue a dialogue with me—a search for a working model of forgiveness that serves real people seeking to survive and transcend the misery of real-life transgressions.

How
Can I
Forgive
You?

Introduction

IS FORGIVENESS GOOD
FOR YOU?

There's a wonderful story about two kids playing in a sandbox together. One gets mad and storms off with his toy truck. As he runs to the swings nearby, he turns and cries out to his playmate, "I hate your guts and I'm never going to talk to you again." About ten minutes pass, and they're throwing a ball at each other, laughing, enjoying the day. As their parents observe this interaction, one father shakes his head and says to the other with a mix of admiration and amazement, "How do kids do that? How can they be at each other's throat one minute and get along with each other so famously the next?"

"It's easy," the other father explains. "They choose happiness over righteousness."[1]

I love this story. It's so filled with the bounty of the human spirit, with affirmation of our ability to adapt, to resolve our petty disputes and focus on what really matters most to us in life. We are social beings who need each other, who inherently prefer to repair interpersonal ruptures than to hate or hold a grudge. Most of us want, and like, to forgive.

The problem with the sandbox story is that it's about children who reconcile after an insignificant grievance. It's not about what happens between two adults when one willfully and maliciously hurts the other, and the hurt party is left to grapple with how to forgive or reconcile with the offender. That's a much more complex story.

Some of us believe we have an obligation to forgive, unconditionally, categorically, and that to do so is central to what it means to be a decent human being. Most of us, however, can't live up to such high moral principles except in theory, or feel that we would compromise ourselves if we did. We can't—and won't—just dust off an injury, pretend that nothing happened, and embrace the person who injured us. Regardless of what we may have been taught, a quick, one-sided, kiss-and-make-up response doesn't seem real or right. For Genuine Forgiveness to take place, we often need much more.

WHAT DOES IT MEAN TO FORGIVE?

Most of us have been raised on several dubious assumptions that need to be debunked. Let's look at them.

Questionable Assumption #1: Forgiving is good for you. When you forgive, you get rid of the poison inside you and restore your health. When you refuse to forgive, you get sick and suffer.

Forgiving has been marketed as the new mental and physical panacea—a healing balm that cures every ailment: depression, anxiety, chronic hostility, high blood pressure, heart disease, stroke, cancer, and immune deficiencies. It has also been said to repair broken hearts, broken relationships, a broken sense of self. "Forgiving is the only remedy for the pain the offender left us with, the only way to heal the hurt he caused,"[2] writes Lewis Smedes in *The Art of Forgiving*.

My patients have taught me otherwise. Watching them recover from interpersonal injuries has shown me that:

- you can heal yourself and clear your head of emotional sludge—resentment, rage, hurt and shame—with or without forgiving;

- you can release your bitter and obsessive preoccupation with getting even—with or without forgiving;
- you can make peace with yourself and come to terms with what happened—with or without forgiving; and
- you can get back together if you choose, without selling yourself short—with or without forgiving.

You can do all this for yourself and by yourself, even if the offender is unapologetic, even if he refuses to acknowledge your pain or apply a drop of salve to your wound—even if he has passed on.

How Can I Forgive You? shows you how.

Questionable Assumption #2: Forgiving is the only spiritually and morally sound response to violation.

We grow up assuming that forgiving is key to a caring, principled life. But I've learned that you don't need forgiveness to be merciful and feel empathy, even compassion, for the person who hurt you. You can see him as a flawed human being, treat him with unmerited benevolence, and try to understand why he acted the way he did—all without forgiving him.

Morally and spiritually, you're no more required to forgive an unrepentant offender than you are to love him. You're free to reserve forgiveness for someone who has the fortitude to admit his culpability and the decency to help release you from the pain he has made you suffer. I would go so far as to say that you don't restore *your* humanity when you forgive an unapologetic offender; he restores *his* humanity when he works to earn your forgiveness.

Questionable Assumption #3: You have only two choices— forgiving and not forgiving.

Most self-help books reinforce the conventional assumption that even when the offender is unrepentant, you have only two options: Forgiving and Not Forgiving. Forced to choose between them, you either dismiss your pain and forgive those who don't deserve it, or you say no to forgiveness and find yourself trapped in a "prison of hate."[3]

For years I listened to patients caught in this dilemma and realized that there had to be another solution. The language of forgiveness needed a vocabulary to describe what real people with real injuries do when they make peace with a person who won't apologize. As Rabbi Susan Schnur points out, such rigid categories—forgiving and not forgiving—"make a mockery of the complex continuum or resolution in the aftermath of a betrayal. We may partially forgive, vengefully forgive, contingently forgive, not forgive yet reconcile. We may mourn yet not forgive, achieve understanding yet only forgive certain parts of the betrayal; become indifferent; become detached."[4]

I began wondering, wouldn't it be wonderful if there were a way for us to release all the hate and hurt bundled up inside us, enjoy all the physical and mental health benefits of forgiveness, and live a just and humane life—all without having to forgive a recalcitrant offender? Isn't there something between the all-too-warm fuzziness of forgiving and the impenetrable coldness of Not Forgiving? Something that says "You don't have to hate the offender or exact a pound of flesh, but you don't have to forgive him either?"

How Can I Forgive You? describes this radical, new "something." I call it Acceptance.

Acceptance is a responsible, authentic response to an interpersonal injury when the offender can't or won't engage in the healing process—when he's unwilling or unable to make good. It's a program of self-care, a generous and healing gift to yourself, accomplished by yourself, for yourself. It asks nothing of the offender.

Acceptance helps you:

- place a premium on your own health and clear your head of emotional poison;
- be true to yourself and honor the full force of the violation;
- overcome fantasies of revenge while seeking a just resolution;
- ensure your emotional and physical safety;
- restore and integrate your valued self;
- see yourself and the offender with objectivity, honesty, and equanimity;

- forge a relationship with the offender that satisfies your personal goals; and
- forgive yourself for your own failings that caused you harm.

What I'm suggesting is that we can get back in the sandbox if we choose, even when the other person does nothing to right the wrong he has done. We can opt for no relationship with this person, or a partial and imperfect one. We don't have to dwell on the injury, but we don't have to forget or minimize it either. We don't have to love or even like this person, but we can see him fairly and choose to get along, if that's in our best interest. We can be ourselves in his presence and accept that he'll never be anyone other than who he is. We can even give him a chance to do better and earn Genuine Forgiveness if he chooses to rise to the challenge.

Questionable Assumption #4: It is up to you, the person who was violated, to forgive.

So much of the literature on forgiveness has been written specifically for you, the hurt party, telling you what *you* need to do to *grant* forgiveness, rather than telling the offender what *he* needs to do to *earn* forgiveness. This single-minded focus, I believe, has compromised, twisted, and cheapened the process of forgiveness and created a saintly, abstract concept that many of us feel pressured to accept at any cost.

The rest of us, however, are likely to choke on this idea and reject it as unrealistic, disingenuous, and unjust. We refuse to believe that it's real or right to have to shoulder the burden of forgiveness alone. We'd rather not forgive than forgive unilaterally.

I'm reminded of my patient's response when, in trying to help her recover from her partner's affair, I suggested that she consider medication to control her obsessions. "I have to deal with my shattered sense of self, my jealousy, my contempt," she raged. "And now you want *me* to take drugs? What does *he* have to do? Let *him* take the drugs!"

Many of you feel the same way about forgiveness. How unfair it seems that the person who hurt you is typically not addressed by moralists or forgiveness experts. How odd that he's rarely called upon to make repairs. At the very least, shouldn't both of you be invited to do the work of forgiveness?

My book speaks mainly to you, the hurt party, about what you can do to recover from a profound injustice when the offender is unwilling or unable to make amends. But it also speaks to you, the offender, when you want to be involved in the healing process. There is, in fact, an entire section devoted to you and to what you must do to earn forgiveness—and perhaps, in the process, forgive yourself.

Questionable Assumption #5: Forgiveness is an unconditional gift. It does not need to be earned.

The idea that you, the hurt party, should gift the offender your forgiveness, even when he's unapologetic and undeserving, is rooted in Christian ethics. In the New Testament, there are numerous exhortations to "love your enemy," to pardon those who hurt us because that's the merciful and compassionate thing to do. Christian or not, most of us grow up believing that forgiveness is required of us, without conditions.

Behind these teachings is an assumption that if you need something back from the offender in order to forgive—if you believe that forgiveness must be earned rather than gifted—you haven't fully developed as a moral being. The lesson is that you should feel small and ashamed for thinking you are entitled to restitution.

It's not my place to debate the ethics of unconditional forgiveness. But my clinical experience working with patients over the past twenty-nine years, observing how people heal and what they need to heal, has taught me that they tend to react in one of three ways:

- They reject the idea that when you forgive you ask for nothing in return, and then turn their back on forgiveness because it seems so skewed in favor of the offender.
- They subscribe to the religious concept of forgiveness and

"gift" it to an unworthy offender, but then feel unresolved, perhaps even cheated or compromised.

- They say that they subscribe to the ideal of forgiveness, but then, when presented with a real-life situation, they refuse to forgive.

I've noticed that, whatever their reaction, people struggle to forgive in a way that allows them to maintain a sense of integrity and self-worth, and that they would like support, not just from a higher power, but from the offender himself. The popular notion that they're somehow inferior or undeveloped because they want the offender to redress the chaos he has inflicted on their life is particularly damaging to those who lack a healthy sense of entitlement. These are people who forgive too cheaply. For those with a stronger sense of themselves, the idea of forgiving unilaterally and unconditionally often seems misguided—a kind of self-sacrifice or self-immolation.

As I've said, you can choose by and for yourself to release an unrepentant offender from your hatred and your desire to harm him. You can gift him your good-will. You can work to see him objectively, fairly, even compassionately. You can accept him and ask nothing of him. But if you're going to offer him what I call Genuine Forgiveness, he's going to have to pay a price and join you in an intimate dance. In this unconventional approach to forgiveness, a hard-won transaction takes place as the two of you redress the injury together. Forgiveness is no gratuitous gift from the heart; it must be earned. As you, the offender, perform costly, humbling, heartfelt acts of repair, you, the hurt party, create opportunities for him to come forward and make good.

Questionable Assumption #6: We all know how to forgive. If only we open our hearts, forgiveness will flow.

Most self-help books talk abstractly and inspirationally about forgiveness as a "moral gift,"[5] "a desire of the heart,"[6] "a quality of life"[7]—but leave you wondering what exactly it means and how to make it happen. Often forgiveness is defined in such lofty, absolute terms that people can't grasp it, so they throw up their hands instead and conclude, "It takes a person with a big heart to forgive—bigger than mine." Or they feel compelled to embrace the concept and make some meaningless, robotic gesture of goodwill.

The concept of forgiveness carries a heavy weight—more than it can bear. It means so many things to so many people who consider it from different frames of reference—from academicians influenced by grand theological teachings to secular researchers trying to reduce abstruse concepts into manageable, bite-size units that can be studied in laboratory settings. What has evolved is a mishmash of concepts that often do nothing more than confuse and pressure those who are seeking relief from suffering. What is missing is a concrete, down-to-earth vision of forgiveness—one that is human and attainable.

I've had the opportunity to observe people firsthand in my clinical practice and to witness their struggles to forgive and be forgiven. The model I developed has grown organically as I've listened to and observed how real people heal after real interpersonal injuries. The examples you will read ring true because they are true.

Questionable Assumption #7: Self-Forgiveness doesn't require you, the offender, to make amends to the person you harmed. It's a gift to yourself.

The topic of Self-Forgiveness takes us deep into uncharted waters. Advocates of Self-Forgiveness often describe it as an internal act, an offering of compassion and love that allows you to feel better about the wrong you inflicted on others. As I define it, Self-Forgiveness, like Genuine Forgiveness, is not a free gift to yourself. Nor is it a process that goes on privately within your mind. I believe that for Self-Forgiveness to be substantive, heartfelt, and genuine, it must be earned. If you, the offender, want to forgive yourself, you must acknowledge your wrong and make amends directly to the person you harmed. If that's not possible, you must perform other acts of repentance and restitution that in effect speak out against your offense and demonstrate your commitment not to repeat it.

Self-Forgiveness is not something you do just to make yourself *feel* better. It's something you do to make yourself *be* better. Forgiving yourself and working to win forgiveness from the person you violated go hand-in-hand. As you earn her respect and forgiveness, you come to respect and forgive yourself.

TWO DYSFUNCTIONAL APPROACHES TO FORGIVENESS

How Can I Forgive You? describes four different approaches to forgiveness: Cheap Forgiveness, Refusing to Forgive, Acceptance, and Genuine Forgiveness. The last two we have already touched on. Both are adaptive. The other two are dysfunctional.

Cheap Forgiveness

Even if the offender ignores your pain, you may be so frightened of his anger or rejection, so desperate to preserve the relationship, that you're willing to do anything—even forgive him. But this forgiveness is premature, superficial, undeserved. I call it cheap because you offer it before you process the impact of the violation, ask anything of the offender, or think through what lies ahead.

Refusing to Forgive

You may refuse to forgive (1) when you want to punish an unremorseful offender; (2) when you associate forgiveness with reconciliation or compassion, neither of which you're prepared to offer; and (3) when you use retaliatory rage to protest a violation and see anything more conciliatory—particularly forgiveness—as a sign of weakness. Not Forgiving makes you feel powerful and in control, but it's a reactive, often rigid and compulsive response to violation that cuts you off from life and leaves you stewing in your own hostile juices.

THE FOUR APPROACHES TO FORGIVENESS: A COMPARISON

The accompanying chart summarizes the differences among the four approaches to forgiveness.

	The Hurt Party Comes to Terms with the Injury	The Offender Participates in the Healing Process	This Leads to Reconciliation
Cheap Forgiveness	No	No	Yes
Refusing to Forgive	No	No	No
Acceptance	Yes	No	Yes or No
Genuine Forgiveness	Yes	Yes	Yes (often) or No

HOW THIS BOOK IS WRITTEN AND ORGANIZED

How Can I Forgive You? provides concrete, detailed, step-by-step instructions for both of you as you cut a path to forgiveness. It's divided into four parts: (1) Cheap Forgiveness, (2) Refusing to Forgive, (3) Acceptance, and (4) Genuine Forgiveness. The first, second, and third parts are written mainly for the hurt party. The fourth part (Genuine Forgiveness) is divided into two sections: The first shows the offender what it takes to earn forgiveness; the second shows the hurt party what it takes to grant forgiveness.

For the sake of clarity I refer to one of you as the hurt or injured party and to the other as the offender, fully aware that with interpersonal injuries we are seldom completely guilty or completely innocent. Also, I speak of the hurt party as "she" and the offender as "he." Gender does not determine guilt, of course, but identifying each of you in this way makes for a more readable book.

All the case studies I describe are true in the sense that they're based on my work with patients or my conversations with associates and friends. Some people may be hurt or insulted by the way I modified their stories; others may be relieved. The reader should know that I've always changed names and details, and that I've developed composite portraits to protect people's identities and illustrate certain points.

My clinical examples run from the serious to the profane—from a deliberate, predatory act of sexual abuse to a clumsy act of spilling wine on a countertop. However, I don't quantify the magnitude of the harm that was done for two reasons. First, the basic critical tools that are needed for healing are largely the same for all injuries. Second, the severity with which someone experiences an injury is highly subjective—a slap to one of you may be a deathblow to another.

Many of you have asked for a follow-up to my first book, *After the Affair*. I appreciate your loyalty and have included here many case studies related to infidelity. But I've now widened my scope to include all significant "violations of human connection."[8] Examples include:

- a spouse who treats you with contempt for not living up to his or her own impossible standards;
- a friend who turns away from you when you develop breast cancer;
- a sibling who refuses to help you care for an elderly parent;
- a parent who is too depressed or too drunk to take interest in you; and
- a therapist who traumatizes you as deeply as the offender himself.

A RADICAL CHOICE

When I give professional training workshops, I invite therapists to come to the microphone and talk about someone who has offended them and how they're coping with the violation. What I find over and over is that we're all struggling to forgive someone, and hate feeling fractured within our significant relationships and within ourselves. We are all searching for an answer, some new approach, that frees us from the corrosive effects of hate, gives voice to the injustice, and helps us to make peace with the person who hurt us and with ourselves.

Most of us are also struggling with the knowledge that we have mistreated others. We, too, are looking for a way to feel more human and integrated, less alienated and embattled. We can make ourselves feel right by feeling wronged—buying into our biased, self-righteous version of the truth, and blaming the person we hurt. But we won't feel good about ourselves until we clean up the damage we caused.

For those of you who have done wrong, I encourage you—in fact, I hope to help you—to muster up the honesty, maturity, and strength of character to reach out to the person you have hurt and make an earnest, bighearted effort to win her forgiveness. If you accept the challenge, I doubt you'll be sorry.

For those of you who have been wronged, I encourage you to take care of yourself, be fair, and seek life-serving ways to cleanse your intimate wound. By providing two adaptive alternatives—Acceptance and Genuine Forgiveness—I hope I can give you the courage to forgive, and the freedom not to.

Part One

CHEAP FORGIVENESS

*C*heap Forgiveness is a quick and easy pardon with no processing of emotion and no coming to terms with the injury. It's a compulsive, unconditional, unilateral attempt at peacemaking for which you ask nothing in return.

When you refuse to forgive, you hold tenaciously to your anger. When you forgive cheaply, you simply let your anger go.

When you refuse to forgive, you say "no way" to any future reconciliation. When you forgive cheaply, you seek to preserve the relationship at any cost, including your own integrity and safety.

Cheap Forgiveness is dysfunctional because it creates an illusion of closeness when nothing has been faced or resolved, and the offender has done nothing to earn it. Silencing your anguish and indignation, you fail to acknowledge or appreciate the harm that was done to you.

If you forgive too easily, you're likely to have what personality expert Robert Emmons calls "a chronic concern to be in benevolent, harmonious relationships with others."[1] The character trait that defines you could, in fact, be called "forgivingness." While some people would regard "forgivingness" as a virtue—Emmons calls it "spiritual intelligence"—I would suggest that it can rob you of your freedom to respond to an injury in an authentic, self-interested way. It can also be bad for your health, as we'll see later. When you feel compelled to forgive regardless of the circumstances, you're offering not Genuine Forgiveness but a cut-rate substitute.

PEOPLE WHO FORGIVE TOO CHEAPLY

Cheap Forgiveness comes in several forms. You may recognize yourself in one of them.

The Conflict Avoider

This is the most common type. Overly compliant and forgiving, you tend to dismiss an injury for the sake of protecting a relationship, as mutilating as it may be. On the surface, you act as though nothing is wrong. Inside, you may be hemorrhaging.

Conflict avoiders remain in relationships without voice and without a healthy sense of entitlement. Your submissive behavior—your tendency to subjugate your needs to those of others—is often based on one of three fears.

1. You fear that the offender will retaliate with anger or violence.

If you grow up with rageful parents, you may learn to keep silent—to go along in order to get along. This pattern is likely to persist into adulthood, as it did for a patient named Marsha. "My parents' anger was frightening," she told me. "I remember the day my mother threw over the Ping-Pong table and my father, drunk, chased her with a gun. I locked myself in my room and couldn't eat or sleep for days. Living with them, I learned to pick my words carefully, to lie low. I hated them both and got married at sixteen just to get out of the house. To this day I'm not good at anger. It scares me. I never even allow myself to feel anger. God knows where it goes."

2. You fear that the offender will reject or abandon you.

You may also resort to Cheap Forgiveness because you fear being cast off by someone whom you depend on for a sense of self-worth. This "morbid dependence"[2] is like insulin to a diabetic. It is not optional. It is a necessary lifeline.

Kathy, a forty-seven-year-old massage therapist, is a case in point. Desperate to hold onto her husband, Jack, she left herself no space in which to negotiate her needs. "I think of myself as a love junkie," she told me. "Why else would I stay in such a sick relationship? Jack drinks too much, he cheats on me, he lashes out at me verbally and sometimes physically. What happened last week should have been a wake-up call, but I shut off the alarm. We were on vacation, watching a video, and Jack was drinking. I asked him, 'What do you want to do for dinner?' and he blurted out, 'You've ruined my life!' and then slapped me and told me how much he hated me, and started in about how I was making him miss the end of the movie and how he wanted to kill me. A little over the top, wouldn't you say? And then he started to cry and tell me he hated himself and didn't know why he was so cruel to me. I know if I were healthy, I'd leave. But I'm stuck here, trying to be good enough for him, the way I tried to be good enough for my mother. She used to tell me, 'If it weren't for your younger sister, I'd have no reason to live'—that's how much I meant to her. I guess I'm still trying to get her—someone—to love me, even if they're as messed up as I am."

Needing to stay connected to Jack in order to affirm her own worth, Kathy constantly made excuses for his behavior. "It's the alcohol," she told me once. "The alcohol makes him violent." Or, "It's his low self-esteem—that's why he drinks. He projects his self-hatred on me, but he doesn't mean to be so mean." And shortly after he slapped her and told her how much he hated her, she told me, "We're closer than we've ever been."

Making excuses for Jack's violent, uncontrollable behavior and deluding herself about his capacity for change kept Kathy trapped in a dangerous relationship. But without Jack she was without a self, and that felt more terrifying than his degrading words or his physical abuse.

3. You fear that by speaking up for yourself, you may harm the offender.

Another reason for Cheap Forgiveness is your fear that you'll wound the offender if you confront him with the truth. Overprotective of his feelings and dismissive of your own, you exaggerate his fragility and your capacity to cause harm.

A patient named Peggy was driven by this concern for others. For seventeen years, she satisfied her husband Ted's need for sexual novelty and tolerated his voyeuristic obsession with pornography. She allowed him to see what he called a "sexual enhancement counselor" naked in the woman's office. She agreed once to group sex with neighbors. "This way I'll have no reason to cheat on you or leave you," he told her.

One day, Ted asked Peggy to dress up like a hooker, go to a bar, and try to pick up other men while he looked on. Reluctantly, she played along. She never actually left the bar with anyone, but in the following

days and weeks she found herself feeling increasingly depressed and
disgusted with herself. She was still determined to forgive Ted, though,
as she always had forgiven him, and went in search of confirmation
from her twenty-nine-year-old daughter, Rose. "I stayed with your
father all these years to keep the family together, and I would like your
sympathy and support," Peggy told her.

Rose's cold response was a rude awakening. "I'm almost thirty,"
she said. "Don't lay this on me. Whatever you're doing is for your
sake, not mine. Do you really want me to be grateful that you sacri-
ficed your life for me, that you gave up your happiness for mine?
That's a gift I don't need, thank you. Is this what you've wanted to
teach me all these years—that I should stay in a marriage and try to
make it work, no matter how awful my partner treats me? Is that the
lesson I'm supposed to come away with?"

Shaken by her daughter's response, Peggy entered therapy and
began to question why she failed to draw a line—why she felt so
desperate to keep Ted happy that she would sacrifice every shred of
self-respect for him. "Do I tolerate too much?" she asked me. "Why
don't I speak up about what matters to me?"

Delving into her past, Peggy answered her own questions. "My
parents separated when I was ten," she told me. "It was a bitter divorce
that tore the family apart. And I got caught in the middle. They asked
me which one I wanted to live with. I knew my mother would never
forgive me if I left her, so I chose her, but it killed my relationship with
my father. Frankly, it killed my relationship with my mother, too. I
vowed that when I grew up I'd create a different climate for my own
family. I swore my marriage would be different. . . ."

Peggy's idea that she needed to preserve her marriage for her
daughter's sake, or for some greater good, no longer made sense to
her—if it ever had. "Rose is grown up and has a life of her own,"
Peggy told me. "My vow to create a loving home is ridiculous—I
can't make a good marriage alone."

I'd like to give this story a happy ending, but Peggy decided to
drop out of therapy rather than tolerate the anxiety caused by her
growing self-awareness. She's still with Ted, forgiving his behavior

too easily, too cheaply. The coping patterns she learned in early childhood are too deeply ingrained for her to give them up—a reminder that having insights into our self-defeating patterns doesn't mean we have the will or the courage to change them.

Of course, something might still happen to give Peggy the clarity and conviction she needs to exorcise her devils and act on her own behalf. But first she would have to learn the value of a healthy selfishness and retire from her role as peacemaker.

The propensity to forgive may be shaped not just by interactions with parents, as it was for Peggy, but by conformity to popular social and religious beliefs, such as, "If you can't say something nice, don't say anything at all" and "Forgive and you shall be forgiven." These lessons get wired into us at a young age and influence our behavior as adults. What we're often not taught is what to do with our anger or with other unruly emotions that surface when someone tries to hurt us. No one tells us what Harvard psychologist Carol Gilligan found in her research with adolescent girls—that when we stop speaking up about violations in our relationships, we lose not only our voice, we lose ourselves.[3]

The Passive-Aggressor

If you're a conflict avoider, you readily forgive others at your own expense. If you're a passive-aggressor, you're also quick to forgive—subjugating your needs, silencing your voice, and conveying the false impression that all is well. Inside, though, you're probably not resigned but defiant and bitter, and busy sabotaging the peace you paid for with your shallow, deceptive words of forgiveness.

Operating indirectly, even subversively, you rebel through sins of omission. Instead of protesting your mistreatment openly and directly, you detach and get even in underhanded ways, effectively frustrating others by ignoring their requests and withdrawing from them physically and emotionally. Your decision to act forgivingly is manipulative; it's your way of getting even, feeling powerful, in control, on top. Though you may pretend to turn the other cheek, privately you seek an eye for an eye. As psychologist Scott Wetzler writes, "The passive-aggressive man may pretend to be sweet or compliant, but beneath his superficial demeanor lies a different core. He's angry, petty, envious, and selfish."[4]

Passive-aggressive types tend to develop covert patterns of relating in their early years. If your parents reproached you for challenging their authority, you may learn to give lip service to what others ask of you, while secretly defying them and getting your own way. If your parents humiliated you for showing vulnerability—crying, asking for help—you may as an adult be terrified of becoming dependent on anyone but yourself. Believing that a relationship is nothing more than a power game, you may keep your moves to yourself and reveal nothing about your inner workings. You may confuse cooperation with submission,[5] and attachment with loss of control.

Dan is a good example of a passive-aggressive peacemaker who masks his hostility. He and his wife, Emily, spent four years trying to conceive a child using infertility drugs. Finally they succeeded with in vitro fertilization, and Emily gave birth to a healthy boy. As Dan explained it to me, Emily then cut him out of her life and transferred all her attention to their son. Dan retaliated by turning his attention to his young office assistant.

A year later, in therapy, Dan acknowledged how testy and diminished he felt when the baby was born. "The angrier I got, the quieter I got," he told me. "Last Mother's Day I told Emily I had confused the date and scheduled a golf game with an old college buddy. The 'buddy,' of course, was the girl I was seeing. I promised I'd be home by three, but walked in at six, apologized, gave Emily a big hug and some roses, and proceeded to fall asleep in front of the TV."

Like a conflict avoider, Dan achieved only the illusion of peace—at a very dear price. Afraid of being overpowered or canceled out, he asserted himself in the only way that felt safe to him—by being secretly oppositional. Today, like most compulsive peacekeepers, he continues to struggle to be himself in relationships, but lacking both the strength of character and the interpersonal skills to negotiate conflict, he doesn't know how. He smiles, but secretly he seethes. On the surface, he forgives everything; underneath, he forgives nothing.

The passive-aggressor's pattern of making peace is to give with one hand and take with the other. Outwardly he humbles himself and accepts blame; inwardly he feels innocent and gloats over the success of his ruse. "My father and I engaged in a battle of wills," a patient named Jim told me. "But I learned to beat him at his game. Whatever I did, he demanded an apology. Once when I came home late he stormed up to me and said, 'Are you sorry? Tell me you're sorry!' He kept at it. Finally I told him, 'I am . . .' and then whispered silently under my breath, 'not.' That 'not' became the magic word, my way of being, my way of surviving that tyrant."

The Self-Sacrificer

The self-sacrificer is someone who, by conviction, puts others first. He enjoys acting with a generous heart and tries not to bear grudges. He may try to emulate saintly qualities of mercy and forgiveness, usually valuing other people's needs more than his own. In contrast to the conflict avoider, who often feels subjugated and conscripted into making peace, the self-sacrificer feasts on forgiveness.

As Jeffrey Young and his colleagues point out in *Schema Therapy*, if you have self-sacrificing tendencies, you tend to "listen to others rather than talk about yourself, take care of others yet have difficulty doing things for yourself, focus attention on others yet feel uncomfortable when attention is focused on you, and [be] indirect when you want something versus asking for it directly."[6]

So what is cheap or false about a self-sacrificer's willingness to forgive? Nothing, if it's a considered response to a specific injury and not a blind, instinctive stab at martyrdom; nothing, if you've wrestled with the alternatives and allowed yourself some freedom of response. Forgiveness becomes cheap or false when it's a rote, generic response, with no nod to content or circumstance.

Let me mention, on a lighter note, how my dear friend and colleague Michelle and I often exhibit a self-effacing altruism when we try to make plans to get together. This is how it might go. Michelle calls and says, "How would you like to meet me at the new Indian restaurant for dinner?" I pause and say, "Great. When's good for you?" She replies,

"I can meet you anytime after seven, but if that's too early for you, I can make it later." I say, "Fine. Let's do seven-fifteen" (which is actually much too early for me). We hang up, and she calls me back within minutes. "I heard you hesitate," she says. "What's wrong? Do you want to go somewhere else?" I reply, "Well, the truth is, I got sick the last time I went to that restaurant, but I'd be willing to give it another try." She replies, "No way. Let's go to that Italian restaurant you like," and she hangs up. I call her back, "Really, I'm happy to try the place you suggested. . . ." And on it goes. Put two self-sacrificers together, and they won't be able to come up with a plan of action in time for dinner.

There's nothing seriously harmful or dysfunctional about two people wanting to take each other's needs into account, and both feeling good about it (except that it's exhausting)—unless they're unable to respond in a more inner-directed, self-serving way when the circumstances warrant it. Both Michelle and I would be cheap forgivers if, when it really mattered, we couldn't say, "I'd really like to do X, not Y." This requires what Robert Karen calls "a natural self-ishness"[7]—an ability to speak up for what you need and set limits on what you're willing to do for others, relative to what you're willing to do for yourself.

Is the self-sacrificer on a higher moral plane than others? I wouldn't presume to answer this delicate question, but I would say that what's good for one individual may be poisonous for another. I also know from my clinical practice that people who are categorically committed to self-sacrifice but have not themselves wrestled with its meaning are often significantly distressed. A person's first, unconsidered response is not always his best.

Gretchen, a fifty-three-year-old Catholic school administrator, struggled to live a righteous life, filled with acts of goodness, without sapping her vitality or sacrificing her basic needs. When her mother died suddenly of leukemia, Gretchen's infirm ninety-year-old father asked if he could move in with her. Gretchen was recently divorced, working part time, and still caring for her three children at home, so she found herself torn. But she readily agreed. "I've been taught my whole life to give of myself, to be kind to others," she told me. "It's what I believe and what I teach my children. How could I not let him stay?"

Three months after her father's arrival, his sister Janice—Gretchen's aunt—was diagnosed with Parkinson's disease and asked Gretchen if she could move in, too—"Only for a month," Janice insisted, "while I get my things in order and arrange to move to an assisted living facility."

Gretchen went along. Thirty days passed, then sixty, then ninety. Gretchen offered to take Janice around to visit some local homes, but Janice snapped, "No. I can't possibly leave now. I'm not ready."

Gretchen assured Janice that she could stay as long as she wanted. "How can I kick her out—my own flesh and blood?" Gretchen told me.

But Gretchen felt used, depleted, and angry at herself. She knew, at some level, that she was being taken advantage of, but she was unable to draw boundaries or speak up for herself. Unlike Janice, she couldn't say no.

"It's not just that they make demands on me," Gretchen complained. "It's that I have no time to do anything for myself. If I take the kids out to dinner, I can't enjoy myself, thinking I should have brought Dad and Janice along. If I bring a date home, they sit in the den with us until he leaves. It doesn't occur to them to go back in their rooms, and I don't feel right telling them to. Dad doesn't make me feel guilty; I make myself feel guilty. My aunt's a different story. She feels entitled to have me take care of her and gets annoyed when I don't. And I buy into it. I feel bad. I *am* bad. I want to make everyone happy, but where does that leave me?"

Gretchen's problem, like that of other self-sacrificers, was not her humility, her tolerance, or her magnanimity. Her problem was her inability to act on her own behalf, to allow herself a range of responses that took account of her personal needs. Her aunt was as insensitive to Gretchen as Gretchen was to herself. And so, like others who automatically make peace, Gretchen remains today caught in a web of moral imperatives—a swamp of "musts" and "shoulds" from which there is no apparent escape.

ADVANTAGES AND DISADVANTAGES
OF CHEAP FORGIVENESS

What Are the Advantages of Cheap Forgiveness?

Here are five reasons why you may gravitate to Cheap Forgiveness:

1. It may keep you connected to the offender.

Cheap Forgiveness may allow you to maintain an appearance of harmony and keep your relationship alive, or at least intact. Some researchers support the idea that partners who can forgive a spouse for serious emotional injuries tend to be more happily married,[8] a notion I question.

2. It may make you feel good about yourself, even righteous
and superior.

As Ben Franklin said, "Doing an injury puts you below your enemy; revenge makes you but even with him; forgiving sets you above him."

3. It may protect you from confronting your own complicity in the
conflict, and wipe your slate clean, too.

Self-awareness can be painful. Cheap Forgiveness keeps you blissfully in the dark.

4. It may nudge the transgressor toward repentance.

Your conciliatory behavior may inspire him to treat you in equally benevolent ways—apologizing, making amends for the way he mistreated you. Your pardon may also exploit his sense of guilt and indebtedness, so that he becomes more friendly or respectful.

5. You believe that it's good for your health.

Cheap Forgiveness may seem to reward you with significant health benefits—releasing you from obsessions, reducing your anxiety and depression, and lowering your blood pressure and heart rate. As we'll see, these benefits are highly debatable.

What Are the Disadvantages of Cheap Forgiveness?

Let's look at how each of these advantages is linked to a disadvantage.

1. Cheap Forgiveness may preserve your relationship, but quash any opportunity to develop a more intimate bond.

When I first started working with issues of infidelity and an injured spouse would tell me, "I've forgiven my partner, I just want to move on," a part of me would secretly thank her for making my job easier. But I've since learned to be wary of such facile gestures and not to take the bait. Compulsive peacekeeping may allow you and your partner to stay connected, but nothing more—you don't get closer. When a violation is not talked out or resolved—when you gloss over his responsibility to restore trust and safety—no healing takes place. The underlying issues sit silently between you.

This was the case with a couple I interviewed on *Good Morning, America*. John had just learned that his wife, Mary, had had a brief affair shortly after their only child went off to college. In front of an audience of several million, Mary expressed deep remorse for hurting him. John, a retired air force lieutenant, quickly accepted her apology and extended a hand in peace. "I don't need to talk about this anymore," he told her. "I've forgiven you and just want to move on."

My immediate advice was, "Be careful not to forgive so fast." It seemed to me—and of course on these shows, the expert gets to analyze the complexities of a lifelong relationship in a four-minute time slot—that an instantaneous display of forgiveness was the last thing that would help this couple. The reason Mary had the affair to begin with was that she felt lonely and cut off from her husband, a situation exacerbated by her child's departure. *Forgiveness was the cheapest gift John could give her.* It cost him nothing. What Mary needed now was not a quick fix but conversation—plain honest talk about who she was and what she needed from him so they could develop an intimate bond. She wanted to be known, and she wanted to know him better. John's perfunctory peace offering could only produce more of the same—more silence, more alienation—and perpetuate their dysfunctional way of relating.

Some research does suggest that spouses who forgive their partners have happier marriages, but perhaps it's not the *act of forgiving* in and of itself that creates the better marriage, but the *transaction* that takes place between two people when forgiveness is earned. When the offender demonstrates that he understands and is sincerely disturbed by the harm he has caused you, and when he works to make repairs, you may be more motivated to release your resentment and invite him back into your life.

2. Cheap Forgiveness may make you feel morally superior to the offender, but your sanctimonious high is likely to prevent you from getting closer.

Some of you may deceive yourselves into believing that your generous gift puts you on a higher spiritual plane than the offender. "I, the humble, charitable one, have the capacity to forgive and am therefore closer to God," you tell yourself. "I can forgive someone even as defective as you."

Your benevolence may be on shaky ground, however, and may hide your true motivation. You need to ask yourself, "Is my forgiveness an act of exquisite humility or merely a manipulative gesture meant to establish my superiority?" If it is the latter, you rob yourself of the opportunity to have the offender tend to your wounds, make you feel cared for, and earn your goodwill.

3. Cheap Forgiveness blocks personal growth, denying you insights into yourself that would help you develop more satisfying relationships.

When you forgive too quickly, you never learn the lessons that come from confronting your own complicity. The couple I spoke to on *Good Morning, America* illustrate this point. The husband, John, simply let his wife—and himself—off the hook. End of story. He never faced how *he* may have failed her and contributed to her loneliness. Instead of negotiating a permanent peace, he offered a temporary cease-fire.

4. Cheap Forgiveness may give the transgressor a green light to continue mistreating you.

Cheap Forgiveness may not only *not* lead to the offender's contrition, it may increase the probability that he will harm you again. It has been found that among abused women, those who reported being the most forgiving toward their partners were more likely to suffer continued abuse.[9] If the offender never suffers the consequences of his transgression and can always expect you to be a fountain of mercy, why wouldn't he repeat his crime?

5. Cheap Forgiveness may make you sick, emotionally and physically.

We often hear about the physiological benefits of forgiving—of letting go of anger and making peace—but most of these findings are easy to misinterpret. What they show is that there's a *relationship* between forgiving and better health, not that forgiveness *causes* better health. What does make you feel better, studies indicate, is a reduced level of chronic hostility and distress,[10] and that comes from Acceptance or Genuine Forgiveness, not from Cheap Forgiveness. With Cheap Forgiveness, you bury or deny your resentment, you don't resolve it.

In *The Type C Connection: The Behavioral Links to Cancer and Your Health,* Lydia Temoshok and Henry Dreher maintain that Type C persons—those who are chronically unaware of their negative feelings and therefore quick to forgive—are more likely to be candidates for cancer than those who attend to these feelings and learn to cope with them. Temoshok and Dreher contrast Type C people, who exhibit "compulsive, unyielding niceness in any situation—no matter how stressful, insulting or dangerous"—with Type A persons, who are hostile, less forgiving, and more susceptible to heart disease than others.

Temoshok and Dreher go on to say that the absence of anger in Type C individuals "did not stem from a sense of inner peace. . . . Underneath their facade, there was a great deal of *unexpressed* anger, carefully guarded feelings of anxiety, and in many cases . . . a deep-seated feeling of despair."[11]

How the mind and body interact remains a mystery. We don't know if or how repressed emotions can cause tumors. But it has been hypothesized that a lifelong tendency to repress anger and other strong emotions wreaks havoc on our cellular organization and weakens our immunity to certain diseases. Woody Allen made this point in his inimitably nutty way in the film *Manhattan*. When his girlfriend (played by Diane Keaton) dumps him for his best friend and Allen refuses to get ruffled, Keaton shouts at him, "Why don't you get angry so we can have it out, so that we can get it out in the open?"

"I don't get angry, OK?" Allen replies. "I mean, I have a tendency to internalize. That's one of the problems I have. I—I grow a tumor instead."[12]

When we succumb to the notion that anger is evidence of weak moral character and poor emotional control, we make nice on the outside and sickness within.

UNDERSTANDING CHEAP FORGIVENESS

Acknowledging Your Pain Allows You to Address It

Feeling anger can be a healthy, adaptive reaction when your rights have been stomped on. It arouses you and stimulates you to act. Without it, you may lack the courage to speak out, to seek a just resolution, to protect yourself from further harm. If you don't allow yourself to feel indignant when someone hurts you, who will protect you from buying into his contempt? If you don't know that you're bruised or enraged, who will encourage you to question what the relationship is worth, to draw a line and say, "Enough. I've had enough."? Who's home? Who's there for you? Who will be your voice? Who will ask for your fair share? The inability to feel anger is as dangerous as the inability to feel pain, and leaves you just as defenseless.

A patient named Laura was a model of the cheap forgiver. When her husband, Tom, promised to be faithful after his third affair, she took him back, virtually chanting, "Tom's my husband. I married him for good and bad. I made a commitment. I keep it for the sake of the boys. Tom's weak. He needs me. I'm the only one left who believes in him. If I leave, he might kill himself. Where would he go? He'd drift from woman to woman and lose everything he's worked for."

Laura felt right upholding her moral and familial duties, but she could not say, "I want"—ever. She could not feel her own outrage, value it, or act on it—ever. Even when Tom continued to cheat on her, even when he passed on to her a sexually transmitted disease that made her infertile, she felt sorry for him, made excuses for him, and took him back into her heart.

Laura had to make peace. There was nothing saintly or noble about her response. If she had probed her feelings, I think she would have discovered a need to be both humane to Tom and true to herself. If she had known that Acceptance was an option, she could have worked toward it, empathizing with Tom rather than humiliating or judging him, while also honoring her own needs. She didn't have to forgive him or reconcile with him. She didn't have to jeopardize her children's well-being or her own.

If your pattern is to forgive at any price, it will take courage and a conscious effort to tune into your feelings and let your voice be heard. The payoff is that you'll give the offender a chance to know you are bleeding inside and to step forward and bind your wound.

The ability to speak up about who you are, how you're hurting, and what you need is an essential part of what it means to be intimate. As Harriet Lerner writes so eloquently in *The Dance of Connection*, "Through words we come to know the other person—and to be known. This *knowing* is at the heart of our deepest longings for intimacy and connection with others. How relationships unfold with the most important people in our lives depends on courage and clarity in finding voice."[13]

Of course, the offender may not respond to your anguish in a supportive way, but, as Lerner goes on to counsel, "Even when we are not being heard, we may still need to know the sound of our own voice say-ing out loud what we really think."[14] If you're too aware of the danger of speaking up and too unaware of the cost of remaining silent, you'll treat yourself with the same disregard the offender showed you, and end up feeling just as discounted and disenfranchised as he made you out to be.

Was I Violated—or Am I Imagining It?

What makes it nearly impossible for some peacekeepers to speak up is their uncertainty about whether a violation actually took place. Children of alcoholics and victims of physical or sexual abuse in particular often grow up in a world that tries to convince them that *the injury never happened.* In *The Courage to Heal,* Bass and Davis discuss how victims of trauma are re-traumatized when oth-ers, even their immediate families, dismiss their memories of sexual abuse as vindictive lies or misguided, crazy imaginings.[15] Victims whose recollections are questioned often spend their lives doubting the truth of their own experiences—pretending they were never hurt and learning not to trust their own intuition or their own version of reality. This reaction can be as damaging as the violation itself.

A patient named Nancy grew up in a family that denied the reality of her mother's alcohol abuse. "Most of the time Mom stayed in bed, depressed and shut off from the world," Nancy told me. "But then she'd go on an alcohol binge and come ripping through the house, screaming, throwing things. The next day, no one would say a word. We'd be sitting around the dinner table—my father and five kids—and my mother would be out cold in the bedroom. It was eerie. I'd look around and wonder, 'Did what happened really hap-pen? Am I losing my mind? Why isn't anyone talking about it? Why is everyone pretending we're a normal family?'"

You've Got It All Wrong—the Problem Is You

Some people may deny what happened to you or convince you that *you're* the guilty one—that *you're* the one who's wrong or bad. You may soon learn that to live in peace with them you need to silence your voice and swallow their scorn.

"When a nun in elementary school whacked me with a geography book for playing the wrong note during my piano lesson, my mother made me practice more," a patient named Denise told me. "When my boyfriend slammed his fist through our den wall, my mother asked me, 'What did you do to provoke him?' When I told her Dad put his tongue in my mouth, she told me to shut up, that my tongue was more dangerous than his. Whatever happened to me, she made me feel I deserved it, I caused it. I learned not to make waves. I assumed I had no right to complain."

Origins of Cheap Forgiveness

If you want to break out of your pattern of mindless peacemaking, it may help to look back at your early life and identify the critical experiences that shaped you. Did you grow up so frightened of conflict that you couldn't acknowledge when you were violated, let alone expect the offender to make repairs? Were you so traumatized by a parent's abandonment that you desperately held on to relationships, no matter how superficial or unhealthy the bond? Were you taught to be so other-directed that you couldn't appreciate yourself except when you were serving someone else? Did you grow up with an excessive sense of responsibility, a hypersensitivity to others' needs and feelings?

Perhaps a family member was physically ill or emotionally disabled, and you were thrust into the role of a "parentified" child who readily sacrifices herself to care for others. Perhaps your parents were critical or controlling, and you learned to surrender your needs in order to avoid humiliation. As disparate as these two experiences are, both may lead you to subjugate your needs as an adult,[16] and forgive too quickly and automatically for your own good.

The roots of your behavior may also go back to the moral and religious exhortations of your family or community. You may have been taught that decent people forgive, that if you aspire to behave in a godlike way, you have no other choice.

Pressure to forgive at any cost may be drilled into you through seemingly innocent messages. One of my patients was told again and again, "Birds in their little nests agree; why can't we?" These family mandates get deeply embedded in us at a young age and stay with us throughout life.

Your biological imperatives are another variable. Low levels of testosterone, for example, may contribute to passivity or shyness and make you more likely to lay down your arms and avoid conflict than to seek revenge or even acknowledge the harm that was done to you.

A patient named Phyllis traced her pattern of Cheap Forgiveness directly to her relationship with her mother. Phyllis must have told me the same story ten times in therapy—it captured a formative experience in the development of her adult self. "My mother used to pick out my clothes for me," she would recall. "She said she knew what looked good on me, and what I liked, better than I did. Even as a child I sensed how badly she needed me to love her, to merge with her. She told me how mean her mother had been to her, always favoring her sister—and how important it was that we be close. Her idea of 'close' was to take over. My idea was to let her dominate me. I came to doubt my ability to know what I felt or thought as a separate human being. I couldn't say no to her. It's the same with my husband, Steve. For years I've tried to be his good little wife, eviscerating myself, mastering the art of staying attached to a difficult, overbearing person, while ignoring my resentment, my despair. After two kids and thirty years of marriage, I just found out he's been carrying on with his personal trainer for ten years. He put her through a Ph.D. program—in psychology. I've told him I need him to get into therapy with me to make sense of it all, but he insists the affair is over. 'My honey, my baby,' he says, pleading with me not to leave; and on some level I ask myself, 'Why can't I just believe him? Why can't I just give up my tantrums, forgive him, and move on?' A part of me wants to scream and another part wants to make him happy. It's so hard to separate myself out from all this. And that's what I'm here to work on with you."

If, you, like Phyllis, have a propensity to forgive too easily, you may be responding not to a particular interaction but to early childhood patterns. To access them, I encourage you to look closely at how you routinely react to injury. Ask yourself:

- Do I compulsively seek to repair relationships, regardless of the circumstances or my feelings?
- Do I beat up on myself when someone mistreats me?
- Do I make excuses for the offender?
- Do I repress or deny a violation?
- Do I fail to know my anger or my despair?
- Do I fail to voice my objections or my needs?
- Do I often feel powerless, trapped, manipulated, snuffed out?
- Do I pardon the offender as a way of asserting my control, dominance, or moral superiority?
- Do I extend a generosity of spirit to everyone, and therefore to no one?
- Is Cheap Forgiveness my typical, robotic response when someone hurts me? If so, does it serve me in this particular situation, or should I consider another tack?

What you may discover is that your characteristic response is not necessarily your healthiest—that it makes more sense, sometimes, to offer the offender an opportunity to apologize and seek forgiveness.

That's what a high school teacher named Ruth did when her son Josh insulted her. "I E-mailed him, asking if his girlfriend Andrea would like some Chanel perfume for her birthday," Ruth told me. "His response was short and to the point. 'Isn't that the perfume you and your mother used to wear? Why would I want my girlfriend smelling like the two of you?' I felt slapped—not just because of the insult but because Mom died just a few months ago."

Ruth revealed her hurt to me but said nothing to her son. Having grown up taking care of a mentally handicapped sister, she was a perfunctory peacekeeper—unfailingly considerate, sympathetic, programmed to deny her own hurt feelings. Oversolicitous and desperate for affection, she defined herself through the approving eyes of others, even those who violated her.

Ruth was prepared to shake off her feelings, as always, and go back to grading papers, when she remembered how her father—"a

sweet, soft-spoken man who never confronted anyone"—had repri-
manded her long ago for behaving abominably toward her mother.

"I was a sophomore in high school, going out on a first date with
a real catch—at least he seemed that way at the time," Ruth said,
"and I was terrified that Mom, with her lack of education, would say
something stupid and spoil my chances with this guy, so I instructed
her to stay in the kitchen and not come to the door when the bell
rang. My father overheard me and let me have it. 'You're totally out
of line, insulting your mother and hurting her feelings,' he scolded
me, in a voice sterner than I had ever heard before. 'This woman
kills herself for you—you owe her nothing but gratitude. Don't you
ever speak to her that way again.'"

The incident happened more than thirty years before, but when
Ruth told me about it, she still flushed with shame. "Dad was right,"
she said. "And I respected him for saying so. It couldn't have been
easy for him. It was so uncharacteristic."

Ruth's thoughts went from her parents to her son Josh. "I know
I'm not doing myself a favor by not disciplining him," she said.
"Why am I so anxious to forgive him? Do I think he'll get so mad
that he'll stop loving me? Do I think he'll be so crushed by my anger
that he'll never recover?"

At her next session, Ruth told me, "I did something out of character. I called Josh and left him a message that his comment hurt me
deeply. I told him that a more appropriate reaction would have been,
'Thanks for the offer, Mom. I'll find out if Andrea is into Chanel.' I
waited a day for his response. Nothing. I was rattled. But the next
morning I got a very thoughtful apology. 'Mama, got your message.
Sorry you took my comment about the perfume the wrong way. I
was joking. I guess it wasn't that funny. It was nice of you to think of
Andrea. Love, J.'"

Ruth went from feeling totally cut off from her son to feeling
deeply proud that he had the character to admit being wrong and
apologize. She also felt good about herself for not offering her typical gift of Cheap Forgiveness. "Josh came through," she told me. "So
did I."

If you, like Ruth, are a compulsive peacekeeper, I encourage you not to shrug off your feelings but to pay attention to them, share them with the offender, and give him a chance to understand how he wronged you and make good. This process shows respect not only for you but for the resilience and substance of the offender, who may relish the opportunity to make amends. I invite you to find the courage to do this.

"Healthy relationships," writes Dana Crowley Jack in *Behind the Mask*, "require mutuality (being with), but they also require positive aggression (being opposed)." In other words, you must challenge "devaluing patterns of interaction" and experience your right to be an "I" within a "we."[17] Cheap Forgiveness bypasses the injury—as well as any possibility of developing a healthy relationship with yourself or with the offender.

Part Two

REFUSING TO FORGIVE

*W*hen someone deliberately hurts you, you may refuse to forgive him because Not Forgiving seems the most self-affirming thing to do. The only other response you know—forgiving—may feel far too generous. Giving voice to your rage, you proclaim, "My feelings matter—if not to you, then to me. And to prove it I'll offer you no cheap pardon, no opportunity to repay your debt, no out. Whatever you say or do, I'll continue to despise and denounce you. I'll show you that you can't hurt me with impunity, that what you did was unforgivable."

RESPONDING WITH AGGRESSION OR DETACHMENT

Refusing to forgive usually takes one of two forms. First, you may strike out aggressively at the offender, heaping on him the full weight of your "condemnatory fury,"[1] deriving an almost sadistic pleasure from the power, the thrill, of subjecting him to the pain and indignity you believe he inflicted on you. Second, you may turn your back on him and try to destroy him with your indifference. Your silence will speak volumes about your contempt.

Either way—through aggression or detachment—your goal is to teach him a lesson and keep him in your punishing grip. Either way, you hope to strip him of his humanity, recalibrating the balance of power and restoring your place in the sun. "Vindictive triumph," notes the distinguished psychoanalyst Karen Horney, becomes "the only goal worth striving for" and is achieved through the acquisition of power to frustrate, humiliate, or exploit the person who has offended you.[2]

So long as you're in an unforgiving mode, your anger is non-negotiable; there can be no emotional resolution, no letting go, no letting in. Should the offender show remorse, you won't soften your rage. Should he refuse to repent, you're likely to feel trampled on twice—once by the injury and again by his failure to acknowledge it. His disregard for your suffering may wound you more deeply than the injury itself. "Why should I forgive someone who refuses to apologize?" you protest. "Why is it up to me to make peace? If I don't want to be hurt again, shouldn't I seal the boundaries around me and cut him out of my life, out of my psychic space?"

ORIGINS OF NOT FORGIVING

All of us refuse to forgive at times, but our response is usually proportional to the provocation. Our anger flares up and later subsides. For some of us, however, Not Forgiving is not an isolated reaction to a single violation but a lifelong pattern of response. This pattern could be innate—a basic personality trait. Or it could be learned, largely from damaging early life experiences but also from negative assumptions about the meaning of forgiveness.

Innate Factors That May Stop You from Forgiving

I know of no formal study that has found a chemical basis for Not Forgiving. Preliminary data suggest, however, that a tendency to react with hostility is associated with such neurochemical variables as "excessive hormones, like testosterone, or a deficiency of neurotransmitters, such as serotonin or dopamine."[3] Recent research suggests that those of us who have "a highly reactive sympathetic nervous system and a slow-to-respond parasympathetic nervous system" may experience and react to offenses with heightened anger and hurt, leading to an unforgiving response.[4]

In his research on the origins of hatred and violence, Aaron Beck, M.D., University Professor of Psychiatry at the University of Pennsylvania, finds an adaptive, evolutionary explanation for our guided instinctive response to imagined or real threat. In prehistoric times, he points out, there was survival value in overreacting to any noxious stimuli. A quick, unfettered response to danger could spell the difference between life and death.[5]

Researchers who study forgiveness have postulated a personality trait they call "vengefulness"—a tendency to act aggressively against a perceived offender. People who exhibit this trait are likely to be more negative, more easily offended, less empathic, and less likely to forgive.[6]

Learned Factors That May Stop You from Forgiving

If you tend to say no to forgiving, it may be that you continue to perpetuate dysfunctional interactions from your past. Here are three examples:

- If you were physically or emotionally battered at an impressionable age, you may grow up seeking to empower yourself by feeling contempt for others. You may permanently sever ties with anyone who makes you feel weak or helpless in the slightest way.
- If you grew up in a family where ruptures and grudges were a way of life—for example, your mother banished her sister from her home forever—Not Forgiving may become your calcified response to conflict, even with someone who deserves better treatment.
- If you grew up in a strict, repressive family where you were subjected to cruel humiliations, you may become punitive and unforgiving as an adult. Pressured to live by the rules, to abide by uncompromising ideas of right and wrong and unrealistically high moral principles, you may evolve into someone who is emotionally restricted, lacking in spontaneity and warmth, and impatient with anyone, including yourself, who can't meet your exacting standards. If you are reluctant "to consider extenuating circumstances, allow for human imperfection, or empathize with anyone else's feelings,"[7] your natural response is to Not Forgive.

Parents are not the only ones who may teach you never to forgive; popular culture can play a role, too. If you're taught that "only sissies forgive" or that "when you forgive, others walk all over you,"

you may be loath to make peace with anyone—even if the offender tries hard to redress your grievance—even if your perception of the grievance is exaggerated or wrong. So long as you see forgiveness in terms that discredit you, Not Forgiving is likely to be your only viable option.

It's often *the personal meaning* you ascribe to a perceived offense that ultimately colors your emotional and behavioral response to it. As Beck points out in *Prisoners of Hate: The Cognitive Basis of Anger, Hostility, and Violence*, your "catastrophic" distortions and misperceptions of what happened may create a frame of mind that encases you in hostility or impels you to lash out.[8]

PEOPLE WHO REFUSE TO FORGIVE

Let's look now at two types of people who tend to be unforgiving—the narcissist and the Type A personality. Does one describe you?

The Narcissist

Individuals who routinely refuse to forgive often have what is called a narcissistic personality disorder. Narcissists believe that they're "entitled to special rights and privileges, whether earned or not. They're demanding and selfish. They expect special favors without assuming reciprocal responsibilities and express surprise and anger when others don't do what they want."[9]

If you're a narcissist, you may frequently feel wounded and enraged when others refuse to comply with your agenda. Your exaggerated sense of entitlement leads you to assume that people are mere instruments for your self-enhancement, placed on earth solely to serve you. Since others don't exist to you as separate individuals with needs, desires, and feelings of their own, you're likely to exploit them and not see how this exploitation may set up the conflict you blame them for creating.

If you recognize some of these qualities in yourself, you may be someone who is dependent on the admiration of others to keep your self-esteem afloat, and hypersensitive to anyone who threatens your sense of specialness. Any experience of degradation or personal failure may cut you so deeply that you feel not just slighted but annihilated. Rather than admit how much you need others to fill the emptiness inside you, you may devalue them and assume an air of superiority. Forgiveness is not an option for you—you have too great a sense of self-importance and too little humility.

"Humility," writes Robert Emmons, "is the disposition to view oneself as basically equal with any other human being even if there are objective differences in physical beauty, wealth, social skills, intelligence, or other resources. . . . It is the ability to keep one's talents and accomplishments in perspective, to have a sense of self-acceptance, an understanding of one's imperfections, and to be free from arrogance and low self esteem."[10] Without these qualities, you're unlikely ever to forgive.

It's hard to forgive someone if, lacking humility, you believe that he's totally at fault and that you're perfect and can do no wrong. If you could accept a degree of complicity, you might respond more charitably, but that would shatter your grandiose view of yourself and ask more of you than you have to give.

When most of us feel wronged—when our sense of fairness is violated—we usually vacillate among three responses: acceptance, forgiveness, and retribution. When a narcissist feels wronged, however, he believes that his only choice is retribution.[11] He can see no alternative but to strike back and settle the score with anyone who dares to defy his power, weaken his control, or threaten his belief in his own perfection.

The narcissist is unlikely to be affected by these words, because he's unlikely to read them. Incapable of tolerating the discomfort of self-scrutiny or criticism, he seeks admiration, not self-knowledge. He attaches to those who flatter him and discards those who don't. People who get into therapy are often those who are desperately clinging to a narcissist, trying to be good enough, trying to apologize and make peace with someone who is chronically unrepentant and unforgiving.

The Type A Personality

Several researchers have found a link between the Type A personality and the narcissistic personality. Like the narcissist, the Type A individual is power-oriented, hostile, condescending, over-reactive to minor frustrations, defensive, and incapable of close relationships.[12] If you're a Type A person, you have an impatient, self-centered, demanding manner that's likely to push people away and make it hard for them to apologize to you or care about your hurt feelings. Blaming them for your own offensive behavior, which you lack the insight to see, you lock the door on forgiveness.

Paul, a hulking forty-five-year-old Wall Street trader, was both a Type A personality and a narcissist. Every day for him was an opportunity to settle scores. Easter was no exception. On a family trip to Boston to see the Celtics, he stopped in a crowded deli for a quick bite before the game. Dressed in black, with his hair punked up, he was a tough and formidable presence. He and his children finally reached the front of the line when an older couple slipped in front of them. Paul called over the seating clerk and jabbed at his watch. "No problem," the clerk assured him, "you're next." But when a table freed up, the couple took it. Paul saw red. He pulled a wad of hundred-dollar bills from his pocket and waved it in the clerk's face. "You see this?" he said challengingly. "This is lunch money for me. You know how I make a living? I kill. And you've made me very unhappy." Within minutes, Paul and his family had a table.

"I knew my kids were watching, so I tried to keep my voice calm," Paul told me later. "I don't know what I would have done if they hadn't been there. This guy just sent me over the edge. He made me feel invisible, like I didn't exist—just like my father did."

I encouraged Paul to peel back the layers of emotions he had experienced in the deli and try to understand where his reaction was coming from, how it repeated deep-seated patterns of response, and how he might deal with conflict differently in the future—still conveying annoyance without losing control or frightening his children. He began by responding to the following questions. If you, like Paul, have an unforgiving style of coping, you're likely to answer yes to many of them, too:

- Do I get insulted and offended too easily?
- Do I have too many confrontations with people?
- Do I jump to conclusions, take what people say or do too personally, and react with arrogance or indignation?
- Do I tend to harbor grudges forever?
- Do I cut myself off from those who hurt me without wrestling with the truth about what actually happened?
- Do I find that an apology is never good enough to warrant my letting go of an offense?
- Do I take comfort in the role of victim and fail to see that an injury wasn't simply something done to me but something I may have been partly responsible for?
- Do I dream of ways of crushing my opponent? Do I fill my time with retaliatory fantasies that make me feel powerful, superior, and in control?

ADVANTAGES AND DISADVANTAGES OF NOT FORGIVING

Why Not Forgiving May Seem Attractive to You

Not Forgiving may come across as an appealing option for at least three reasons.

1. It makes you feel invulnerable.

Not Forgiving gives you an aura of invincibility and allows you to convert "a feeling of impotence into a feeling of omnipotence."[13] When you refuse to forgive, you gather strength by humiliating the person you accuse of humiliating you. In your eyes, a "nonforgiver" is a hammer; a forgiver is an anvil begging to be hit.[14]

The strength you feel from striking back at someone who hurt you may not be entirely illusory. You may force him to think twice about re-injuring you and reduce the frequency with which he tries.

Of course, you might inflame the conflict and provoke him to attack you again; but your tough, retaliatory stance may also intimidate him and show him who's the boss.

2. It lets you blame others for your own failures.

Not Forgiving lets you blame others for your own failures and transfer to them whatever it is you curse (and eventually need to confront and forgive) in yourself. It helps you ward off the shame and humiliation that come when someone gets too close to the unflattering truth about you. "The source of my problem lies in you," you insist, "not in me. *You* made me miserable. *You* made me fail. Because of you, I don't have a better job, more friends, more money, more happiness, more freedom, more laughter, more stuff. Because of you, I drink, take drugs, have affairs, can't get out of bed in the morning, can't find my way, can't get a life." Living in a "grudge state,"[15] you insist that you're innocent and that the person who hurt you deserves every imaginable punishment. You conveniently blame him for all your troubles, when the problem may be *you*—*your* inability to take the initiative, ask for help, say no.

3. It replaces the emptiness inside you with a surge of elation.

Whether you boldly retaliate or hold yourself aloof, Not Forgiving makes you feel alive and kicking, and at one with yourself. As Robert Karen notes ironically, "No one is immune to the joys of victimhood and revenge."[16]

Why Not Forgiving Is a Dysfunctional Response to Violation

When you say no to forgiving, what started as a self-protective solution to pain—a way of coping with your indignation—ultimately leaves you feeling cold and bitter. What held out the promise of restoring your self-regard, creating emotional and physical safety, and providing a just resolution to the injury, doesn't deliver—or delivers at a dear price. The presumed rewards of Not Forgiving, which initially seemed so attractive and healthy, turn out to be maladaptive in at least three ways.

1. Not Forgiving cuts you off from any dialogue with the offender and any positive resolution of the conflict.

When you exorcise the offender from your life, you deny him the opportunity to respond to your grievances and earn forgiveness. Refusing to consider what he meant to you in the past, and could still mean to you today, you also deny yourself any possibility of reconciliation. In human relationships, there are so many unintended slights and misunderstandings. If both of you could only air your differences, it might change the face of the violation and soften your response. Remember, if you choose to open a dialogue, you're not required to reconcile or forgive, but you may let the offender in and your sorrow out.

2. Not Forgiving may restore your pride, but it cuts you off from an opportunity for personal growth and understanding.

When you refuse to forgive, you transfer all the blame to the offender and make yourself unassailable. This proud pretense of perfection, however, is likely to mask a shaky interior. As Karen Horney writes, "Neurotic pride is an exalted self-esteem that is built not upon existing assets but upon an imaginary superiority."[17] Wrapped in sanctimonious anger, never questioning how you may be wrong, you cut yourself off from an opportunity to look into yourself—to learn, change, and grow.

Behind your refusal to forgive may be a fear of facing your own frailty and failures. You may blame someone for excluding you, for example, and not see how your belief that you're not worth knowing causes you to distance yourself. You may accuse someone of subjugating you and not see how you fail to speak up and set boundaries. You may feel tyrannized by the demands of others but not know how to relax and create balance in your life.

Blinded by rage, you become an expert in how others let you down. You can write volumes on how your parents, children, or friends have failed you, but you often know little about how you have offended others, who in turn defend themselves or strike back at you in equally combative ways. And you fail to see others with the same generosity you insist that they extend to you.

*3. Not Forgiving may make you feel less empty, but it poisons you
   physically and emotionally and cuts you off from life.*

The venom that pours into your bloodstream when you refuse to
forgive may make you feel less hollow, more vital, and more ener-
gized, but it may also leave you "psychically sterile"[18]—detached
from life, blind to those who deserve your gratitude, cut off from
tenderness, beauty, and joy. You may seek the solace of solitary plea-
sures—a book, a walk—or shared moments with old friends, but
rage is likely to be the only feeling that resonates inside you.
Obsessed with getting even, you fulfill your basic need for protection and self-preservation,[19] but leave no time to gratify your
"higher" needs for peace, creativity, love, and connection.

Though hating may make you feel alive, it may also make you
physically sick, or more susceptible to illness. A growing body of
research demonstrates that chronic negative emotions such as bitterness, cynicism, mistrust, and hostility—all expressions of Not Forgiving—sap your energy and undermine your mental and physical
well-being.[20] A recent study found that subjects who were
instructed to rehearse unforgiving responses to a violation experienced elevated blood pressure and increased arousal of the sympathetic nervous system.[21] If these physiological effects are chronic
and intense, they could compromise your immune system, increasing the risk of cancer or infectious diseases, or building calcifications
in the coronary arteries leading to cardiovascular disease.

Refusing to Forgive may isolate you not just from the person
who hurt you but from those who have done you no harm. Mistrust
is like blood seeping from a wound, staining everything it touches.
Morbidly absorbed in the injury, you may push everyone away, even
those who care for you and want to help you heal. Unable to open
up to them, or even admit that you welcome their support, you're
likely to stand firm but alone.

Stabilizing and strengthening yourself requires more than a shot
of indignation. You need to turn inward and make sense of the
injury so you can go on with your life. You need to reach out and

develop more nourishing connections with those who are there for you, or who would like to be there for you. There's a difference between nursing your wounds and binding them, a difference between destructive rage and constructive anger. When you don't know the difference, Not Forgiving becomes your raison d'être.

Giving up the brute arrogance of Not Forgiving is hard work. You need to dismantle your pride, learn humility, and stop blaming others for your share of the problem. As Horney so colorfully points out, "taking this road would mean—heaven forbid—becoming more human. It would mean giving up [your] isolated grandeur, [your] uniqueness, and becoming an ordinary human being like everyone else without any special privileges; becoming part of the swarming mass of humanity."[22]

Most of us have suffered violations that seem unpardonable. Refusing to Forgive seems to demonstrate our courage and wisdom—our strength, our self-respect, our right to justice. The truth is, however, that Refusing to Forgive offers only a superficial balm for our wounds. It may give us a temporary rush of power, but it doesn't permit a clear, measured, self-sustaining response. It doesn't release us from our preoccupation with the offender or provide anything more than hatred to rebuild our injured pride. It gives us a veneer of protection but doesn't really make us any less fragile or more fulfilled as human beings.

In the end, Not Forgiving is just that—a negative force, a way of *not* being engaged in life. It is a sorely limited, constricted, hard-hearted response to injury that feeds on hate and humiliation and diverts us from the greatest challenge of all—to make peace with ourselves so we can feel whole and happy to be alive.

Part Three

ACCEPTANCE

*A*cceptance is a gutsy, life-affirming response to violation when the person who hurt you is unavailable or unrepentant. It asks nothing of anyone but you. Unlike Cheap Forgiveness or Refusing to Forgive, it is based on a personal decision to take control of your pain, make sense of your injury, and carve out a relationship with the offender that works for you.

Judith Herman points out in *Trauma and Recovery* that you aren't responsible for the harm that was done to you, but you are responsible for your recovery.[1] In other words, your freedom lies not in protesting the unfairness of the violation or in getting the offender to care. Your freedom—perhaps your only freedom—is in deciding how to survive and transcend the injury. Don't underestimate this freedom: it's enormous. With it comes the power to decide how you're going to live the rest of your life. As you take the task of healing into your own hands, you empower yourself and make peace with the past.

THE TEN STEPS OF ACCEPTANCE

When you accept someone:

- Step 1: You honor the full sweep of your emotions.
- Step 2: You give up your need for revenge but continue to seek a just resolution.
- Step 3: You stop obsessing about the injury and reengage with life.
- Step 4: You protect yourself from further abuse.
- Step 5: You frame the offender's behavior in terms of his own personal struggles.
- Step 6: You look honestly at your own contribution to the injury.

- Step 7: You challenge your false assumptions about what happened.
- Step 8: You look at the offender apart from his offense, weighing the good against the bad.
- Step 9: You carefully decide what kind of relationship you want with him.
- Step 10: You forgive yourself for your own failings.

A Case Example

Let's look at a patient named Sam, who learned to accept, but not forgive, his emotionally stunted father.

"For as long as I can remember, Dad ignored me," Sam recalled. "The only use he had for me was showing me off to his friends—like the time our lacrosse team won a championship and instead of giving me a big hug he went around bragging that his son was Number One. When I was eleven, he told me Mom had arthritis. It was cancer. I was playing lacrosse when one of his salesmen called out from the sidelines, 'Go home. Your mother's dead.' I never felt so alone. Even at the funeral, Dad never reached out to me. He didn't have a clue what I was feeling."

Sam finally got his father's attention the only way he knew how—through crime and drugs. Outwardly, he projected toughness and resolve. Inwardly, he felt lost, unlovable. He didn't ask himself why. He was a married man when he finally confronted his father about his mother's death. "Why did you send a stranger to break the news?" he asked. "How could you have been so insensitive? What were you thinking?"

"What did I know?" his father said, shrugging him off.

It was a sad, shallow response—the throwaway comment of a man who was unable to tap into his son's pain.

Sam now began to work on developing a view of himself independent of the way his father treated him—to begin valuing all that was likable and special about himself. In his search for validation, he turned inward and learned to take his father's behavior less personally. "Dad's been self-absorbed and self-congratulatory with virtually everyone, not just me," he reminded himself.

Sam stopped focusing on how neglected he had been and began investing his energy in taking care of himself and in doing things that would build his self-respect. He worked on getting closer to his wife, his sister, his friends. He took up marathon running. He developed a love of music.

In therapy, Sam struggled to understand his father's limitations. "Dad's father abandoned him," he told me. "Dad was one of five kids left at home with their grandmother while their mother worked. Maybe he was telling the truth when he said, 'What did I know?' Maybe he didn't know how to comfort me. Maybe he didn't even know what comfort was."

I asked Sam to think about how he may have contributed to his father's behavior. "I was a tough kid with a terrible temper who didn't let on that he had any emotional needs," he admitted. "I wasn't easy to parent. I probably sent him messages that said, 'Take care of my sister instead.'"

Sam thought through what kind of relationship he would like to have with his father. He weighed the advantages of hating him and amputating him from his life, against the disadvantages. Where would mercy lead him? Where would staying in touch? Was it doing Sam any good to protest how his father had mistreated him? Did he really want to spend his life feeling betrayed and abandoned?

Before his father died, Sam visited him in the hospital and learned to value his admirable qualities—his humor, his stubborn refusal to submit to liver cancer or to burden others with his pain.

Near the end, Sam said to him, "Dad, it would help me get closer to you if you could acknowledge how alone I felt as a child and how, after Mom died, you were never able to give me much of yourself. His father looked at him and said, "For Christ's sake, get off the cross."

At the cemetery, Sam was overcome with compassion for himself—for all the losses and deprivations he had endured, for all the wrong turns he had made; and he forgave himself for losing sight of his inner goodness and his potential as a human being.

He wanted to forgive his father but couldn't. The man was incapable of grasping the harm he had done or showing remorse for Sam's pain. But Sam was determined to stop agonizing over it and get on with his life. He was determined to take the power of healing back to himself.

Sam had finally reached an inner, emotional resolution that was realistic and authentic, given his history. What he could offer his father—Acceptance—fell short of Genuine Forgiveness, but it allowed him to reach out to the man, respect his strengths, tolerate his limitations, and enjoy a relationship that felt comfortable and real.

Let's look now at how, through Acceptance, you, too, can rehabilitate your injured self and settle your account with the offender.

Step #1: You honor the full sweep of your emotions.

With Acceptance, you appreciate the magnitude of the wrong that was done to you and give full voice to the violation. You refuse to let go of your grievance until you've grasped its meaning and understood its effect on you. You may need to replay the injury again and again until the whole truth sinks in.

You're likely to experience many losses at this time—losses regarding the way you know yourself and the person who harmed you, losses regarding the way you think about people and the world you live in. Whatever is gone or changed has to be acknowledged and grieved.

Some of you are experts at anger but can't feel sadness. For you, anger is easier to access and leaves you feeling righteous and safe. Often, however, anger doesn't tell the whole story, or even the most important part. As James Baldwin wrote, "I imagine one of the reasons people cling to their hates so stubbornly is because they sense, once hate is gone, they will be forced to deal with the pain."[2]

Others of you tend to block out anger but feel depressed. You may minimize what was done to you, telling yourself, "Many people have been hurt much worse than I've been. Who am I to complain?" But life is not a contest, and your pain counts as much as anyone else's. You need to know and value your feelings in and for themselves. Failure to acknowledge them is not humility, it's self-denial.

It helps to create a place within you where your emotions are safe—an empathic, holding environment where you do not judge, deny, or dismiss whatever is going on inside you. Once you acknowledge your feelings and give yourself permission to have them, you can begin to normalize them. All your life you may have been taught that emotions are dangerous, a sign of weakness. You may have learned to cut yourself off from them. But now you need to embrace them, secure in the knowledge that when someone violates you, you are not crazy or alone in responding with intense, even conflicting emotions.

In his study of grief, psychologist Jay Efran[3] tells the story of a young boy who got separated from his mother in a grocery store. Frantically, the child ran up and down the aisles, searching for her. When he finally saw her, he threw himself into her arms and started to weep. Efran poses the question, "Why did the child cry only then, *after* he had found his mother?" and explains that at that moment of reunion the boy got in touch with his terror and was overcome with sorrow for himself. For him, as for all of us, the ability to empathize with ourselves—to feel our own suffering, to know what we have endured—is a critical step in becoming whole again.

For ten years, from ages five to fifteen, a patient named Kate was sexually molested by her stepfather. Now she is twenty-five and engaged to Bruce, a man who professes to care deeply for her. "I love him," she told me, "but when I let him have sex with me, which isn't often, I find myself crying afterward. I don't know what's wrong with me. I get furious just thinking how screwed up I am. I don't know why I have these feelings."

I told her that I thought she does know. "You're angry because your stepfather stole your innocence," I said. "He took away your ability to respond naturally to human touch, to appreciate your body.

When you cry after sex, you appreciate, at that moment, all you've been robbed of. You see how you've been damaged through no fault of your own. You feel resentment and you also feel sad for yourself. When you cry, you let go. It's a way of holding yourself and feeling your pain—of having compassion for yourself. Please try not to be so self-critical. It's healthy, allowing yourself these feelings. It's part of the process of accepting. In time I hope you'll come to accept not just the violation but your own natural response to it."

Like Kate, most people never forget traumatic wounds. Nor should they. The mind has a mind of its own. It never forgets. And this is adaptive. From past experiences, we learn lessons, recognize the enemy, anticipate harm, and avoid it. Health comes not from exorcising painful events from our minds but from bearing witness to our pain, acknowledging its impact, commiserating with ourselves, mourning our losses, and then giving new meaning and creating new connections with people—including, perhaps, the offender.

Step #2: You give up your need for revenge but continue to seek a just resolution.

When somebody deliberately wrongs you, it's not unusual to want to inflict on him the pain he inflicted on you. But you should remind yourself that what usually brings lasting satisfaction is not hurting someone but having your own hurt understood and validated. And that's unlikely to come from a recalcitrant offender, no matter how brutally you punish him.

Retribution is also bound to provoke the offender and set up an endless cycle of reprisals and counter-reprisals, with escalating bitterness and violence. Your mind is likely to become a battleground, overrun with fruitless fantasies of revenge that block you from living your life in ways that generate pleasure or meaning.

With Acceptance, you learn to let go of this reflexive white rage—this blind need to wound or get even. You realize that though revenge may give voice to your pain, it will not douse your inflamed thoughts or feelings, or restore your place in the world. In the end, you'll find that your wound remains unhealed, and that stoking your anger has brought neither peace nor resolution.

The goal of revenge is to crucify the offender. The goal of Acceptance is to resurrect your best self. Revenge is other-directed; Acceptance is inner-directed. When you contain your obsessions, the offender becomes less important to you than *you* are to you. Getting back or getting even becomes less important than getting well.

Keep in mind that when you accept someone, you don't necessarily relinquish your need for justice or just punishment. Deciding to accept a partner who cheated on you or divorced you for your best friend doesn't stop you from seeking legal recourse—hiring a competent attorney and going for the best financial and child custody settlement you can get. Acceptance doesn't demand that you seek justice or restitution, but it doesn't preclude those options either. In the final analysis, the critical issue is not whether the offender gets his due but whether you free yourself from your emotional dependence on him and move beyond his transgression. It may help to take Nietzsche's advice and reduce the offender to such insignificance that you have no need to waste energy on him.[4]

When Mary, a middle-aged fiction editor, discovered through E-mails that her husband was sleeping with a neighbor's wife, she decided to let everyone know—including the neighbor's kids. She called and left a message on their answering machine: "Hi, kids. Do you know your mother is a whore?"

"Why shouldn't I destroy her family the way she destroyed mine?" Mary asked me. It was a very understandable human response. The problem was that it violated Mary's moral code and did nothing to ease her pain. She felt shamed twice—once by her husband and once by herself.

"I knew it was the wrong decision," she told me later, "because it made my skin crawl."

Like Mary, you may want to settle scores, but I recommend that you first ask yourself:

- In the end, what am I after? Do I want the offender to feel my pain? If I hurt him back, how will I benefit? Are there ways other than retribution that will get me what I want?
- Ultimately, does it matter what happens to this person who violated me, so long as I restore my self-esteem and my capacity to live a good life? What response will best help me recapture my dignity, my self-respect, my sense of control over the world?
- If he refuses to acknowledge my pain, where else can I go for comfort and support?

There is no single or best way to respond to a violation, so I encourage you to slow down until you find a solution that honors your principles and dignifies your pain. I also suggest that you balance your quest for revenge against your quest for personal healing. Your sense of power and protection is likely to come less from acts of retribution than from feelings of wholeness and safety. Your goal is to feel less scared, less scarred, more in control. If you want your life back, you need to take care not to become so focused on punishing the offender that you ignore how this process punishes you.

Step #3: You stop obsessing about the injury and reengage with life.

Obsessions are dominating, intrusive, repetitive thoughts that cause distress and compromise the quality of our lives. If you're struggling to contain them, you might ask yourself, "What purpose are they serving? I've re-lived what happened a thousand times; if I re-live it another thousand times will I be any happier or less tangled inside? I'll never have this moment again—is this how I want to spend it?"

What you're likely to discover is that your obsessions trap you inside your own head and distract you from the business of living. They impair your health and mood, raising your blood pressure and heart rate and increasing your feelings of anxiety, anger, and depression. They also reinforce a narrow, perhaps warped perspective on what happened, making it difficult for you to understand or accept it.

With Acceptance you make a conscious decision to break loose from your nagging thoughts and reclaim the energy you've spent on feeling betrayed—to dismantle your rage and reach out to life again. With Acceptance, you refuse to be infected with shame or resentment. Your personal well-being becomes paramount. You come to like yourself more than you hate him.

If you're having too many conversations with yourself, you're probably not having enough conversations with the person you should be talking to—the one who hurt you. But if he can't or won't hear your pain, you can rein in your obsessions without him. I'll discuss how to do this in the exercises below.

It's important not to confuse the act of letting go of your unproductive ruminations with the idea that the injury doesn't matter. When you work to curb your obsessions, you affirm the impact of the injury, but you also affirm your commitment to health. You don't necessarily replace negative feelings with positive feelings, but you do refuse to dwell on negative feelings or let them dominate you.

Here are some concrete strategies for controlling or limiting your obsessive thinking:

- *Challenging your negative thoughts.* One way to break free of negative thoughts is to confront them head on and actively talk back to any that are mistaken or maladaptive. This is what a patient named Diane did after her dinner plans with her close friend Marie fell through. The day before the dinner Diane left a message on Marie's answering machine, asking her where she would like to meet. Marie replied with a message of her own: "I'm really sorry, but I can't make it tomorrow. I'm helping my son fill out his college applications—we've got three weeks left before they're due—and I'm totally overwhelmed. Let's make another plan next month." Charted below are Diane's negative thoughts, how they made her feel, and how she tried to respond more constructively.

Negative Thought	The Feeling It Produced	A Constructive Response
She doesn't value my friendship.	Hurt, shame	I'm taking Marie's rejection personally and jumping to conclusions. She told me when we made the plan that she might not be able to keep it because of all the pressures in her life. She has trouble doing things for herself and feels responsible to her son. She's always been friendly and warm in the past.
I shouldn't have to call her to find out she has no intention of meeting me.	Anger, hurt	This is a "should" statement; it is my idea about how relationships should work, not necessarily about what's right or real. This thinking could cut me off from a good friend. I can talk this out with her.

This exercise helped Diane correct her dysfunctional ideas[5] and put them to rest. It may help you, too.

- *Questioning your habitual response to injury.* You may be responding to this injury in ways that are typical of you—ways that say more about your pattern of response to violation in general than about what the offender actually did, or meant to do, to you. I encourage you to ask yourself, "Do I tend to have an obsessive style of thinking? If I weren't stewing about this offense, would I be stewing about another? Am I replaying the details not just because I was so badly hurt but because I'm mentally trapped in my pain and don't know how to let it go?"

- *Medication.* Certain medications clear your head, help you concentrate, and reduce your irritability and depression. They may also help you sleep so that you can be more functional and resourceful during the day. The depletion of certain chemicals in the brain is known to translate into obsessive thinking, so you may get relief from medications that restore this chemical imbalance. Psychiatrist Laurence Lorefice recommends a group of SSRI's (selective serotonin reuptake inhibitors such as Prozac, Zoloft, and Paxil) which often help to diminish obsessional thinking.[6]

  You should know that medication is not meant to take away your pain or give you a deceptive sense of happiness or benevolence, but rather to stabilize you and allow you to respond to the injury in a healthier, more balanced way. You can ask your internist for a prescription or consult a psychiatrist, particularly one who specializes in psychopharmacology.

- *Distraction.* Instead of remaining trapped in your own head, you can open up your senses and actively turn your focus outward to what is happening in the world around you. You might see two people interacting in a restaurant, for example, and entertain yourself by imagining their conversation. You might divert yourself by playing a game like Scrabble, taking up a musical instrument, or reading aloud to a child. The point is to take part in activities that lift you above painful thoughts and memories and give you a renewed sense of control, pleasure, and well-being.

- *Thought Stopping.* This is another technique for actively interrupting your obsessive cycle. You may be driving along when suddenly you realize that you've wasted the last fifteen minutes reliving some upsetting incident from the past. With Thought Stopping, you ask yourself, "Am I figuring something out for the first time? Am I solving a problem?" If you find that you're only recycling old material that brings back bad feelings and accomplishes nothing, try directing your attention elsewhere. Some of you may find it helpful to tell yourself, in the gentle, compassionate voice of a friend, "Stop! Give me your hand. We're out of here. What else could we focus on that would be more interesting or uplifting?"

- *Social support.* Obsessive thinking takes place in the privacy of the mind. It's terribly isolating. To get outside, you might seek the company of caring friends who can provide positive feedback and remind you that you're not as worthless or contemptible as the offender made you feel. Even if you think you're too self-absorbed to be good company, you should push yourself toward people who help you feel better about the world and about yourself. There's enormous healing power in being listened to, in having your pain held and validated. The offender may not be willing to reach out to you, but others may—others who can honor your truth and goodness by embracing your pain.

- *Normalizing your response.* It helps to know that your obsessions may be adaptive—that there's nothing shameful or crazy about your preoccupation with the offense. "What's wrong with me?" you may ask. "Why can't I move on?" You may feel that your mind is under siege, that an enemy has taken up residence in your brain and you have no way to dislodge him. What you need to remind yourself is that obsessive ruminations about a traumatic event are commonplace. Knowing that you shouldn't be doing better may help you to accept yourself, feel more normal, and put the injury to rest—on your own timetable.

- *Relaxation, visualization, and meditation.* Another way to control your obsessions and achieve stasis (equilibrium) is to slow down your breathing, relax your muscles, and fill your mind with peaceful thoughts or images. These techniques are described in several excellent books, including *The Relaxation Response* by Herbert Benson, *Forgiveness: A Bold Choice for a Peaceful Heart* by Robin Casarjian, and *Chi Fitness: A Workout for Body, Mind, and Spirit* by Sue Benton and Drew Denbaum. In *Wherever You Go There You Are,* Jon Kabat-Zinn teaches Buddhist exercises that awaken the mind to the present moment and deepen "your capacity to dwell in stillness."[7]

- *Stimulus control.* With this technique, you allow yourself to obsess, but you set limits on where, when, and for how long. During the time allotted, you go at it, full tilt. At the designated moment, however, you pull yourself together and turn your attention elsewhere—but not before asking, "How productive, how satisfying were these ruminations?" You may find that your time would have been better spent focused on the present, not the past.

- *Self-care.* One way to cut through your obsessions is with a program of self-care. As the saying goes, "Living well is the best revenge." Ask yourself, "How can I make myself feel cared for and whole?" Activities might include getting into therapy, connecting with friends, going back to school, exercising, praying—anything that makes you feel valued, empowered, steady, competent, happy, and proud.

Step #4: You protect yourself from further abuse.

Accepting someone who is physically threatening doesn't mean you have to open yourself to further abuse. In fact, the process of Acceptance urges you to take precautions to ensure your safety, and to set up physical barriers if necessary—changing routines so that you and the offender don't cross paths, switching jobs, moving out of your house or town, even obtaining restraining orders to keep him out of your physical space.

Acceptance, as we know, does not necessarily mean reconciliation. You can accept someone and ban him from your life.

When You Forgive Too Easily

With Cheap Forgiveness, your fear of rejection takes precedence over your need for protection, and you fail to cushion yourself from future harm, physically or emotionally. To demonstrate your humanity and smooth out the conflict, you sidestep such basic questions as, "Is this person healthy for me?" "Should I trust him with my well-being?" "What makes me think that someone who hurt me once won't hurt me again?" If you need to restore the connection at any price, you can't afford to process your feelings or look too clearly at the offender or at the offense.

Like the psychotherapist Karen Olio, I take issue with the author of *I Can't Talk About It: A Child's Book About Sexual Abuse*,[8] who insists that a child must forgive her unapologetic father for sexually molesting her. Olio argues that survivors "who already must struggle with the feelings of self-blame caused by the abuse" are effectively re-traumatized when they are made to feel guilty or deficient for not being able to forgive.[9]

This was Sandy's problem. She grew up with a father who battered her and a mother who raged. Her parents divorced when she was nine. The man she married, Ed, tended to keep things inside, then explode, just as his own father had done. He threw plates. He made scenes. When he punched his hand through a screen door, she cringed. Would she be next?

Sandy wanted nothing more than to keep her family together, but she also needed to provide a safe haven for herself and her autistic son. She knew firsthand the danger of living with violence, but she loved Ed and learned to gloss over the truth about him—to make peace and get along.

One night she called me in a panic. "Ed just slapped our son," she blurted out. "Ed yelled at him to put his pajamas on and get ready for bed, and I guess he didn't 'snap to' fast enough. I'm scared. But maybe I'm making too much of this."

Sandy was bad at feeling anger. It frightened her. But splintering her family frightened her more. I advised her to be careful. "If you ignore what's going on, you could put yourself and your son at serious risk," I warned her.

Eventually, Sandy stopped questioning her right to protect herself and her child. She saw that she was contributing to the problem by making excuses for Ed and discounting the threat of danger. Ed had many lovable qualities, but she could never feel safe with him. "I don't know where it's going to end up," she told me, "but in the meantime I've contacted an attorney and gotten an injunction barring him from the house."

When You Refuse to Forgive

When you say no to forgiving and fail to resolve the wrongs of the past, your wound continues to bleed and may infect your relationship with others. If, for example, you cut yourself off from a cold, uncaring parent and never come to terms with your pain, you may project your "emotional sensitivities and yearnings"[10] onto your children, unconsciously burdening them with your unmet need for validation, and causing them, in turn, to feel unsafe with you. You risk imposing on the next generation a "revolving slate of injustices."[11]

Step #5: You frame the offender's behavior in terms of his own personal struggles.

Your journey into the heart and mind of the offender doesn't excuse his behavior, but it may free you from the mistaken assumption that you caused or deserved it. When you accept someone, you remind yourself that, yes, this person did something *to* you, but what he did was not necessarily *about* you.

When Gloria Steinem spoke at a private girls' school in Connecticut, the young interviewer admitted that she had never heard of the well-known feminist. Asked whether she was insulted, Steinem replied, "It's not important whether she knows who *I* am, so long as she knows who *she* is."[12] Bless the self-possessed Steinem, who reminds us not to let others dictate how we feel about ourselves.

Replacing Shame with Empathy

As you trace the offender's story and see how he was damaged, and how he subjected you to the same abuse or neglect he may have experienced himself, you begin to understand why he acted the way he did. You realize that he was born with a deck of cards, that over time he was dealt a few more, and that today he is playing out his hand with you. If you weren't there, he might be playing the same hand with someone else. The more you know about him as a person distinct from you, the less likely you are to take his behavior personally. And the less personally you take his behavior, the less likely you are to experience shame.

Shame comes when you think that his behavior is about you—about your unworthiness, your defectiveness, your unlovability. Shame lifts when you realize that his behavior is about *him*—his innate disposition, his traumatic experiences, his responses to life's stress. You may not have access to this information about him, but in order for you to fight shame, it helps to come up with some hypotheses. This chapter will help you develop them.

Stepping back and seeing him wrestle with his own demons is likely to be a restorative, centering experience for you—one that lets you regain your equilibrium and self-esteem, become the author of your own experience, and let go of your obsessive thinking. I'm reminded of a patient named Norma whose paranoid schizophrenic mother used to beat her and her sisters. Understanding that her mother treated her so inhumanely because the mother was ill—not because Norma was trash, as her mother led her to believe—gave Norma the strength to survive and let go of her shame.

Once you understand the offender's limitations, you're likely to stop expecting more of him than he can give. No longer fighting the ghosts of his past, you can give yourself the care and love he couldn't provide. Seeing his personal history spread out before you, you can free yourself from those obsessive questions, "How could he?" "How dare he?," and understand that what he did follows seamlessly from who he is.

When you look at him clearly and honestly and see how he, too, has suffered, you may come to view him as a fellow victim. You may realize, perhaps for the first time, how deeply and irreversibly damaged he may be. No longer is he the mere perpetrator of an unforgivable act. He becomes a real person whose internal battles—whose anxieties and insecurities—triggered his hurtful behavior. Armed with this wisdom, you may be able to release yourself from his grip and walk away.

Factors Underlying His Mistreatment of You

Let's look first at those life events, those external factors, that may have upset his emotional balance at the time of the injury. You might begin by asking yourself, "What was going on in his world that affected his sense of self and made him feel so fragile, so self-absorbed, that he treated you the way he did?"

People can be harsh or insensitive because something terrible has just happened to them. I remember attending a fundraising dinner where I was introduced to a woman who seemed inexplicably cold. I later learned that her husband had just left her for a lap dancer, and she felt publicly humiliated meeting me, knowing I had written a book on infidelity.

There are countless reasons why someone might hurt you that may have absolutely nothing to do with you. One person may have been anxious or short-tempered because of financial worries—a drop in the stock market, a loss of retirement funds. Another person may have just had a fight with a sister or a lover and been too preoccupied to attend to you. Someone else may have snapped at you because he was stressed out trying to meet a deadline on a book contract or was worried about a friend who was being treated for cancer.

There are also *internal* factors to look for. Some have to do with the offender's cognitive errors—mistaken assumptions, such as "You think you're better than I am" or "You want to control me," that may have led him to misinterpret your behavior and respond inappropriately.

Another factor to consider is his personality. Is he usually shy, or sociable? Anxious or easy-going? Cranky or contented? Passive or aggressive? It's normal to see others in relation to ourselves, but the person who hurt you has a cluster of enduring attributes that were formed largely before you met, some of them biologically based, others ethnic or cultural. You can choose to take his behavior personally or not, but you're not going to change who he is and who he has always been.

A third factor to explore is his health. Was he feeling dizzy or sick? Was his behavior altered by alcohol or medications? Is he hard of hearing? Any of these extenuating factors could have affected his behavior.

What about his learned patterns of response—patterns of coping with stress that he developed in reaction to formative life experiences, usually in childhood? Seeing him in the context of his own damaged life won't necessarily make his behavior more palatable, but it may keep you from shouldering more than your fair share of blame. I invite you to read more about these coping strategies in the Appendix.

Keep in mind that Acceptance is a gift to yourself, not to the person who hurt you. It is a process you enter into primarily to free yourself from the trauma of an injury. Your goal is not necessarily to feel sorry for him, to feel compassion or pity for him, to excuse him, to develop positive feelings for him, to wish him well. It is certainly not to sugar-coat what he did to you or compromise the authenticity of your response.

I can't say this often enough: Your attempt to understand his mistreatment of you in no way frees him from responsibility for his behavior or entitles him to hurt you. Nor does it obviate your need to seek justice or a just punishment, should you believe it's warranted. Knowing what motivated him doesn't mitigate the wrong he did or make it less painful. What such knowledge may do, however, is help you respond in ways that are more proportional to the violation, less vengeful, obsessive, or apologetic. Your new insights into his behavior may also help you feel less devastated, more solidly in control of your life. But you should never confuse your willingness to understand him with the act of forgiving him.

When You Forgive Too Easily

When you forgive too easily, you're likely to be the master of extenuating circumstances, dredging up whatever you can about the offender's injured past as evidence that his behavior toward you is no fault of his own.

"He was victimized by circumstances he didn't deserve or control, so how can I hold him responsible for what he did to me?" you tell yourself, ignoring the fact that, though life may have loaded the gun, someone pulled the trigger. When you dwell on the fact that he inherited a genetic predisposition to alcohol, say, or was born with a physical disability, you fail to see that biology is not always destiny. By writing off his injurious behavior, you free him from any obligation to treat you with the same respect he's likely to expect of you.

Excusing a person's behavior because of his personal damage is pseudo-forgiveness. So is over-identifying with him, and reasoning, "We're all wounded. We're all sinners who need to be forgiven. We're all products of our upbringing. No one has it easy. Everyone has a story to tell. Who am I to judge?"

I'm not suggesting that there isn't truth and wisdom in this charitable approach to forgiveness. But compassion needs to be balanced against a full appreciation of the harm he did to you. I ask you to have as genuine a concern for yourself as for him, to care as much about how *you* have been wronged as about how *he* has been wronged. Setting these priorities will free you to consider Acceptance as an alternative to Cheap Forgiveness.

When You Refuse to Forgive

Those of you who refuse to forgive will balk, "Don't ask me to waste my time picking through someone else's garbage. Why should I care *why* he hurt me or how his parents neglected him? Is it my job to dredge up compassion for someone who has deliberately wronged me, and make excuses for his transgression? To hell with his story."

This response is understandable. When you view him as a victim, not just as a perpetrator, you risk feeling empathy and compassion for him. Seeing him in one-dimensional terms—as evil, as bad—makes it so much easier to keep your distance, feed off your self-righteous anger, and dismiss him. When you frame him in more complex ways, as a flawed human being struggling to survive his troubled past, you make it more difficult to pigeonhole or condemn him.

To those of you who are determined never to forgive, let me ask: If by learning more about the offender you come to feel compassion for him, must you feel compromised? Is there anything dangerous in deepening your understanding of him? You can be softer without feeling weak or foolish or allowing yourself to be stepped on. You can know with certainty that what he did to you was wrong, yet be touched by whatever hardships he has personally endured.

Step #6: You look honestly at your own contribution to the injury.

When we feel hurt or angry, it's easy to fault someone else. "*You're* to blame," we insist. "*You* made me feel this way." But the fact that we feel upset at someone doesn't necessarily mean he's guilty. Sometimes our rage is our own, forged in our own hearts and minds, fed by our personalities, our provocations, our exaggerated response to conflict. Yes, this other person may have done something to offend us, but perhaps not to the degree that our intense response would suggest. Our reaction may be entirely inappropriate or even dangerously misguided.

Owning up to your issues—tearing down your defenses and looking honestly at yourself—can be painful work. The process may teach you that you were more than just a victim, and that, perhaps, there is no one to forgive but yourself.

The same factors that influenced the way the offender treated you may have influenced the way you treated him. Again, some of these factors may be external. You might ask yourself, "What was going on in my world at the time of the injury that may have affected me emotionally, making me feel more vulnerable, less in control, less resilient, so that I reacted inappropriately? Did these life events throw me off-balance and lead me to act in ways that were callous or otherwise offensive?"

Internal factors may also shape your response. It helps to ask such questions as, "How did my personality affect my reaction? How did it influence the way I was treated?" If you're innately shy, say, and the offender took this personally and assumed you didn't like him, that was his mistake, not yours. You didn't hurt him; his mistaken assumptions about you hurt him. But if you're shy and didn't speak up and then felt offended that someone didn't show interest in you or respect your position, you need to confront how you contributed to your own pain. It may be that your own silence—not his behavior— set a trap for you.

What about your dysfunctional ideas about yourself and the world, ideas that may have been based on damaging early life experiences?[13] Did they play a role in your mistreatment? These fixed ideas often pre-date the offense and even your relationship with the offender, and create what I call *channels of psychological vulnerability*. What happens is that your heightened sensitivity—to being abandoned or ridiculed, for example—leads you to misperceive or misreact to events today.

How You Incite Others to Mistreat You

It's intriguing how, when we treat others according to our assumptions about ourselves and the world, we induce them to treat us in kind, creating a self-fulfilling prophecy. For example, if you believe, "Nice guys finish last; my strength is in my toughness," you may act aggressively and provoke antagonistic responses, confirming your belief that you need to be "hard" to function in this mean-spirited world.

A "hurt party" named Patrick is a case in point. He learned to fight his father's verbal and physical abuse with a combativeness of his own, a pattern that carried over into his marriage. After fending him off for seventeen years, his wife, Maggie, said "enough" and left. A year later, he called and asked her to talk out what had led to their divorce. "For my own personal growth, I'd like you to tell me how I pushed you away," he said. "If you'd like, we can do this in front of my therapist. I won't argue or defend myself. I promise just to take notes."

Maggie chose to talk on the phone. She rattled off the following list of complaints, which he transcribed and brought into therapy: "Patrick, you were intimidating, not only to me but to the kids. You didn't actually hit me, but the threat was always there. Your words can be harsh and mean. You think people owe you, and that by being tough you'll get your way. And you may, but at a huge cost to your relationships."

Patrick knew that Maggie used criticism to deflect attention from her own failings, which he believed were numerous. But by opening himself up to hear her story, he moved beyond the role of helpless victim which he had been conscripted into by his bullying father, and faced how he had driven her to reject him.

Owning Up to Your Share of the Problem

You may refuse to accept even the smallest share of ownership in what happened. You may be convinced that you've *been* wronged, not that you've *done* wrong. But the assignment of blame is rarely binary—as in, "I'm innocent, you're guilty." Injuries are more often systemic, each person's behavior ricocheting off the other's, each misstep pushing you both further toward the edge.

You're likely to want the offender to undo his damage first: "You change, and then I will," is the name of the dance. Or, "You hurt me, so you make it right, and then I'll decide if I want to warm up to you." This attitude often leads to marital meltdown, as it did for Arnold and his wife, Jill.

Arnold complained that Jill rejected him sexually. She complained that she was too exhausted for sex because he never helped with the kids. Both felt angry, hurt, and sanctimonious. What Arnold needed to understand was that for Jill, as for many women, sexual intimacy is inseparable from emotional intimacy and must be cultivated outside the bedroom. His giving the kids a bath would have romanced her. His emptying the dishwasher without being asked would have lubricated her libido. Until he helped out more,

Jill was going to shut down. She in turn needed to see that if she embraced Arnold sexually, she would make him feel wanted and would kindle in him a willingness to pitch in more around the house.

When you're locked in confrontation, you can easily get caught up in the moment and in your own self-serving version of the truth. For a more honest look at yourself, you need to step back and observe what you may have done to trigger the offender's objectionable behavior.

This is exactly what Martha needed to do to salvage her relationship with her twenty-seven-year-old son. She constantly grumbled that he never called her or sought her company. What she failed to see was that every time they got together, she assaulted him with questions on the very topics he felt most anxious and inadequate about—his dating situation and his job. The more silent he became, the more advice she gave, until, guess what?—he turned away and found excuses not to meet. Caught in her own hurt, she was unable to see how she pushed him away.

Challenging Your "Official Story"[14]

Why is facing our own issues so challenging at times? Why is it so hard to admit culpability, not just to the person we hurt but to ourselves? One reason is that it forces us to contradict our "official story." This is our personal, predigested take on the truth that protects us from knowing what we fear or despise in ourselves.

"Perhaps the most universal form of solace for the frailties we need to deny," writes clinical psychologist Robert Karen in *The Forgiving Self,* is "the stories we tell ourselves about our lives. We soothe ourselves, consciously and unconsciously, with fairy tales tinged with grandiosity that leave us feeling less vulnerable than we really are."[15]

An example of an official story might be your view of yourself as a great parent, certainly better than your parents ever were to you. Perhaps your father worked incessantly and rarely gave you the attention you craved. Now, as an adult, you consider yourself more empathic, more available than he ever was. But then one day your twenty-year-old son gets furious at you and calls you selfish, the most selfish person he has ever known, and suddenly you're forced to choose sides—his or yours. You may want to blame him for grossly distorting the truth, for being so remarkably unappreciative—and you may be right, to some degree. But you also may be disavowing another piece of the truth: that perhaps you haven't been there for him as reliably as you would like to believe you were, that perhaps you, too, have been self-involved and neglectful. Hit with the unvarnished truth, your precious core belief about yourself is likely to crumble.

How dare you make me confront the ugly truth about myself?

A child isn't the only one who may threaten your fantasies about yourself. A partner may, too. You may think of yourself as a very attractive mate—a great catch—then, suddenly, he leaves you for someone else. For years you told yourself you weren't happy and should move on. But now he has left you, and you somehow have to absorb that reality. It challenges your official story of yourself as the deprived, neglected one. You want to blame him for his selfishness and his weak, unsteady character. But now he tells you he's leaving because you make him feel invisible. Suddenly, you're experiencing the sense of abandonment you felt as a child. You hate this person for dredging up those painful moments buried in your past. But is there some truth in his accusations? Could it be that because of what happened to you as a child, you never fully committed yourself to him and injured him in ways in which you felt injured? Is there a powerful lesson here, and are you willing to open yourself up to learn it?

The person you accuse of hurting you is sometimes guilty of nothing more than bearing witness to your faults and vulnerabilities. You're likely to feel assaulted by him, but you might at the same time feel grateful for the insights he forces you to confront—insights into how you were hurt in the past and how you continue to get hurt today.

When Karen writes, "To mourn is to love again,"[16] I take this to mean that when we look at ourselves unflinchingly and face our imperfect selves, we open ourselves to the possibility of healing.

Mourning the injuries of the past frees us to love again and to give others what no one gave us.

Questioning Your "I Am an Abused Person" Story

One of the most difficult "official" stories to go back and rewrite is the "I am an abused person" story. As the injured party, you fancy yourself the victim, pure and simple. You excel at recalling all the ways you were harmed over your lifetime, all the people who exploited you, denigrated you, let you down. What you may fail to see is that you feel abused too easily. You resent too freely. You twist the truth and imagine that someone meant to harm you when no one did.

What gives rise to this "official" response? It could an inborn tendency to be negative or passive. It could be a cognitive error such as "personalization" (you assume someone meant to hurt you when he had no such intent). Or it could be your early life experiences, which taught you that people will betray you. Whatever the source, you end up feeling chronically and pervasively abused—"a feeling," psychoanalyst Karen Horney says, "which in its extent and intensity goes beyond, and is out of proportion to, actual provocations and may become a way of experiencing life."[17]

Embracing your "official story" of abuse lets you:

- see yourself as good, right, fair, and virtuous;
- disavow the destructive impact your behavior has on others;
- hold others responsible for whatever goes wrong in your life; and
- hide behind a veil of oppression when it's you who fail to protect or promote yourself.

Questioning your "official story" is a daunting business because of what it may reveal about you. But it can also bring rewards, helping you to:

- clarify what happened—untangle who did what to whom;
- sort out your feelings about the offense and the offender;

- decide what you want to correct in yourself that would foster more authentic, gratifying interactions; and
- transcend the traumatic effects of your childhood.

The challenge is to face your flaws honestly while still having compassion for yourself—still liking, even forgiving, yourself.

Step #7: You challenge your false assumptions about what happened.

We all give meaning to the drama of our lives. Unfortunately, we don't always distinguish our version of the truth from what really went on. Identifying distortions in our thinking—separating the facts from what they signify to us—is a critical part of the Acceptance process. It requires much hard work—much self-scrutiny, much information-crunching—but it will help you respond with greater objectivity and ease your anger or pain.

Here are a few of our most common cognitive errors.

Dichotomous Thinking

This cognitive error is also known as "all-or-nothing" or "black-and-white" thinking. Here you tend to view others in terms of rigid, polarized categories: You're perfect or horrible. You're right or wrong. You're good or bad. Cataloging someone in this way fails, of course, to do justice to his complexity. An overly critical portrait leads to character assassination and reinforces your decision not to forgive. An overly positive portrait leads to idealization and reinforces your decision to forgive at any price.

Mind Reading

When you engage in mind reading, you assume, often incorrectly, that you know what the other person is thinking. Marsha's response to her husband, Dave, is typical. After he ended his affair, the couple entered therapy to rebuild their marriage. One day Marsha found an old photo of them taken at a family picnic. "How happy we look," she said, nostalgically. She waited for Dave's reply, but he said nothing.

Later, when Marsha and I were alone, she said, "He's angry at me for bringing up the affair again. But what does he expect? He's got to know that for every time I bring it up, I must think about it a hundred times. Why can't he be patient with me? Does he think I'm made of iron? He's probably still in love with that other woman."

The truth was that Dave wanted nothing more than to restore his wife's faith in him. He had said nothing not because of the reasons Marsha conjured up, but because he was overwhelmed with guilt. "I hate myself," he told me. "I destroyed her trust in me and much of the joy we once shared. I feel evil."

Marsha misinterpreted Dave's silence, and her false assumption significantly altered her response to him. I suggested she ask herself, "Am I misreading what he's thinking and feeling? What do I know, and what do I only assume? Can I check out my ideas by saying to him, 'You seem annoyed, upset. I'm wondering what you're thinking'?"

Like Marsha, you need to get the facts straight and not fill in the blanks with your own homemade assumptions. Before you can respond fairly to the offender, you need to examine whether your ideas say more about you than they say about him.

Overgeneralization

When you overgeneralize, you make too much of a single detail and get caught in the belief that "he always does this; he never does that."

Jill's response to her husband, Dean, is illustrative. She was irked when he chose to finish up a mailing for a charitable organization and missed the awards ceremony for their daughter's swim team. "I've got to question whether I'm married to the right guy," she told me. "We seem to have completely different values. I want a spouse who cares about his family and enjoys being part of it. Dean's always busy when I need him."

Jill's emphasis on this one particular offense prevented her from seeing the bigger picture—that her husband coached their daughters' field hockey teams, attended parent-teacher conferences, and regularly helped the girls with their homework. Her relationship to

Dean became hostage to a single negative memory. To gain objectivity, she needed to ask herself, "Am I seeing this one moment in the context of our whole life together, or am I isolating it and drawing sweeping conclusions?"

With Acceptance, you consider all the data, not just those facts that prove your point but also those that contradict it. You also look at the whole person, not just at his flaws or virtues. You may decide that his behavior toward you is so egregious that it wipes out anything good about him. Or you may decide the reverse. Whatever you conclude, you'll make a wiser, more self-interested decision if you view the full person, not a single act.

Personalization

Personalization is when you see someone's behavior only in terms of yourself and ignore all other explanations—explanations that might leave you feeling more neutral and less scarred.

When you personalize, you put yourself at the center of the universe, so to speak, and act as though all things revolve around you. The truth may be that you're not quite so important to the offender, and that you're flattering yourself to think you're the sole target of his anger or scorn.

I saw personalization in action one day when I walked into an upscale boutique on Madison Avenue, dressed for theater. A salesperson approached and asked if she could help. I told her no thanks, I'd like to look around, and she walked away. Another woman, standing close by, turned to me and complained, "I guess I'm not worth being waited on."

There was no way to know whether the woman was a serious shopper or whether the salesperson had even seen her; if the salesperson had, my guess is that she would have been delighted to earn a commission on anyone who came through the door. What was clear was that the woman had applied her own personal meaning to an ambiguous situation and created unnecessary emotional distress for herself. It's possible, of course, that the salesperson *did* think the customer wasn't worth her time, but if so, the customer would have to question why the salesperson—someone she didn't know and probably would never see again—mattered so much to her.

Jumping to Conclusions

Here you make assumptions about an injury without getting the full story, and wound yourself unnecessarily. Faced with vague or incomplete data, you fill in the gaps and respond to issues of your own making.

When the World Trade Center was attacked, Sally and Max were traveling in Europe. For what felt like an eternity, they didn't know the whereabouts of their daughter, who lived in lower Manhattan. As they raced back to their hotel, hoping to find a message, Max launched into a tirade on how the disaster would ruin the economy and undermine the dollar. Sally told me, "I felt sick listening to him. Who was this unfeeling monster? How could he care so little for our child?"

Max explained later, "I saw Sally flipping out. There was nothing we could do until we reached the hotel, so I just tried to fill the air with conversation. I must have sounded ridiculous, but the truth is, I was in a state of shock myself."

As Sally learned, you can't respond to an injury in a constructive way unless you know the "offender's" intentions. The process of Acceptance asks you to look for various plausible, less hurtful explanations and not jump to easy conclusions.

"Should" Statements

Your response to the offender's behavior will be deeply affected by your rules about how people should act, what you expect of them, and what you believe is right for the world. Aaron Beck refers to these as "should statements."[18] Albert Ellis refers to them as "musterbations"[19]—the *musts* and *ought to's* which we impose on others and on ourselves. Fred Luskin calls them our "unenforceable rules."[20] Judith Beck calls them "imperatives." "You have a precise, fixed idea of how you or others should behave," she writes, "and you overestimate how bad it is that these expectations are not met."[21]

"Should" statements include: My mother should be able to provide emotional comfort for me when I need her. My father should take interest in my sports and attend my games. My son should thank me for all the things I buy him. My daughter should want me to be highly involved in her wedding plans. My daughter-in-law should spend as many holidays with us as she does with her family. My boss should realize how hard I work and fight to get me a raise. My brother should spend more time with our elderly parents. My sister should call me on my birthday. My neighbors should keep their animals on their own property and see the reasonableness of my argument.

Most "should" statements are a set up for disappointment because they ask people to deliver more than they have to give. When someone fails to meet your exacting standards, you're likely to feel bruised and self-righteously blaming—pointing a finger at him rather than at your own unrealistic expectations.

To correct this tendency, you need to recognize that your rules are exactly that—*your* rules, not necessarily anyone else's. They represent your morality, your needs, your values. The rest of the world is not required to go along. When you insist that people should be different from the way they are, you're bound to cause yourself frustration and anguish.

Albert Ellis, founder of Rational Emotive Therapy, was once asked, "How do people plagiarize your work without the slightest compunction? How do they feel so comfortable stealing your ideas without referencing you?" His response was vintage Ellis: "Eee . . . asily!" If only more of us could be like Ellis, a man without "shoulds" who substitutes humor for indignation and accepts people for who they are, not who he wants them to be.

In his provocative book *Man's Search for Meaning*, Viktor Frankl suggests an existential response to the world's injustices. A Holocaust survivor, he argues that we cannot dictate how people treat us, but we can control how we choose to react to their treatment of us. This may be our only freedom, but it's a profoundly important one, for it helps us to maintain a sense of mastery in a chaotic world.

The point to remember is that your pain or sorrow may come

not from someone else's behavior but from your own attitudes and beliefs. Would you get less hurt, then, if you expected less? That's obvious. When you insist that someone be just so and don't allow for a range of human responses, you're more likely to experience him as inadequate, even despicable, and feel cheated. If you can convert a demand into a wish and learn to distinguish what you think you need from what you merely hope for, you may end up feeling less rattled by others when they fall short.

Correcting Your Cognitive Errors

To cut through your cognitive errors, it helps to speak to the offender and consider what he has to say. You don't need his input to accept him, but if he's willing to talk, and not abusive or blindly self-righteous, why not hear him out? You may find that your pain is grounded in a misunderstanding, and that there's nothing to repair and nothing to accept or forgive.

In "A Boy Named Sue," a song with lyrics by Shel Silverstein, Johnny Cash tells the story of a boy who spent his life nursing a false assumption: that his father named him Sue to make his life miserable. Vowing revenge, the boy hunts down his vagrant father and knocks him to the ground.

The father explains himself, saying that he called the boy Sue not for any malicious reason, but to make him tough so he could survive in a mean world. The truth is an awakening for the son and drains away his years of bitterness. He throws down his gun and embraces his father, but not before swearing that if he ever has a son, he'll name him Bill or George—anything but Sue.

The lyrics of this song are sheer fun, but they teach a profound lesson about human interactions—that we get hurt at times because our assumptions about others are dead wrong. Confronting his father with his pain, Sue stumbled on the man's true intentions and got to see him as a real person, not as the "dirty, mangy dog" he thought him to be.

Like Sue, we often lock our interpersonal injuries away in deep storage for years, only to find out they were based on misunderstandings that could have been straightened out in a heartbeat. Too bad Sue didn't talk to his father sooner.

An Exercise to Correct Your Negative Thoughts

To check out whether your ideas are valid and useful, write out your "automatic thoughts"[22] about what happened. Let yourself get into your anger or hurt. Don't try to think rationally or calmly. Don't edit. Then, taking each idea separately, ask yourself:

1. Is this idea true? What cognitive error might I be making?
2. Is this idea useful? What feelings and behaviors does it generate in me?
3. Is this idea typical of the way I think? What's my pattern?
4. Do I need more information about what happened? Where can I get it?

Here's how a patient named Sandy challenged her unproductive thoughts.

One day when she returned home from work, she was furious to find an unsightly pile of used pipes on her immaculate lawn. The man who had replaced the underground drains had finished his job and failed to take them away. Steaming, Sandy called and left a message for him to remove them immediately. A day passed. Then another. Sandy called twice more, to no avail. To gain control of her response, she tried the following exercise. First she wrote down her automatic thoughts: "What a sleaze ball. I can't believe he'd try to get away with this. It was so stupid of me, paying him before I checked out his work. You can't trust anyone today."

She then talked back to these ideas:

1. My cognitive errors are dichotomous thinking, jumping to conclusions, and overgeneralization. "Maybe something happened that I don't understand. I've hired this man before, and he's always been reliable and decent."
2. My ideas aren't useful. They make me feel taken advantage of,

vindictive, betrayed, stupid. They solve nothing. They make me want to strike back.
3. My ideas are typical of me. I distrust people and assume the worst about them. This is an attribute I probably picked up from my mother, who always thought people were ripping her off.
4. I can call him one more time and appeal to his decency.

Sandy took her own advice and left a strong but conciliatory message. "I don't understand what happened," she said. "You've always done such good work and been true to your word. Please call and explain why you're not returning my calls."

The next day she heard from him. "I'm sorry," he explained. "I was out of town and didn't check my messages. I left the pipes because I thought you'd want to show them to the person who installed your sprinkler system. He ruined them. Of course I'll come and pick them up."

Sandy hung up, having been reminded of something all of us should keep in mind—the value of checking out our assumptions so that we don't unnecessarily injure ourselves and others.

Step # 8: You look at the offender apart from his offense, weighing the good against the bad.

When somebody hurts you, it's normal to have negative feelings about him. With Acceptance, you honor these feelings, but you also try to separate the offender from the offense and view his behavior in the context of your relationship. You don't just look at the moment when you were mistreated; you look at all the moments you've shared, weighing the good against the bad. The process demands that you be true to your memories, not letting one obliterate the rest. Of course, this is possible only when the two of you have a shared history. Without one, you have nothing to respond to but the injury.

When he has been good to you in the past, and you have experienced his kindness first-hand, you're likely to feel less critical and condemning. But if he has been good to others but not to you, why should you care? If your mother is mean to you, will it matter that she's sweet to your brother? The offender may have likable attributes, but if you've never enjoyed or profited from them, they're unlikely to soften your response to him. In fact, knowing he has a benevolent side reserved for others may only fuel your anger and heighten your sense of injustice.

Acceptance doesn't require you to feel any particular way toward the offender. It asks only that you try to see him objectively. It also asks you to be on guard against the propensity to think in absolutes—to see only the negative in him if he has been good to you, or to shut out everything but the good if he has harmed you. As the Austrian-British analyst Melanie Klein points out, it's natural for us to want to split the world into opposing camps—good and evil, right and wrong. Unable to hold an "ambivalent view,"[23] we demonize or deify people. Choosing sides feeds the illusion that we see things more clearly, but the opposite may be true.

For most of his adult life, John resented his mother for being cold and unnurturing. "I don't remember her ever hugging me, even when I was a kid," he told me. "When my best friend died, you'd think she would have comforted me, but she kept her distance."

John went on feeling deprived and resentful long after his mother's death, not realizing that his memory of her captured only part of the story. I encouraged him to make one list of the qualities in her he disliked, and another of those he liked. One list reinforced his image of her as tough and unfeeling. The other showed that she had loved him unconditionally, had supported him in his search for himself, had challenged him intellectually, and had been there for him in times of sickness and celebration.

Weighing the lists against each other, John was able to see his mother in a more complex, multi-dimensional light. Freed from his fixation on her shortcomings, he could process all that she had meant to him. "She was never very good in the physical affection department," he told me wistfully. "But I believe she still loved me in her own way."

Listing someone's positive and negative qualities can be a

relationship-enhancing exercise for you, as it was for John. It could also draw you further apart. Wherever the process leads is fine. The purpose is not necessarily to undo the damage but to respond to it in a controlled and thoughtful way, without minimizing or exaggerating its seriousness.

It may be informative to interview others who know, or knew, the offender in a different light and can offer evidence that challenges the way you view him. You may ask yourself, "Why bother? He hurt me and isn't worth another second of my time." But if you want to fight your obsessions and continue the relationship—if you want a reality check and are curious to know more—why wouldn't you consult others for their insights?

This is what Mike did. He had always viewed his mother in negative terms—"She dressed in high heels and a girdle," he told me dismissively. "She hated grass and rain. When the 'girls' came over for canasta, she brought me out and showed me off to her friends like I was some sort of diamond brooch, or a new dress from Saks."

Mike was in his second marriage and on the far edge of middle age when he met his aunt—his mother's sister—at a family wedding and asked her to share her memories of his mother, who had died many years before. What began as table talk with a relative turned into a corrective experience that led to Acceptance.

"Yes, she showed you off to her friends," his aunt recalled, "but you *did* excel, and she was very proud of you. She wasn't big on the outdoors, like you—she wouldn't have been caught dead in sneakers and probably never even heard of L. L. Bean. But she wasn't afraid of life either. She went to college before most women considered applying, and she graduated in three years. She traveled to Europe with your father and loved seeing new sights. She headed charitable organizations, ran her own business, and had many loyal friends. She took delight in you and your accomplishments, and encouraged you to find yourself. True?"

Mike nodded yes. Like many of us, he had been committed to a biased version of the truth, playing up what he disliked in his mother and dismissing what he liked. He now began to question why he had viewed her so narrowly. It wasn't that his portrait of her was wrong, he realized, but that it was selective and biased, and cut out so much of what was wonderful in her—not just in his aunt's eyes, but in his own.

Continue to Weigh the Good and the Bad.

Acceptance is an ongoing process. Over time, a crisis or a change in circumstances may bring out qualities in the offender that were masked or undeveloped, and make you see him in a different light. You, too, may change and grow. This was what happened with me. The corrective experience was death—the death of my mother.

Throughout my life, she was critical and difficult to please. When I told her about a vacation I was planning, she responded, "It's ridiculous, how you spend money." When I told her about the Ph.D. programs I was planning to apply to, her only comment was, "I don't know why you work so hard."

At the end of her life, however, as she lay in the hospital dying of lung cancer, she changed. Frail and dependent, she stopped competing with me. And I suppose that I, too, laid down my arms. She let me be there for her, feeding her and wiping her on the toilet. She clung to me when she tried to stand. She thanked me. I felt appreciated. The nature of our relationship changed. I became the good daughter I had always wanted to be. Perhaps she became the loving, supportive mother she had always wanted to be.

Shortly after her death, I began questioning my aunts about her, and I realized that emotional support was a luxury she had never experienced as a child—her parents had been too busy struggling to make ends meet. Her father was up at three each morning and on his way to lower Manhattan to buy produce for their grocery store. Her mother, who spoke Yiddish at home, worked a sixteen-hour day, running the store and feeding a family of five. Conversations were brief and to the point. Loving had to do with providing, feeding, clothing. Emotional support? I don't believe my mother understood what this meant. When she talked, she spoke without filters or censors. She wasn't exactly delicate in her choice of words or sensitive to their impact. She was blunt and lacked interpersonal skills—what we call emotional intelligence today.

Over time I've come to understand my mother's toughness in the context of her life experience and to accept that she was unable to expose her softer side—until the end. I appreciate now that she tried her best, working hard to send me to the best camps, the best schools, while running the family business, a fabric store. In some important ways she wasn't there for me. She couldn't comfort me or encourage me. She seldom made me feel that she took delight in me. But she wasn't nasty or mean-spirited either, and her heart was often in the right place. When I think of her, I like to remember those occasions when she greeted me warmly. Because she never apologized for being so hard on me and never seemed to understand or care how insufficient she made me feel, I cannot honestly say, "I forgive you." But I can accept her, and love her, and embrace her in my memory and in my heart.

When You Refuse to Forgive

When you say no to forgiving, you define the offender in terms of the harm he caused you and exorcise all other information about him that might rehabilitate him in your eyes. You invest in hating him, and frame him in ways that support your hatred. The idea of questioning whether you're seeing him fairly strikes you as a form of surrender, an intrusion on your time. Any effort to appreciate the multiple roles he has played in your life—those that harmed you, those that enhanced you—leaves you feeling confused and vulnerable. How much simpler, it seems, to view him through the cold clarity of your anger.

There are many reasons why you may refuse to see him in a more objective and benevolent light, but here's one that may be relevant to you: *You need to see him not as he is but as you need him to be.* You define him by distinguishing him from you: *I am what you are not.* You highlight the wrong in him as a foil to your own rightness. Painting him as evil lets you see your own goodness in relief; if you had to see him more clearly, you would be forced to see yourself more clearly and to acknowledge your own deficiencies, even your own complicity.

The Offering of Collateral Gifts

In sizing up the offender—weighing his good qualities against his bad—it helps to consider what I call *the offering of collateral gifts*. These are the caring, seemingly gratuitous gestures he may make at any time after the injury, with no apparent reference to it. Wordsworth called them "little, nameless, unremembered acts of kindness and of love," and they need to be acknowledged if your evaluation of this person is going to be fair and comprehensive.

Should you see them as peace offerings? Is the offender trying to say in his own oblique way, "I'm sorry; I did wrong; I'd like to make up for it"? Or is there no connection between these gifts and the pain he caused you? You may never know, because he may never discuss the injury, never adequately acknowledge the harm he did. Yet these benevolent acts can have a powerful, positive effect on you and on your relationship.

Lisa received such a gift from her former husband, Ben, after years of estrangement. Their divorce had dragged on for years, with an ugly custody battle over their daughter. "He never showed a drop of remorse for breaking up our family and decimating my life," Lisa told me. "I was so depressed, so lost, I couldn't function. I even questioned whether the kids were better off without me."

The court finally awarded Lisa and Ben joint custody, and both remarried. Years later, while Lisa was in therapy with me, her sister lost her job, and her mother secretly went to Ben and asked for help. Ben came through, finding the sister a position in a friend's company. He never mentioned the divorce or the years of rancor. "Has he suddenly become a good guy?" Lisa asked me. "Or is this his narcissism at work again—his need to experience himself as powerful and universally loved?"

"Does it matter?" I asked.

Lisa thought it over. "I suppose not," she said, "perhaps because I love my sister more than I hate Ben. But whatever his motives, what he did for her makes me feel warmer toward him and offsets some of the damage he caused."

Ben found other ways to be generous. He paid for their daughter's housing until she could support herself. And when Lisa's frail father needed to get into a rehab facility, Ben pulled strings to get him in.

"Ben scarred me for life," Lisa told me. "But in all fairness, he also lent me a hand. At the time of our divorce, I saw him as a monster. Today I accept him as a flawed, complex man who cut me more deeply than anyone I've ever known but who also came through for me. Maybe the qualities I hate and love in him go hand in hand. The same insatiable need for love and approval that made him cheat on me may have motivated him to take care of my family when they needed him."

Ben has still never directly acknowledged his destructive behavior. Until he does, Lisa will never know whether he's aware of, or cares, how profoundly he made her suffer. She stops short of forgiving him because he has never directly addressed the injury. But his offer of collateral gifts continues to resonate with her and has gone a long way toward helping her accept him.

The Flip-Flop Factor

Using the Flip-Flop Factor to attach to someone

As Lisa discovered, the qualities you hate and love in someone may not only co-exist, they may be two sides of the same basic personality, seen from different angles. I call this phenomenon—that the qualities that attract and repel us are incontrovertibly linked and presuppose each other—the *Flip-Flop Factor*.[24] It's a concept you can put to good use when you're trying to come to terms with an injury and sort out your feelings toward the person who hurt you.

Let's say you love your husband for his playfulness and creativity, but hate the way he ducks responsibility and throws himself into the joy of the moment whenever there's work to be done. What the Flip-Flop Factor teaches you is that the same attribute that makes him so spontaneous and so much fun may also make him irresponsible, and that if you're going embrace one side of him, you need to tolerate the other.

A patient named Jane resented her husband Marc for his in-the-face opinions and his intrusive advice about everything she did. She put beef in the stew—he told her lamb would be better. She sliced the carrots—he insisted she use the food processor. To accept him, and to cushion her annoyance, she learned to ask herself, "What is it about this obnoxious trait of his that works for me? What about it do I find attractive?" What she saw was that she loved the way he doted on her and enjoyed doing everything together. Her parents had never been around to give her guidance or direction. What drew her to him from Day One was the way he lavished attention on her, making her feel noticed and cared for in a way her parents never had. Seeing his negative behavior in this positive light made her feel less personally wounded and helped her accept what she considered his shortcomings.

Using the Flip-Flop Factor to detach from someone

The Flip-Flop Factor can also help you detach from someone who injured you when all you see is his positive (flip) side.

This is how a patient named Harriet used the concept. For most of her life she idealized her father because the truth about him was too hard to bear. He had left the family for another woman when she was ten, and he was never heard from again. Forgiving him was her way of escaping the pain of his abandonment. The man she had known was a heavy drinker and a gambler, a profligate who never paid his bills, including child support. Yet her memory of him remained unsullied.

By identifying her father's positive attributes ("He loved life and good times") and matching them against his negative attributes ("He lived off the flattery of women and shirked responsibilities"), Harriet began an inward journey that put her in touch with her real feelings and helped her formulate a more balanced, authentic response to him. "I'm trying to see him as the person he is, not the person I want him to be," she told me.

You, like Harriet, do yourself a disservice when you overlook how someone failed you, forgive him too easily, and assign him qualities he never had. The Flip-Flop Factor may help not by fueling your desire for *reattachment,* but by supporting your quest for *detachment*—helping you see how the qualities you love may be intimately tied to those that destroy you.

What you hate in someone, you may also envy

The Flip-Flop Factor also teaches that what distresses you about an offender may reveal as much about your own unresolved inner conflicts as it does about him. It shows you that you may hate him for what you can't admit you hate in yourself, and that you may envy him for what you lack in yourself. These realizations won't come easily, but they'll help you see how your personal issues color your response to him.

Maggie Scarf, author of *Intimate Partners: Patterns in Love and Marriage,* writing about "the unacknowledged, repudiated, and thoroughly unintegrated aspects of one's own personality," explains the analytic concept of projection. "What was once unacceptable within the self is now what is so intolerable and unacceptable in the partner. The war within each member of the couple has been transformed into a war between them. And each believes that peace and harmony could be achieved if only the other would change."[25]

Scarf could have had a patient named Abbey and her husband, Bruce, in mind. Abbey chronically complained about him. "He lacks passion, fire, enthusiasm," she told me. "I want someone who smiles at me, who's warm and expressive and excited about life." She couldn't see that the qualities she criticized him for were related to those she envied him for, and lacked in herself.

To understand why Abbey was drawn to Bruce, we need to know that she grew up with a father who was emotionally constricted and a mother who was verbally and physically abusive. Abbey's first marriage was to a man who was, in her own words, "exceedingly handsome, dashing—a bonfire." The marriage blazed out after a year, the time it took for her to discover his infidelities. She was just as miserable with Bruce, but though a part of her hated him, another part knew exactly why she had sought him out, and understands why she stays with him today. "I deliberately chose him because I believed I'd be safe with him, and I knew he'd be a responsible, calm force in my life," she told me. "He's boring, but he's stable. When my life is steady, I have trouble remembering how important that stability is to me, but I know I can't live without it. Bruce doesn't sweep me off my feet, but he doesn't throw me to the curb either."

Abbey saw that the qualities she found insufferable in Bruce were intricately bound to the qualities she needed in him. But on a deeper level, she couldn't bear to face the fact that the qualities that drew her to him—his even temper, his basic contentment—were qualities she herself was missing. Unlike Bruce, she felt constantly distraught, empty, cheated. Making him the object of her rage, hating him for being flat and dull, protected her from facing what she lacked—the ability ever to feel content with anyone, including herself.

The Flip-Flop Factor may help you, as it helped Abbey, to think differently about your dissatisfaction. As I said in *After the Affair*, it "challenges you to view your differences in a new way, one in which you reconcile, tolerate, and perhaps, at times, embrace the bright and dark sides of your partner's personality, and your own."[26]

You can apply the Flip-Flop Factor to any relationship. Alison saw the principle at work first-hand when she and an old college friend, Susan, agreed to spend a day together in Manhattan.

Their plan was to leave in the late morning, poke around the Metropolitan Museum, have a spa lunch, and then devote an hour to Bloomingdale's. The night before, Alison's son called to say he was going to be in town the next day. Alison would have loved to see him, but she had committed herself to spending the day with Susan and said nothing. A few hours later, Susan called to say that her own son had arrived unexpectedly from college, and, since she wouldn't dream of leaving him alone at home, she had invited him to join them. Alison was fuming but said nothing. For weeks she had been looking forward to an intimate, relaxing afternoon with an old friend—having either son along would change the dynamic altogether. Trying to make the best of the situation, she called her son to see if he could join them, but it was too late. He had other plans.

The three went to the museum but never made it to Bloomingdale's. "We spent most of the day in an NBA store, looking for equipment for her son," Alison told me. "Susan wasn't a bit apologetic. It never occurred to her that she had done anything she needed to apologize for. Our relationship will never be the same."

What initially drew Alison to Susan was her friend's directness, her self-confidence, her ability to say and do what she wanted—in short, her flip side. Their disastrous day in New York showed Alison the flop side of these same attributes. She now saw her friend as self-centered and insensitive.

Alison eventually acknowledged three truths. The first was that attractive and unattractive qualities go hand in hand. The second was that the qualities she criticized in her friend were related to qualities she envied and lacked in herself. Susan was direct and assertive and made decisions unencumbered by the needs of others. Alison, in contrast, was trapped in her own head, hostage to the needs of others. Her father had died young, and she had grown up learning not to ask for much and not to trouble her overburdened mother. Silencing her voice and putting her own agenda aside were patterns that continued in her adult relationships and compromised her ability to enjoy people and negotiate conflict.

The third truth Alison faced was that people are rarely all virtuous or all evil. When she allowed herself to look at Susan more objectively, she admitted, "She isn't always selfish. She can be a very thoughtful and caring friend. She has sent me gifts on my birthday and brought me meals when I've been sick. She takes charge— sometimes for herself, sometimes for me. If she weren't in my life, my life would be the poorer. On balance, her faults mean less to me than our friendship."

Must there always be a flip side?

Here's an important caveat for those of you who have been seriously violated in a relationship: sometimes the flip (positive) side is irrelevant. It's not that there is no flip side; it's that you've never seen it, or that it has never enhanced you in any way. If your father sexually molested you, you don't have to think well of him because he's capable of tenderness or good at getting his way. Seeing his positive attributes does not have to soften your negative feelings toward him. You can accept him without liking him or seeing him in a glowing light.

Step #9: You carefully decide what kind of relationship you want with the offender.

If the offender is unwilling or unable to make amends, what kind of relationship makes sense for you? Is reconciliation in your interest. If you do reconcile, how do you honor the devastation and anger you feel inside? Can you remain authentic to yourself and still interact with him in a civil, constructive, conciliatory way? Can you forgive someone who is dead or otherwise inaccessible?

Acceptance, as we know, does not require reconciliation. You can accept someone and reconcile, or you can accept him and not reconcile. Whichever path you choose, Acceptance asks only that you start out from that place inside you where you are most secure, most centered, most self-affirming. Cut yourself off from him to take revenge (Not Forgiving), or quickly reattach to him to smooth things over (Cheap Forgiveness), and you're likely to sabotage your future.

Here are three healthy options for you, when the offender can't, or won't, apologize.

1. Acceptance Without Reconciliation When the Offender Is Inaccessible

If the offender has died or is out of reach and you literally can't communicate with him, reconciliation is obviously not an option. But you can still accept him and the pain he caused you. He may be gone from your life, but his memory will continue to chafe, and you need to deal with this discomfort in a way that doesn't disfigure you or ruin your life. You owe this not to him but to yourself.

This work of making peace with an absent offender is the work of Acceptance. It doesn't require his participation (as Genuine Forgiveness does). It doesn't demand an ongoing relationship. What it does ask is that you:

- try to see what happened clearly, without blinders;
- recognize your contribution (if any) to the injury;
- understand his intentions, to the extent that this is possible;
- recognize both the good and bad he has brought to your life;
- forgive yourself for allowing him to hurt you;
- work to remember him without hating him or hurting inside so terribly that you bury yourself in pain.

Reaching out to him after his death, in letters perhaps, or in words spoken silently at his grave, may provide some consolation. It doesn't matter that he can't hear your grief and is no more available to you today than he was before. You don't expect him to change or make up for what he did. But you may achieve a certain peace if you declare the truth to him as you see it, in the clarity, wisdom, and dignity of your own voice. It may also help to imagine his response. Hearing the words you want so badly to hear—the words you know he could never say— can give a language to your pain, and help you heal.

This approach comforted a fifty-year-old psychologist, Kim, who found herself struggling to accept her mother's coldness two years after the mother's death. At a professional training conference I gave on forgiveness, Kim shared her story:

"My mother loved my children from my first marriage but refused to have a relationship with my stepchildren when I remarried," she said. "I'm still trying to overcome my resentment."

I asked Kim what she does to get over her pain.

"Occasionally, I go to my mother's grave and speak to her directly," she confessed to the group, laughing through her tears. "Our relationship is improving because today my mother listens and doesn't talk back. I can say things to her that I couldn't say when she was alive."

"Like what?"

"'Mom, it hurt me that you never recognized my step-kids. John'—my second husband—'has been so good to me, rescuing me from a very unhappy first marriage. Your behavior made me feel you didn't care about my happiness, or me—that you thought I deserved to suffer or be miserable or alone. I feel you blamed me for the problems in my marriage and never forgave me for getting divorced.'"

I asked Kim what she wished her mother could have said to her. Kim replied, "I would have liked her to say, 'Kim, I don't know why I was so nasty to your step-kids. They're really good kids. And I see how good John is to you. I see you're happier. You deserve this. They're all lucky you're in their life. I'm sorry for making you feel I want you to suffer. You've been a wonderful daughter. I love you and wish you great happiness.'"

Kim turned to me and added, "In my heart I'd like to forgive my mother, but I can't."

I told her, "I understand your response. It makes sense to me. Realistically, when someone knowingly hurts you and fails to show even the slightest sign of discomfort or remorse, the idea of forgiving him seems excessively generous. There's another healthy alternative, though, and that's Acceptance. Perhaps that's what you're searching for. The cure lies not in your forgiving your mother, a woman who couldn't earn forgiveness. Nor is it in your imagining her to be more than she was. The cure comes when you learn to live with her failings and relieve the ache in your heart."

I stayed in touch with Kim and over time encouraged her to:

- control her obsession with the damage her mother had done to her;
- make room for simultaneous feelings of bitterness and love;
- release herself from any mandate to forgive her mother, and learn to accept her instead;
- give voice to her injury and allow her own version of the truth;
- refuse to let the feelings her mother generated in her— shame, sadness—undermine her self-esteem;

- feel compassion for herself for all she has endured;
- realize that she didn't deserve to be rejected by her mother;
- accept that what her mother offered her was all she had to give; and
- try to remember what she loved in her mother (such as taking Kim's kids to the movies and doing arts and crafts projects with them when Kim was at work).

Through her unilateral efforts, Kim healed herself and learned to accept her mother. She also came to terms with the limitations of their relationship in a way that felt comfortable and honest, while remembering her mother in the best possible light.

2. Acceptance Without Reconciliation When the Offender Won't Apologize

The offender may want an ongoing relationship. But if he refuses to earn forgiveness, you may choose to accept him and break off all contact, at least until he makes amends. I encourage you to consider this option. When you refuse to either reconcile *or* to accept him, you poison yourself with hatred and end up having more of a relationship with him than you care to admit, even if you never cross paths again. Acceptance lets you restore your balance and maintain your integrity—without him. Acceptance lets you heal—without him.

A forty-eight-year-old radiologist, Deirdre, sought to accept her father without reconciling with him, years after the most terrible of violations. While she was at medical school, in her late twenties, she found herself perversely fascinated, almost consumed, by articles about rectal disease. She began to remember her father, a highly regarded pediatrician, treating her for rectal lesions from the earliest age—perhaps four or five. Memories came flooding back of his asking her to bend over the kitchen table, while he inserted himself into her. She knew now, suddenly, absolutely, that even if he hadn't had anal sex with her, he must have abused her in some awful way. Why else would he have repeatedly, ritualistically, examined her in that manner?

Deirdre confronted her parents with her traumatic memories, but they denied them emphatically and accused her of lying and maligning them. Several months later they invited her to join them for Thanksgiving. "My parents' response to my disclosure was so sensationally inadequate," Deirdre told me, "that I decided I couldn't live with myself and also have a relationship with them."

A part of Deirdre wanted to crush her parents, as they had crushed her. But she relinquished her need to hurt them, to have them validate her memory or console her, and gave voice to her truth in the following letter.

> Gloria and Greg—she refused to call them Mom and Dad—
>
> I've been in therapy for two years trying to piece together what happened to me as a child. You tell me you can't apologize for what never happened. But for me not to have my truth acknowledged throws me into a state of confusion and makes me question my sanity and feel even more detestable than you made me feel when you violated me and refused to love and protect me. I can't have a relationship with either of you under these conditions. There is no relationship under these conditions. It doesn't work for me to get together and share good times. So I'd appreciate your respecting my need to seal myself off from you until the time comes when you're ready to admit and make amends for the terrible damage you did. The whole thing is so sad, so evil. I wish that by cutting you out I could cut out the memories. I know that's not possible. They live on inside me. But what I can do is proclaim my truth, respect it, draw a line, and take care of myself by letting only the people I trust into my life. Good-bye.
>
> *Deirdre*

Deirdre's decision not to reconcile with her parents helped her restabilize her world and feel more safe, more cared for, more in control of her destiny. Her decision to accept them allowed her to distinguish herself from how they treated her, and move forward.

Acceptance without reconciliation may also be a sensible option when you're coming to terms with your partner's lover. When I first started to work with people who were recovering from infidelity, I cringed at what they said they needed in order to heal. "I want to go to his girlfriend's office with my four kids, surround her, put my baby on her desk, and say, 'This is the family you destroyed,'" a patient named June told me. "I want to confront her in church, behind the altar with the priest, and let her know she's destroyed my life, and now I intend to destroy hers."

Behind these gothic visions was a need to give voice to her pain—to speak up directly to the person who injured her, to stand tall and declare, "What you did was wrong. My feelings matter. Whether you acknowledge it or not, I didn't deserve to be treated this way."

What I told June is what I would tell any of you who are thinking of confronting your partner's lover: Don't do anything rash or impulsive. Don't contact her without thinking through what you want to accomplish and how you'll feel days and weeks after you deliver your message. However you choose to communicate—by E-mail, by phone, in a letter, or face-to-face—don't speak up if it's only to elicit a specific response; you can never predict how someone will react. Speak up because you have something that needs to be said. And then, to protect yourself from further pain, think through all the ways in which the lover may respond and how these responses may affect you. Most critically, if you decide to unleash your pain, do so in a way that will allow you to walk away with self-respect.

3. Acceptance with Reconciliation When the Offender Won't Apologize

Here are four sensible, healthy reasons why you may decide to accept him and reconcile, even though he refuses to make amends:

- You have to interact with him regularly and find that it takes too much energy to remain cold and distant.

- When you act cold toward him, you feel cold inside, alienated both from him and from yourself. The rupture between you compromises the quality of your life. Having no relationship with him feels worse than having some, no matter how limited or superficial.
- You benefit strategically from an ongoing relationship. For example, you choose to get along with your boss to protect your job, even though you may not respect him. Or you remain civil to your former spouse for the sake of your kids.
- You hope to have new, corrective experiences that might repair the relationship.

Melissa, a psychiatrist, struggled to accept and reconcile with her parents for all these reasons. For twenty years they had rejected her as a lesbian and refused to acknowledge her partnership with Leah. Melissa finally decided to confront them on these issues. A number of letters passed between them, including this exquisitely sensitive one from Melissa:

Dear Mom and Dad,

Over the past eighteen years I've been hurt many times by your insistence that I pretend not to be in a lesbian relationship. I have tried to be forgiving and loving, hoping that in time you would become more open-minded. I thought that, as you saw how happy I was and how good my life was, you would gradually respond to me in a warmer, more solicitous, parent-like way. I would never ask you to condone my life if it violated your standards. Your opinion about my relationship is your own business. What I care about is how you treat me.

Your insistence that I pretend to be a single person in your company is not helping. When the two of you say to me, "You won't bend, and we can't either," it's clear that you both feel fully justified in your actions and words, and not at all sorry. I realize now that I can't expect my forgiveness and love to have a healing effect if you don't care how you're hurting me.

Let me tell you how I think our relationship could be much better—without your sacrificing your values, or me, my integrity.

When you say, "We don't like Leah," you tell me you mean you don't like what she represents. From my point of view, this is a polite way of saying you don't like who I am. It's like saying, "Only if you deny who you are can we tolerate being around you." The reality is that I'm in a partnership with Leah and have been for twenty years. I'm not a single woman. If I had not met Leah, I'd like to think I'd be in a relationship with someone else, and, if so, I'm certain it would be a woman. I am gay. If you can't acknowledge that (you don't need to condone it, just acknowledge it), then it's tough to figure out what kind of relationship we can have.

From my point of view, visits are hard because I know it annoys you for me to mention Leah's name or say anything with the word "we." Can you imagine how restrictive this is for me? Leah and I work together, share the same dreams, the same friends and home. So what can I talk to you about? My brothers? Yes. But I can't talk about myself, not in any natural way. It feels phony telling you about my trips, my work, the things that make me laugh, without mentioning Leah in the same breath. She is central to everything I do. My life would be a shell without the joy we share; you only want to hear about the shell. And that's incredibly sad to me, because I think you'd very much enjoy participating in our life if you didn't think that meant you were condoning us.

There are millions of parents who don't approve of their children's choice of partners. But they ask about them anyway and try to be cordial to them. If they don't, the families grow apart. I would prefer that didn't happen to us. It already has.

So how could our relationship be better? Here's what I think would help:

1. Acknowledge that I'm in a relationship with Leah. At least when talking with me, but maybe also with your sisters and friends, even your priest. You may get some support. Some people will sympathize with you for having a gay child and see it as a terrible burden. Others will let you know they have gay family members, too, and will talk with you about how they feel. Some may even help you learn to laugh about it, and help you feel less alone.

2. Be courteous to Leah. If she answers the phone, identify yourself, make some cordial, everyday conversation with her ("How's your new job? Is it raining there?"), and then ask if I'm home.

    It's been hard for her, too, these past years. She's wanted to send you birthday cards and chat with you on the phone and get to know you a bit. But she knows how you feel about her, and she doesn't want to say something friendly that turns you farther away from her. She doesn't want to upset my relationship with you, so she says nothing, which isn't her nature. It hurts her when you call me at home and she picks up the phone and hears nothing but, "Is Melissa there?" as if she were a person not worthy of a "hello."

3. Understand that when I talk about my life and use the words "we" and "us," these are invitations for you to be part of my adult life. I'd like us to be closer, but it won't happen if I can't be who I am. And an important part of me is *we*.

4. Instead of interacting the way we have these past twenty years or so—unsuccessfully, it seems—let's try on a new set of principles. Here's what I propose:

You can try to relax and enjoy yourself with me, whether I'm alone or with Leah. In exchange, I will never interpret your laughter, or any joy we share, as meaning that you condone my relationship with her. I will understand that no matter how good a time we have, and how close we become, you still disapprove of us and believe our relationship is wrong. You won't need to remind me of your disapproval. You won't have to feel the constant anxiety of parenting me in this domain. We could all just relax and enjoy each other.

I would like to get closer to you. I hope you want to get closer to me, too, and will take my proposal seriously.

Melissa

Melissa's parents never replied. You can imagine how deeply their silence cut her. What helped her survive her disappointment and keep her equilibrium was her decision to take control of her life, give up her insistence that they accept her, and work on accepting them. Here's what she did:

- She allowed herself to honor all that she felt—her sadness, her disappointment, her anger—as a legitimate response to her parents' behavior.
- She recognized what it was about her parents' personalities that led them to act the way they did. This prevented her from taking their prejudices and rejection so personally. "My mother doesn't see the necessity of doing anything that doesn't center on her or match her immediate needs," she reminded herself. "My father avoids conflict and follows her lead."
- She gave up expecting, or yearning for, more than they could give her. "It helps not to expect or feel a need for anything from them," she told me.
- Unwilling to pretend that their rigid behavior didn't matter, she refused to grant them Cheap Forgiveness. Unwilling to

spend her life sparring with them, she refused to succumb to Not Forgiving.
- She worked at limiting her preoccupation with how they hurt her, and actively reached out to others who made her feel loved and respected.
- She gave up her need to forgive her parents, and arrived at the self-affirming position of Acceptance.

Several months after she terminated therapy, Melissa sent me an E-mail, letting me know that she had decided to continue to interact with her parents, even though her contact with them would have to be superficial. "My older brother is mentally handicapped and lives with them," she told me. "If I'm going to keep in touch with him, I need to go through my parents. I'd also like to stay connected to them because it's the morally right thing to do. They're my parents, and I honor them by keeping up with their lives. I believe they should want to keep up with mine, too, but whether they do or not, it's important for me to stay true to the spirit of my own values.

"I still talk to them briefly on the phone every two or three months. I also send them cards, but ones that don't misstate my feelings. For example, I might choose a card that says, 'I wish you a joyous day,' rather than 'You're the best mother a daughter could ever have.' It helps me feel good about myself, knowing I haven't been vindictive to them, that I've acted in a congenial way. It also helps to know there are other people in my life who love me. I have rich relationships with them. I'm nearly fifty. My parents' love is no longer something I require for my happiness. To be honest, I feel at peace with myself. I'm comfortable where I am."

Melissa chose to reconcile with her parents for reasons that served her own strategic interests. Staying in touch allowed her to enjoy the benefits of a relationship with them, while still being true to herself as a benevolent and intelligent human being. As for getting closer to them, it seemed unlikely, but she would see. The door was open.

How Can I Stay Attached to the Offender and Remain True to Myself?

When you have been physically abused, maintaining rigid boundaries between you and the offender makes excellent sense. But after emotional abuse or other nonphysical injuries, your withdrawal may reveal how tied you still are to him—how much you still need him as the object of your fury.

Acceptance lets you remain in a relationship without feeling controlled, inauthentic, or canceled out. This ability to be yourself in the presence of the offender—this "differentiation"[27]—gives you the freedom to stay physically and emotionally engaged with him because you are no longer defined by his mistreatment of you. Your power comes less from cutting him off than from maintaining a strong independent sense of who you are.[28] As e. e. cummings observed, we can be "both and oneful."

In *The Dance of Anger,* Harriet Lerner reminds us that we can stand back from pain without standing back from the person who hurt us.[29] Robert Karen suggests that we can be angry "in a warm, creative, connected way," without isolating ourselves or setting barriers. "There are degrees to which you let people back into your life," Karen says, "and degrees to which you let them back into your heart—which, of course, are not the same thing."[30]

How Mercy Affects Your Decision to Reconcile

Mercy extends a measure of gratuitous good will to the offender that opens the door to reconciliation. Like other gifts of Acceptance, it is granted unilaterally and demands nothing in return.

For some of you, mercy begins with the realization that the two of you share a common humanity—that you are both flawed human beings who are capable of doing stupid, insensitive, shameful things that need to be forgiven. "If I had been exposed to the same damaging experiences, I may have responded in the same despicable way," you remind yourself.

Others among you may protest being thrown into the same kettle of humanity as the offender. "I could never, ever, do what he did," you insist. But you may still want to show mercy as an expression of your wish to live harmoniously with others, and not demand more than a person can give.

Some Relationships Are More Important to Preserve Than Others

Some relationships matter to us more than others. If your spouse is an alcoholic who refuses to seek help, you may decide to end the marriage and cut him out of your life. But if a sibling has a drinking problem, you may want to maintain ties and work with him to confront his addiction.

A teacher named Gail chose to accept and reconcile with the person who hurt her—her older sister Myra. For Gail, some form of relationship was preferable to none.

"Myra ruined my wedding," Gail told me. "She couldn't have been more sour, more critical, more self-absorbed. I know it's hard for her to be the older sister, thirty-two, and living alone. And you can bet that when she gets married I'll feel like I'm losing her, too. But she spent the whole day whining about her dress, her table assignment, the salad, everything. Nothing was right or good enough for her. I wanted to tell her, 'Sometimes, Myra, you have to put yourself aside and understand it's not your day. You have to be there for someone else.' That's a concept she never got."

The sisters met a few times to talk through what happened, but the tension between them escalated. When they met at a restaurant, Gail ended up throwing a plate of spaghetti at Myra and storming out. Myra refused to discuss the conflict again, so Gail got into therapy alone and worked on accepting her sister. "I can see how I marginalized Myra at my wedding," she told me. "I could have done more to make her feel special. It helps to remind myself that she was an only child for six years before I came along—my wedding probably stirred up feelings of being displaced again. This doesn't excuse her behavior—she hurt me deeply. But she's my sister. We share a lot of history, and I'm not going to let this incident tear us apart. There are too many advantages to staying in each other's life."

This became apparent many times over the following years, including the day when Gail went into early labor and Myra rushed her to the hospital; and five years later, when their father died, and they grieved his loss together.

Acceptance with reconciliation gives you, as it gave Gail, the freedom to choose a level of intimacy that feels authentic and safe. You can't get close to someone you don't trust, but you can choose to interact in a circumscribed way.

That's what friends of mine, Steve and Miriam Carson, chose to do in dealing with their neighbors, the Singers.

Steve and Miriam invested a large chunk of their life savings in a summer house on Cape Cod, with a partial view of the bay. The Singers were planning to raise the south side of their roof and maintain the integrity of the view, but they raised the opposite side instead, leaving the Carsons with nothing to look at but the Singers' attic window. The Carsons wrote a seething letter to the local zoning board. The board sent a copy to the Singers, who seethed back. The town resolved the issue in favor of the Singers.

Feeling powerless, the Carsons began to obsess, transforming their summer home from a place of refuge into an emotional battlefield where they played out their spiteful ruminations. They rehearsed all the nasty, cutting things they could say—how cheap and tasteless the Singers were for planting suburban grass on the edge of the dunes, how loud and obnoxious their kids were. At night the Carsons stayed up scheming about how to get even.

Over time, however, they began to realize the corrosive impact their behavior was having on themselves. Selfishly, intelligently, they began to accept what they couldn't change. "What do we want to accomplish here?" they asked themselves. "What's important? Where do we want this to end up?" Self-righteous rage wasn't the answer, they realized; it was poisoning them. So they decided to pack it up and work at making peace. Seeing the conflict through their neighbors' eyes, they slowly, reluctantly accepted the Singers' right to enhance their home in a way that served them. They believed that the Singers had an exaggerated sense of entitlement and would never recognize how inflammatory their behavior was, or apologize for it. But they knew that nothing would bring back their view, and that no one was being hurt by their anger but themselves. So they swallowed their pride and wrote the following letter:

> Dear Christine and Hank,
>
> The fighting that's going on between us is terrible, and Steve and I are very upset about it. The world is such a frightening place these days, it seems sad to be on such terrible terms with our next-door neighbors. The idea of hating each other or not talking to each other for the next twenty years is depressing. We're not happy about having our view blocked, but you had the legal right to do what you wanted. We may never be best friends, but I'd like to see if we can get rid of the anger between us and make amends. Steve and I will do everything we can.

Within an hour of receiving the letter, the Singers called and said, "We were just about to write the same letter. We want to move on, too."

The Carsons' response to the injury was complicated, as yours is likely to be. Was the letter merely expedient? Strategic? Did they write it only because they believed they had no choice but to make peace? Were they coerced by circumstance, with no freedom to respond in an honest, authentic way? Did they really accept their neighbors, or did they play the only hand they were dealt, and offer Cheap Forgiveness?

I would argue that in many important ways the Carsons' response was a model of Acceptance. Unlike the conflict-avoider, they actively reached out to their neighbors and dealt with the dispute head-on. Unlike the self-sacrificer, they allowed themselves to feel angry and violated, saw the Singers as undeserving of forgiveness, and made peace with them to satisfy their own agenda. And unlike the passive-aggressor, they saw the conflict from their neighbors' point of view, worked to free themselves from their bitterness, and confronted the Singers in direct and respectful ways in order to reconcile.

Step # 10: You forgive yourself for your failings.

You may ask, "Why should I forgive myself? I did nothing wrong. It was the offender who violated me." But the issue here is not how you wronged him. It's how you may have allowed *him* to hurt *you*.

How did you do this? What do you need to forgive yourself for? In *After the Affair*, I list a number of injuries that pertain to infidelity,[31] including:

- trusting blindly, and ignoring your suspicions;
- having such a stunted view of yourself that you feel unentitled to loyalty or love; and
- making unfair comparisons by idealizing the lover and degrading yourself.

You may also want to forgive yourself for such self-effacing, self-destructive behaviors as:

- dismissing your suffering and failing to appreciate how deeply you've been wounded;
- believing you got what you deserved; viewing your mistreatment as punishment, and allowing it to shatter and shame you;
- tolerating the offender's abusive behavior;
- refusing to forgive yourself, even when you're innocent;
- making peace at any cost, no matter how superficial or spurious it may be, or how unsafe or miserable the offender makes you feel; and
- losing time and energy engaging in imaginary, vindictive dialogues with him.

For all these self-inflicted wounds you may need to forgive yourself.

How Does Forgiving Yourself Help You Accept the Offender?

When you judge yourself too harshly, you absorb all your criticism and have little or none left for him. Unable to see your role clearly, you cannot see *his* clearly. That was Kathy's dilemma. She had been sexually molested by her stepfather but could not accept him until she first forgave herself.

I learned about this twelve-year-old girl from a colleague who was seeing her in family therapy. In an early session, the therapist asked her bluntly, "Do you blame yourself?" Kathy nodded—yes. "Sometimes I acted too grown up," she said. "I wore a nightgown and looked too pretty. I didn't tell Mom he came into my room at night. He told me if I did, he'd kill us both."

As the therapy progressed, Kathy worked to cut away the excess blame she apportioned to herself and direct it at the person who deserved it. Over time she developed empathy for herself as an unprotected, frightened child, and came to recognize her stepfather's behavior as his responsibility alone.

In a later interview, Kathy showed remarkable strength and clarity. "No matter what I did, I was the child and he was the adult," she said resolutely. "Even if I was pretty, he should have backed off."

As long as Kathy despised herself for what her stepfather had done to her, she could not forgive herself. As long as she framed the injury as her fault alone, she could not properly fault him, free herself to accept him, and move beyond the abuse.

When You Refuse to Forgive Yourself

Lifting blame from the offender's shoulders and transferring it to your own may be your way of protecting him and keeping your image of him untarnished and intact. Blaming yourself also simplifies your vision of the world and frees you from the role of victim. It puts you back in charge.

You may want to ask yourself, "Do I have a pattern of 'unforgivingness' toward myself, a lifelong tendency to berate myself for anything bad that happens, even those events over which I have no control? Am I unrelentingly tough on myself, tougher than I need to be or than the facts warrant? Do I ignore extenuating circumstances that aren't my fault? Were my parents or guardians excessively punitive, shaming, or unforgiving? Did they go for the jugular and make me feel rotten about myself? Did I buy into their criticism?" Understanding these pernicious childhood patterns may help you grow out of them.

When a patient named Mary caught her husband, Sam, in bed with a neighbor, she could no longer deny what was going on. Sam seemed genuinely sorry, even relieved to be discovered, and worked hard to regain her trust.

"For twenty years I knew he was cheating on me," Mary told me. "Now that it's out in the open and Sam is reaching out to me, I think I can forgive him. But what's harder, much harder, is forgiving *myself*. How do I do that when I've been so stupid, so not there for myself for twenty years?"

What Mary found is that it's sometimes easier to forgive others than to forgive yourself, sometimes simpler to accept their mistreatment than to confront your own self-denying behavior.

Like Mary, you may fear that if you forgive yourself, you'll lose track of your mistakes and repeat them. But with Self-Forgiveness you don't ignore or minimize what you did, or lighten your sentence; on the contrary, you commit yourself to changing your ways, so that your response to violation will be more self-protective, more self-affirming the next time around.

IS ACCEPTANCE GOOD ENOUGH?

Forgiveness has been held up as the gold standard of recovery from an interpersonal wound. Unfortunately, as it's currently defined, its reach exceeds its grasp. For many of us, forgiveness fails to provide the emotional resolution and physical health benefits it promises.

By dividing the concept of forgiveness into two adaptive options—Acceptance and Genuine Forgiveness—you have the freedom to choose two different itineraries. One, Acceptance, is a healing journey you make by yourself, for yourself. The other, Genuine

Forgiveness, is a healing journey you make with the offender, as you honor his reparative efforts to make amends. Each is a hard-won achievement. Each is a healthy response to a very different set of circumstances.

Acceptance is not a failure to forgive but an equally powerful way of healing an injury when the person who hurt you fails to participate in the process. Acceptance is not an inferior, immature, or morally deficient reaction. It is a wise and proactive alternative. You can't draw blood from a stone, but you can accept an unrepentant offender.

Acceptance is a process you enter into primarily to free yourself from the trauma of an injury. *Your goal is not necessarily forgiveness. Your goal is emotional resolution, the restoration of your best self, the rekindling of meaning and value in your life.* Acceptance is not only a good enough response; in my view, it is the only honest and healthy response when the offender can't or won't apologize. However, because Genuine Forgiveness requires his caring involvement, it is likely to feel more deeply satisfying and complete than Acceptance.

LOOKING AHEAD

Acceptance supports not only your resolution of the past but your vision of the future. When you understand what motivated the offender and how you may have provoked or permitted his behavior, you're less likely to believe that the conflict will repeat itself with others. This wisdom frees you to forge new connections with a degree of optimism and a sense of safety and purpose. What happened to you once does not have to happen again.

That's what a patient named Kathleen came to realize. When she was a child, her baby brother would hold up his arms to her and say, "Kiss, kiss." Kathleen's schizophrenic mother would smack her, deluded by the paranoid belief that Kathleen was sexually molesting him. When Kathleen got married and had a baby girl of her own, she saw her husband hold up his arms to their child and say lovingly, "Kiss, kiss." Her first response was to go numb with terror. Memories of violence collided with this image of pure, innocent love, caus-ing her to feel disoriented and unmoored.

"It's hard to trust that today is real and that what happened to me won't happen to my baby," Kathleen told me. "Sometimes I'm afraid I'll do something horrible to her. But I've come to understand that for many years my mother was insane and not responsible for her behav-ior. Years later, when she was stabilized on medication, I asked her what happened, and she accused me of being the crazy one. I accept that she's incapable of acknowledging, never mind apologizing for, what she did to me. I've finished the old business of wanting more from her than she can give. I don't wish her harm, but I don't want much contact with her either. I've also come to trust that I'm not my mother. If anything, I'm overly protective of my child. In so many ways, my mother has taught me what I don't want to be."

Through the process of Acceptance, Kathleen learned to differ-entiate "then" from "now," her mother from herself, so that she could invest in her new family. As she relived and made better sense of the nightmare of her childhood, she began to work toward a new life and stem the destructive effects of her past.

"My life is so different today," she told me recently. "I'm moving forward cautiously, but with enough confidence that I'm safe, my baby is safe, loving is safe. I say this with a mix of guilt and awe—I'm no longer just a victim; I'm a survivor. And a pretty good parent."

The process of Acceptance can help you, as it helped Kathleen, not only to survive trauma but to learn from it and grow. It's not, as some people say, that *the injury* changes you for the better, it's that *your under-standing* of the injury changes you for the better. As you resolve old con-flicts and confront how they contaminate your responses today, you cre-ate new possibilities that integrate and empower your most resilient self.

Part Four

GENUINE FORGIVENESS

*R*obin, a married woman in her late thirties, came into therapy hoping to redress a terrible hurt that sat between her and her mother.

"When I was twelve, my father deserted us," Robin told me. "That was a relief, because his only interest in us was sexual. A few years later, my alcoholic mother went after him and abandoned us, too, leaving me and my sister to take care of our two young brothers. She reassured us that she'd be back, and she did bless us with an occasional drunken visit, but basically we were left to fend for ourselves, long before we were ready. Last year, I heard that my father died. It felt like the end of a chapter, so I decided to write Mom and tell her I was married and had just given birth to my second child. She wrote back, 'I'm so happy to hear from you. I'd like to meet your family.'"

Robin replied immediately. "Mom, there's so much to talk about. I'm holding a lot of pain inside me. If you'd like me to forgive you, there are some things I need you to do. I need you to apologize for abandoning me. I need to know if you know how much you hurt me, and if you care. I need you to try to understand, and help me to understand, why you left your family to run after a no-good father. I need to know that if I let you back into my life, you're not going to disappear again. And there's one more thing. When I told you Dad sexually abused us throughout the years, you called me a liar. I need you to take that back. I look forward to hearing from you. Robin."

Robin showed me her mother's response.

My dear daughter Robin,

I hope you and your babies are getting stronger each day and of course that Aaron [your husband] is well and happy, too.

I'm so sorry for any way I caused you heartache. You are so right about me, leaving you and just going crazy. But I never tried to hurt you. In fact, I never knew I had hurt you so deeply—you were a grown-up girl at the time. I didn't realize you still needed me so much. But I can't go back and change things. If I could I would. I say, Lord, give me the strength to change the things I can and the wisdom to know the difference. I don't think I said that right, but you know what I mean.

Robin, revenge belongs to God, and God doesn't like the idea of people judging others, because we all have sinned in the eyes of God. Remember when the people wanted to stone a prostitute to death as she drew water from the well, and Jesus said, "You who have not sinned, let him throw the first stone," and no one threw a stone.

And also, Robin, people who don't forgive, God will not want to forgive. Forgiving people are much happier people and stay younger longer. Forgiveness is good for the soul. What do people gain that hold revenge—nothing but a frown, and that's not pretty. The one who holds revenge has lost so much happiness and hurts themselves the most— wallowing in self-pity and anger, thinking meanwhile that they are making the other person suffer. They think they're getting sweet revenge. Let's take a deep breath and admit that none of us is perfect. Life is so short. Let's make the best we can with what years we have left. Let's go forward, not backward. There is nothing there if we go backward.

My dear, I have to get this in the mail. I've missed you so much in my life. I love you so very much and I always will. I want you to know, if I don't ever get to see you, I carried you inside me and our hearts beat the same. Yes, you were once my baby.

Mama

Robin was disheartened by her mother's letter. "It's filled with platitudes," she told me. "It's not what I need, not what I prayed for." She wrote back:

Dear Mom,

I received your letter, and although I was glad to hear from you, I felt disappointed when I read it. I don't think you understand what I need from you. You talk about what *I* need to do for *you*. I told you I need you to sincerely apologize for not being there for me as my mother. You left for Florida when your job as my mother wasn't over yet. Of course I still needed you. I need you now. I certainly wasn't grown then. You left when I was in high school. I'm sorry you feel I'm judging you. It's not my intention. I don't believe I'm being vengeful. This separation has been hard on me, too. I'm going to these lengths because I need to. I need for you to be the mother. I don't want to be your mother. If my boys ever felt I had hurt them, I would do whatever I could to make it right. I'm hoping you understand better this time. You mention we should not go backward but should look to the future. I need to look in the past and heal the hurt. It's important to me.

Robin

P.S. If you are angry at me for something you felt I did to you, we can talk about that. I need you to take responsibility for running out on me, and the part about dad. Maybe you can't do that. Let me know.

A few months passed, and several more letters were exchanged. Then Robin's mother arranged to come and stay with her daughter for a week. I was out of town, but I called Robin the day before her mother was planning to return home to ask how the visit was going. Robin said, "My mother has really tried to come through for me. She stays up all night with the baby. Seeing how much she loves him and delights in him makes me love her even more."

I told Robin, "You don't know when you'll see your mother face to face again. Are there things you still want to say to her to try to clear the air?"

"I haven't wanted to bring up the things that are bothering me," Robin said. "Everything is going so well. But the hurt lies buried deep inside me and—it's big."

I encouraged Robin not to let the opportunity pass. "I suggest you help your mother locate your pain," I told her. "I suggest you tell her exactly what you need to hear from her and not assume that because she hasn't put her feelings into words, the feelings aren't there, or that she doesn't want to share them with you."

The next week, Robin came in for her session and told me what happened. "Just before my mother left, I sat down with her and said, 'There's something still on my mind that I'd like to talk about. I'm not bringing it up to hurt you or punish you or make you feel guilty. I'm bringing it up because I need to talk it out with you in order to feel closer to you—to heal me, and us. I'd like you to listen, and if you believe what I'm saying, I'd like you to tell me. OK?'

"My mother agreed. I told her, 'I need you to say two things to me. First, I need you to acknowledge that you left me when I was still a kid, when I still needed you, and that that was wrong. Second, when I told you about Dad and you called me a liar, you hurt me as much as he did. I'm not asking you to confirm what happened if you don't know the truth, but I need you to apologize for what you said to me.'

"My mother looked at me with tears in her eyes. 'Robin,' she said, 'I've been such an awful mother. There's so much I haven't been able to face. Yes, I left you when you needed me. Yes, you're not someone to lie about being raped. I'm so sorry. I hope some day you'll forgive me.'

"I reached out to her. 'I do,' I said. 'I do. It's time to start again.'"

Robin and her mother provide a poignant illustration of the regenerative power of earned forgiveness. The mother began the process when she told Robin she loved her and regretted the past. Robin continued it when she told her mother she wanted to forgive her but couldn't, and wouldn't. The issue was not that Robin was unforgiving, but that she first needed her mother to come forward, take responsibility for the specific harm she had done, and apologize for it. Together they demonstrated that when those who hurt us reach out to heal us, reliably and repeatedly, and we support their efforts to bind our wounds, something extraordinary takes place—something transformative, something redemptive.

WHAT IS GENUINE FORGIVENESS?

Unlike Refusing to Forgive, Cheap Forgiveness, or Acceptance, Genuine Forgiveness is essentially interpersonal. It requires the heartfelt participation of both of you. Here are its three core interpersonal features.

1. Genuine Forgiveness Is a Transaction

Genuine Forgiveness is not a pardon granted unilaterally by the hurt party. It's a shared venture, an exchange between two people bound together by an interpersonal violation.

2. Genuine Forgiveness Is Conditional

Genuine Forgiveness must be earned. It comes with a price that the offender must be willing to pay. In exchange, the hurt party must allow him to settle his debt. As he works hard to earn forgiveness through genuine, generous acts of repentance and restitution, the hurt party works hard to let go of her resentment and need for retribution. If either one of you fails to do the requisite work, there can be no Genuine Forgiveness.

A patient named Jane made this point to her husband. Shortly after he admitted his affair, he told her, "I'll never do it again, and I don't want to talk about it—or your grievances—any more. It's ancient history." Jane's response cut to her bottom line: "If you don't want to hear my pain, I can't get close to you. I'm not trying to punish or manipulate you. I'm just telling you what I need to forgive you. It's a simple formula."

With Genuine Forgiveness, both of you address the question, "What am I willing to give in order to create a climate in which forgiveness is possible?" While the offender is never *entitled* to be forgiven, he is more likely to earn this currency if he attempts to repair the harm he caused. While the hurt party is never *obligated* to forgive him, she is more likely to do so, and resuscitate the relationship, if she gives him a chance to make good. This provisional exchange, this "giving in order to get," lies at the heart of Genuine Forgiveness.

3. Genuine Forgiveness Requires a Transfer of Vigilance

After a traumatic injury, you, the hurt party, are likely to become hypervigilant, patrolling the border between you and the offender, making sure you'll never be violated or fooled again. You may live and breathe the injury, obsessed with its grubby details. The offender, in contrast, may want to repress, deny, or minimize his wrongful behavior.

With Genuine Forgiveness, a profound shift in preoccupation takes place. You, the offender, demonstrate that you're fully conscious of your transgression and intend never to repeat it. You, the hurt party, become less preoccupied with the injury and begin to let it go.

Here's how one couple engaged in this process.

After Julia learned about her husband Evan's affair, he gave up the lover, recommitted himself to his wife, and worked hard to earn back her trust. On their twenty-fifth anniversary, he took her out to dinner to celebrate. The waitress came to the table and announced, "Hi. My name is Sandy, and I'm going to be your server tonight." Sandy happened to be the name of Evan's ex-girlfriend. Julia's mood plummeted, but Evan reached out to her and said, earnestly, "I'm sorry this is happening. I really wanted this to be a special evening for us. How are you doing?" Julia paused, then responded, "You just made it easier."

This is an example of a transfer of vigilance. Evan paid attention to Julia's suffering, and Julia in turn worked to let it go. If he had remained silent and let the moment pass, she might have sunk into depression. If she had bludgeoned him with reminders of his affair, he might have become cold and sullen. Over time, as Evan displayed a continued interest in her pain, mixed with compassion and contrition, and she responded with encouragement, they arrived at a place where she could say, "I believe you're sorry and will look out for me. Your efforts allow me to open up to you and feel more trusting."

As forgiveness expert Terry Hargrave points out, "Forgiveness is accomplished when the victimized person no longer has to hold the wrongdoer responsible for the injustice; the wrongdoer holds himself or herself responsible."[1]

Why Is Forgiveness More Genuine When It Is Earned?

I've learned from my patients over the years that forgiveness is more satisfying, more heartfelt, more natural—and therefore more genuine—when it is earned than when it is not. Why is this true? Perhaps for the same reason that when someone buys you a gift that shows he knows you and cherishes you, it's likely to mean more than a gift you bought for yourself. Perhaps also for the same reason that love is more gratifying, more nurturing, when it is embraced by both of you, not by one of you alone.

We are social beings, all vitally interconnected, and we are validated and redeemed when others provide a soothing balm to our wounds and work to release us from the pain they have caused us. Healing, like love, flourishes in the context of a caring relationship. *I would go so far as to say that we can't love alone, and we can't forgive alone.*

What follows is a concrete vision—a series of specific, practical recommendations mapping out exactly what each of you needs to do to achieve Genuine Forgiveness. I hope it will help you embrace the challenging, critical tasks that lie ahead.

WHAT YOU, THE OFFENDER, MUST DO TO EARN GENUINE FORGIVENESS

Let me speak first to you, the offender, since, contrary to what you may believe, it is your repentance and atonement that usually open the door to forgiveness.

I have found that there are six critical tasks you must tackle to earn forgiveness. I can't say that if you don't do all six you won't ever be forgiven, but if you make a sincere attempt, you may give the hurt party the incentive and courage to forgive you. (I'm assuming here that the person you hurt is physically and emotionally available to you; if she's deceased or otherwise inaccessible, you obviously can't earn her forgiveness.)

SIX CRITICAL TASKS FOR EARNING FORGIVENESS

Critical Task #1: Look at your mistaken assumptions about forgiveness and see how they block your efforts to earn it.

Critical Task #2: Bear witness to the pain you caused.

Critical Task #3: Apologize genuinely, non-defensively, responsibly.

Critical Task #4: Seek to understand your behavior and reveal the inglorious truth about yourself to the person you harmed.

Critical Task #5: Work to earn back trust.

Critical Task #6: Forgive yourself for injuring another person.

Healing a relationship takes work—serious, dedicated, noble work—and sacrifice. If you want something as precious, as sacred as the forgiveness of someone you've harmed—if you want to restore order to the chaos you've created and regain your place in her heart—you must be willing to pay, and pay big. Genuine Forgiveness is no gratuitous pardon. It must be earned.

Critical Task #1: Look at your mistaken assumptions about forgiveness and see how they block your efforts to earn it.

Are you unwilling to earn forgiveness because of your erroneous assumptions about what the process entails? Let's look at several common ones.

Mistaken Assumption: I can't begin to earn forgiveness until I feel perfectly safe, comfortable, and ready.

You'll probably never feel completely safe, comfortable, and ready—how could you, when you have to submit to your accuser's judgment? Owning up to her is bound to make you squirm. If not now, however, when?

The Jewish Prayer Book, the *Mahzor for Rosh Hashanah and Yom Kippur*, tells the story of Rabbi Eliezer who advised his congregants to repent one day before their death. "But who knows when he will die?" a follower asked. Eliezer replied, "That's exactly why you should repent today."[2] To this I would add, "Don't live your life as though the person you offended will be around forever, either. Apologize now while you still have a chance."

Mistaken Assumption: I deserve to be forgiven.

So much is written exhorting the injured party to forgive, and so little about what you, the offender, need to do to deserve this offering. It's no wonder that you may think of forgiveness as a gift you're entitled to receive.

We hear the commandment (Leviticus, 19:18) to those who have been hurt: "You shall love your neighbor as yourself." We recall Alexander Pope's famous words, "To err is human, to forgive divine." Jesus enjoined his followers to "Love your enemies and pray for those who persecute you, so that you may be children of your Father in heaven. . . . For if you love [only] those who love you, what reward do you have?"[3]

The hurt party is taught that her act of forgiving will bring her significant emotional and physical benefits. According to the International Forgiveness Institute, "The forgiver discovers the paradox of forgiveness: As we give to others the gifts of mercy, generosity, and moral love, we ourselves are healed."[4] Lewis Smedes, author of several books on forgiveness, writes that as you forgive, "You set a prisoner free, but you discover that the real prisoner was yourself."[5] Elsewhere Smedes writes: "The first and sometimes only person to get the benefits of forgiving is the person who does the forgiving."[6]

We grow up linking human forgiveness with God's grace. "Grace," writes Philip Yancey, "is a gift from God to people who don't deserve it."[7] In his thoughtful book *What's So Amazing About Grace?* Yancey describes "Babette's Feast" as a parable of grace—"a gift that costs everything for the giver and nothing for the recipient."[8] He writes, "Grace came to them in the form of a feast . . . lavished on those who had in no way earned it . . . free of charge, no strings attached, on the house."[9]

From these and similar writings, you, the offender, could easily believe that forgiveness is your due; that when the person you hurt forgives you, you owe her nothing in return.

It's not my place to defend or question biblical concepts of forgiveness or grace. I would only point out what many theologians have reminded us over the centuries—*that grace is not a license for wrongdoing and does not absolve us of our need to seek forgiveness; that whatever mercy God grants us, we are still expected to acknowledge our transgressions and earn salvation; and that when God forgives us, he is not handing us a free ride to heaven.*

When spiritual leaders talk of divine forgiveness, they usually don't mean to imply that God is offering us a gift for which He expects nothing in return, but, rather, that no matter how badly we conduct ourselves, God accepts us into a community of sinners in which we are free to atone for our wrongs.

I can relate to you only what I have observed from my patients as they struggle to heal and forgive:

- If you assume that you categorically deserve to be forgiven—that you possess this right simply because you are human—you make it less likely that the hurt party will forgive you.

- If you don't try to earn forgiveness, the person you hurt can offer you only a cheap substitute.
- If you want compassion, benevolence, love, and forgiveness, you need to act in ways that elicit these feelings in the person you violated.
- What in human terms may be as amazing as grace is your ability to take yourself to task, perform extraordinary acts of penitence, and work to earn forgiveness for your wrongs.

If you look to the New Testament for guidance, there are additional passages you should read. Jesus, for example, tells his followers that their sacrifices to God will mean little if they don't make amends directly to the person they've harmed. Matthew says: "So if you are offering your gift at the altar, and there remember that your brother has something against you, leave your gift there before the altar and go; first be reconciled to your brother, and then come and offer your gift."[10]

The Jewish prayer book says, "Atonement is no mere act of grace, or miracle of salvation, which befalls the chosen; it demands the free ethical choice and deed of the human being. Man is not granted something unconditionally; he has rather to decide for something unconditionally. In his deed is the beginning of his atonement."[11]

Mistaken Assumption: If I admit I was wrong and work to earn your forgiveness, I will seem weak and vulnerable in your eyes and mine.

This assumption is erroneous because you're more likely to come across as strong, not weak, when you admit wrongdoing, and less likely to project strength when you insist that you're always right. You don't relinquish power when you work to earn forgiveness; you give the hurt person back the power you took from her. You restore the balance between you.

Be careful not to confuse humbling acts of apology with weakness and vulnerability. It takes character to embrace the truth. It takes resolve to trade in your pride for something you value more—your integrity, her forgiveness.

If you're courageous enough to say, "I'm sorry," and then work to prove it, you shouldn't assume that the person you hurt will try to shame you and gloat over her victory. It's more likely that your confession will win her respect, diminish her need to punish you, and increase her willingness to accept a fair share of blame for what went wrong.

There are times, of course, when your work to gain forgiveness will get you nowhere. The person you hurt may want you on your knees, begging for mercy, and then walk away, unmoved. Her only goal may be to punish and humiliate you. If she has a vindictive personality, she won't be interested in forgiving you; she'll only want to get even. Another person may refuse to forgive you because to her what you did was too reprehensible, and your efforts to heal her fail to go far or deep enough. If you have a solid sense of self, however, you can choose to do what you believe is right and work to make good, whether your efforts are rewarded or not.

If acts of contrition make you feel weak and defenseless, it may be because of the personal meaning you attach to apologies, not because the hurt party will use your remorse against you. Your fear of being hurt may say more about your formative life experiences than about anything that's happening today. If whenever you apologize you expect to be trampled on, it may be wise to look into your past for the reasons why.

A patient named Donna learned from her toxic parents the danger of accepting blame. As a child, whenever she did something wrong, intentionally or not, her father cursed her and went in for the kill. As an adult, she deflected criticism from herself and refused to admit complicity or imperfection. Her lifelong pattern was to associate apologies with subjugation to a tyrant. Nothing could make her seek forgiveness. Classmates wrote her off as smug and arrogant, when in fact the opposite was true. She couldn't admit mistakes not because she believed she was always right but because she was so terrified of admitting she was wrong.

If you are like Donna, your early experiences are likely to make it hard for you to do the remedial work required to earn forgiveness.

For you, a relationship will not be a place where your wrongs are forgiven, but more like a chess game in which you vie for power and make strategic moves. For you, to say "I'm sorry" is to say "I lose."

A patient named Maxine couldn't apologize for her affair because she believed her husband would abandon her, as everyone else important in her life had. "When I was ten my parents got divorced," she told me. "My mother shipped us off to my father's house without telling us there was no coming back. Then my father got remarried and told me, 'The house is too small. You've got to go live with your older sister.'"

Maxine grew up thinking there was something unlovable about her—why else would both her parents reject her? When she married Andy, she expected that some day he would leave her, too. After she admitted a month-long affair with his best friend, she refused to apologize or empathize with his pain. Puzzled by her response, she entered therapy and came to understand that holding out was her way of holding on—to Andy, to power, to control. "If I show him how sorry I am for hurting him, he'll realize how defective I am and divorce me," she reasoned. "If I don't show him, he may still leave me, but at least the decision will be in my hands, not his." Her twisted logic closed the door on forgiveness.

Mistaken Assumption: I'm not worthy of your forgiveness.

To ask for forgiveness, you must believe you're worth being forgiven. If you assume that you have nothing redeeming to offer, or that you're too evil or empty to make good, you'll have no reason to try.

This was true of Murray, a forty-year-old pathologist, who came to see me after a devastating affair. He was determined to carve out a new life for himself with his third wife, Jill, but he felt so inadequate, so unworthy of her respect, that he made it impossible for her to forgive him. On their anniversary, he tried to buy her a card, but none captured how truly sad and sorry he felt. "I spent an hour looking around, reading the messages, feeling more and more disgusted with myself," he told me. "I finally chose one that made a joke—'If you're unhappy with me, don't worry . . . You can leave!' It was stupid of me, but nothing quite said what I wanted. When Jill read it, she tossed it in the garbage. 'I would have preferred nothing,' she told me." Talking out what happened revealed the truth to them: it was not a lack of love that had made him buy a sarcastic card but his oppressive sense of worthlessness, his belief that he had no claim to her forgiveness. It was not that he didn't want to heal her wound but that he felt too wounded to heal her.

Learning this about Murray gave Jill a reason to stay with him. It also taught him a valuable lesson: that sharing your feelings about yourself, no matter how sordid, may be the most intimate gift you have to offer.

Mistaken Assumption: Nothing can undo the wrong I've done.

Here you fail to do the work to earn forgiveness because you believe that no words or gestures, not yours or anyone else's, can undo the damage. No act of penance matters, you insist, because your offense was too heinous for anyone to forgive.

If you feel this way, I would simply say: don't assume your efforts won't make a difference. There's no way to know unless you try. Even if the person you hurt refuses to reconcile, you may help repair her wounded sense of self and reduce her hostility toward you. Your attempts at apology may not be equal to the crime, but your effort alone is likely to undo some of the damage.

Mistaken Assumption: When I seek your forgiveness, I admit I'm a bad person.

You may think that if you hate what you did, you must hate who you are. This is a crippling assumption. The challenge is to be appropriately critical of your *behavior* without turning against *yourself*. Condemn the whole "you" rather than one particular action, and you'll have no incentive to change or learn from your misconduct.

When Adam confessed his affair to his wife, Lydia, he swore he wanted to repair the marriage. But then he treated her more disdainfully than before. "Maybe I don't love her enough and can't be there for her in the way she needs me," he told me.

I interpreted his behavior differently. What I saw was a man who hated himself for what he had done and was afraid to admit it. The truth was too repugnant to him. His father had been a womanizer, destroying Adam's mother, his family, the family business. "I remember lying in bed, crying and praying, and begging him not to go off on another 'business trip,'" Adam told me.

For Adam to acknowledge that he had behaved just as despicably as his father—that by cheating on Lydia, he was no better than the man he had demonized all his life—would have stripped him bare, forcing him to turn the antipathy he felt toward his father onto himself. Unable to deal with this humiliation, he projected his self-contempt outward at his wife.

If you, like Adam, must deny your guilt to shield yourself from shame, you won't be able to do the work of earning forgiveness. It may help if you distinguish between guilt and shame. Guilt is a response to a specific behavior—one you wish to correct. Shame is a negative response to yourself as a person. You feel guilt for *doing* bad; you feel shame for *being* bad. Psychologist June Price Tangney, a leading researcher in shame and guilt, has found that offenders who are more prone to guilt than shame tend to be more empathetic, more capable of reaching out to the person they harmed, more able to criticize themselves without crucifying themselves. Offenders who are more prone to shame than guilt are more likely to justify or deny their wrongful behavior and insist that they've done nothing that needs to be forgiven.[12] As psychologists Exline and Baumeister point out, "Feelings of shame are more likely to prompt self-protective responses designed to hide the offense, to deflect responsibility, or to make the perpetrator appear innocent, competent, or powerful."[13]

If you can be appropriately critical of what you did (and allow yourself to feel guilt) without hating who you are (and feeling shame), you're more likely to own up to your behavior and make amends.

Mistaken Assumption: You'll never forgive me, so why should I try?

If this is your position, I ask you to ask yourself, "Do I really believe it? Or am I using it to justify my self-doubt and my reluctance to do the hard work of earning forgiveness? Am I speaking the truth or expressing my sense of hopelessness—or helplessness?" Your belief that nothing you do will win her forgiveness can become a self-fulfilling prophecy, saying less about her capacity to grant forgiveness than about your willingness to earn it.

Mistaken Assumption: You should know I'm sorry.

Your assumption that she should be able to read your heart and mind may be no more than an excuse to avoid apologizing. If you checked it out with the hurt party, she might say, "If *I* should know you're sorry, *you* should know I need you to say and feel the words." My experience tells me that if you don't express your remorse, all you can expect for your cheap silence is her cheap forgiveness—or her wrath.

Mistaken Assumption: If I work to earn forgiveness, I'm saying that I'm the only one who did wrong.

Acknowledging your complicity is not the same as declaring that the hurt person is innocent. The forgiveness you seek is only for the damage you caused. At some point you'll want her to accept an appropriate share of blame; but to move the forgiveness process forward, you should acknowledge your own wrongdoing and let your remorse, not your pride, lead the way.

You may want her to admit blame first, believing that she'll then be more humble and forgiving. And you may be right. The problem is that the more you try to deflect attention from yourself, the more defensive and critical she's likely to become. I therefore recommend that you begin by focusing on your own contribution to the injury, apologizing fully and generously, with no ifs and buts. This is likely to create a climate in which she comes forward freely and apologizes on her own. If she fails to do this, you could discuss it with her—but at another time. Insisting on her apology as a precondition for yours will get you nowhere. Your accusations will be all she hears. It may help to heed the advice of Matthew (7:5): "You hypocrite, first take the log out of your own eye, and then you will see clearly to take the speck out of your brother's eye."

Mistaken Assumption: It makes no sense to try to earn your forgiveness if I don't intend to have an ongoing relationship with you.

Most of you won't bother to seek forgiveness from someone you don't plan to see again. But there may be benefit in trying.

A friend named Erin drove home this truth to me. "I rushed over to Eileen Fisher, bought a dress, ran home, tried it on, and then brought it back—all during my lunch break," she told me. "A sales-girl tried to credit my card, but she couldn't get the machine to work. I was late, and exploded. 'If you weren't trained to do this job,' I hissed at her, 'stay away from the front desk.' She took my cue and retreated into the back room. I felt terrible, so the next day I went back and apologized. 'I was in a rush to get back to work,' I told her. 'I'm sorry for being so obnoxious. I know those machines can be temperamental, too.'

"I'll probably never see that salesgirl again," Erin realized, "but what I did left me—and probably her—feeling better. It was totally gratuitous, but I ended up taking some of the meanness out of me, and putting back something kinder. I apologized as much for myself as I did for her."

What we all might take away from this incident is that forgiveness and reconciliation are two separate processes, both for the person you hurt and for you. Like Erin, you don't have to have a continuing relationship with someone to seek her forgiveness and come out ahead.

Critical Task #2: Bear witness to the pain you caused.

To earn Genuine Forgiveness, you need to encourage the person you hurt to open up to you, and listen to her with a caring heart. She can't heal until she releases her pain, and you can't earn forgiveness until you're willing to know what's packed away inside her.

Let's look at what each of these initiatives asks of you.

Encourage the Person You Hurt to Share Her Pain.

To defend against feeling dependent and vulnerable, she may silence herself in a number of ways. She may forgive you too easily. She may go numb. She may go along to get along, as though she has forgiven you, while inside she continues to storm. Or she may retreat into herself and shut you out.

If you're a conflict avoider, her silence will seem preferable to her rage. But don't be fooled. Muffled pain is just as problematic as uncontrollable fury, and perhaps even more dysfunctional. If you don't draw her out and encourage her to talk through her injury, she'll never get close to you or forgive you.

I can't stress this point enough: *no conflict, no closeness.* If you want to rebuild the bond, you, the offender, must regularly invite and embolden her to reveal how deeply you have hurt her. This opening up to you is an act of intimacy, a first step in lowering the barrier between you. Detachment may be her protection. But what may be protective to her is likely to be a death knell for the relationship.

When Vicky learned of Sid's eight-month affair, the couple came into therapy looking like smiling plastic dolls: attractive, impeccably manicured, oh-so-respectfully mannered toward each other. When I asked how things were going, they listed all the nice things that were happening—their child getting into Columbia's MBA program; their bid on a retirement home in Palm Beach that had been accepted. Sid told me in an individual session, "Things are going just fine." Vicky, however, had a different story. She talked about her alcohol abuse, her deep clinical depression, her bitterness over his betrayal. What looked like an absence of conflict was simply a cover-up. Vicky was crackling with resentment. Sid was determined to look the other way.

The couple had spent a lifetime avoiding painful issues. But as the therapy progressed, and Vicky revealed how shaken she was by his affair, and he acknowledged how unsettled he felt about his retirement and a recent bout of prostate cancer, he began to fight for the survival of the marriage.

The challenge for both of them was enormous. "Do you know

how badly Vicky's hurting?" I asked Sid. "You need to prove to her that her misery matters to you. If you want her to heal, you need to emotionally reengage with her and help soak up the anxiety and bitterness inside her."

Sid understood and responded—first by asking Vicky to join him in weekly therapy sessions so that they could learn how to talk out their pain together, and then by following up at home, setting aside time when he encouraged her to open up to him. He began by prodding her with simple, gentle words like, "How are you? Please don't shut me out. I'm serious about reconnecting with you, and that won't happen if you keep your feelings from me. What do you need me to understand? Tell me more. Is there more?"

Gradually, Vicky began to warm up, trust his words, and talk through some of the insufferable moments in their marriage—such as the time she had had a miscarriage and Sid had arranged for a neighbor to drive her to the hospital so that he could go to work. Sid learned to stay present and steady, and to support her efforts to release the sadness in her heart.

When you, like Sid, invite the person you hurt to share her pain and make herself vulnerable in your presence, you build a bridge to her and help heal her brokenness.

Initiate Discussion About the Injury.

Each time you bring up the violation, you let the hurt party know that it's on your mind, too—that she's not alone with it. When you demonstrate that you won't forget what you did and will continue to be mindful of its lessons, you help release her from her preoccupation with the injury. I often say, *If you want your partner to move on, you must pay attention to her pain. If you don't, she will.*

A patient named Jim took the first step when, as Mother's Day approached, he told his wife, Donna, "It was last year at this time that you found out about my affair. I'm sure it's on your mind. It's on mine, too. I've been thinking about how we might spend the day differently this year, to create a new memory, a more positive association. Here are some thoughts I had . . ."

On a personal note, I remember having lunch with my frail, elderly father almost one year after my mother died. Though I wasn't the cause of his distress, I wanted to be a source of comfort. As we sat in a diner sharing a tuna fish sandwich, I wondered to myself, "Does he know we're approaching the anniversary of her death? Should I bring it up? Will I make him feel sad if I mention it?" Finally, I found myself stumbling over the words, "Dad, it's been about a year since Mom died." This man who often seems so cognitively fuzzy, so lost, looked right at me and said, "I know. This Sunday, October twenty-first."

I had assumed that if he had wanted to talk about this, he would have brought it up himself. Or that if I brought it up, I would upset him. Or that if I didn't bring it up, he wouldn't remember. But this trauma—the untimely passing of my mother, his bride of fifty-three years—was all that he wanted to talk about. It was just a question of whether he was going to be alone with his pain or I would share it with him.

Listen to the Hurt Person's Pain with an Open Heart.

You may want to run from the anguish you inflicted on another human being. What good can come from allowing her to pour out her grief, you may wonder, except to punish you and make you feel small? But your listening helps her open up to you and let you back into her life. You can't skip this step. And she can't come forward, trust you, or forgive you until you convince her that you understand and care about the damage you did.

How can a person forgive you if you're indifferent to her suffering? She can't, not authentically—not until you reach out and *hold her pain*. By "hold her pain" I mean that you put aside your own feelings, your own needs, your own agenda; I mean that you dismantle your defenses and justifications, even your version of the violation, and experience her pain as she experiences it, as though it were your own.

You shouldn't try to cheer her up—she's likely to see this as a manipulation to discount or dispel her suffering for your own advantage. Better just listen and allow yourself to be affected by her story. Try to taste her fear, her sadness, her indignity, even if you've never been hurt in the same way—even if you believe your offense isn't as serious as she makes it out to be.[14] Allow yourself to enter her world and resonate with her grief.

A patient named Howard learned to do this, but it didn't come easily or without discomfort. When he left home after a string of affairs, his fourteen-year-old daughter, Alice, tried to cut him out of her life. Occasionally he would stop by and offer to take her to soccer practice or dinner, but she remained sealed off. One day, after listening to her mother screaming at him on the phone, Alice poured out her pain in an E-mail and sent it to him:

> Today you made me realize what a bad and horrible person you have been. The only feeling i have right now toward you is HATE, and i feel it wholeheartedly. Time and time again, ive had conversations with you about how you hurt mommy and how you promised to try and act with dignity and respect. But right now, mommy is crying in the kitchen because you treat her like she is nothing but the dirt on the ground. YOU are the one who is cheating on mommy, don't deny it, so why should mommy try to be nice to you?
>
> The other day, at the tennis courts, Roger [Alice's older brother] called you "Howard" and we all laughed about it. You want to know why? He doesn't even want to be related to you anymore. He doesn't want to call YOU father. YOU don't deserve it and never will. I hate you i hate you i hate you. I tried to keep that hate away, but now i realize that's all i can ever feel toward you. Roger can never forgive you, yet i have never heard you tell him once you were sorry. Are you that much of a coward? What are you good for then—lying and cheating behind people's backs? Dad . . . i know that you are probably really angry and upset because of what im saying, but i cant deny it anymore and i have to get my feelings across to you. Just imagine, in 30 years, when you are left alone in the world . . . who is going to be there for you???

Mebbe one day you'll finally realize everything good youve ever lost. and me and Roger? we'll forget about you and move on.

Alice

Howard came into therapy with a copy of his daughter's E-mail. "I don't know how to react," he told me. "Part of me feels shaken—I've hurt my family terribly. But part of me thinks I should punish her for speaking to me with such disrespect. I never spoke to my father this way, though he did worse things than I've ever done. What do you think?"

My response was, "Your daughter must love you very much. It's probably a lot easier for her to be distant than to share her anguish with you. She's trusting you with her pain. This is a very precious gift. I recommend that you accept it, rise above the harsh language and insults, and try to appreciate the devastation and despair she's feeling. She may be giving you a chance to earn back her trust and love, even her forgiveness."

Howard began to cry. As the weeks passed, he made genuine efforts to reach out to Alice. He sent her an E-mail thanking her for speaking so honestly and arranged to meet with her so he could hear her out. None of this could have happened if Alice hadn't opened up to him and taken the risk of exposing her fury. None of it could have happened if Howard had been unable to bear witness to her pain and absorb what she had to say without defending himself or detaching from her.

A lesson in listening

If you, like Howard, don't know how to listen with an open heart and mind, there are many communication training books that can guide you. Among them are *Healing Conversations: What to Say When You Don't Know What to Say* by Nance Guilmartin; *Why Marriages Succeed or Fail* by John Gottman; and *The Zen of Listening: Mindful Communication in the Age of Distraction* by Rebecca Shafir. These books stress the importance of nonverbal communication, such as:

- listening with both your eyes and ears;
- being respectful of pauses and silences in your conversation and not jumping in to rush away the pain;
- monitoring your tone of voice to convey the sincerity of your concern; and
- using body language (for example, leaning toward the hurt party) to foster connection.

Don't underestimate the power of nonverbal communication. According to one study, your gestures and facial expressions convey 55 percent of the meaning of a message; tone of voice, speech rate, rhythm, and emphasis convey 38 percent; and what we actually say conveys only 7 percent. In other words, "nonverbal cues communicate the bulk of the message."[15]

Listening to both soft and hard emotions

If the person you hurt expresses her pain with "soft" emotions such as sadness, shame, or grief, I suggest that you try to mirror (reflect back) what she needs you to understand. You might say, for example, "What you need me to take in is that when I was unfaithful to you, I destroyed your belief in the goodness of people and robbed you of the way you knew yourself. You used to think of yourself as capable, attractive, funny, full of life. Now, no matter what you do, you can't recapture your familiar self, and you're angry about that."

If she expresses her pain with "hard emotions"—bitterness or rage—it may help to see past her tough exterior and connect with the scared, bruised person crouching inside. Though you may experience her as trying to push you away, she may want nothing more than for you to come closer. If she's relentless in her fury and you find your patience wearing thin, I recommend that you gently try to redirect the conversation away from the details of her argument to what is happening between you on an emotional level. For example, if she is screaming at you and all you want to do is explode or run away, you might pull yourself together and say, "I want to know your pain, but I need you to talk to me in a way that helps me hear it. I'm not asking you to sugarcoat what you feel, but don't shut me out, either. I'm here. I'm listening."

Listening nondefensively doesn't necessarily mean that you agree with her version of what happened. It shows only that you care deeply about the pain you caused and want to be an integral part of her recovery.

Listening, you help her heal and feel human again. "We listen one another into speech," notes Harvard psychologist Judith Jordan. "We're listened into being."[16]

Listening is one of the most powerful healing gestures you can make. It cuts through the hurt party's sense of denigration and isolation and encourages her to reattach to you. Your being fully present to validate her pain is what trauma expert Mary Jo Barrett calls "compassionate witnessing." This exchange in which she entrusts you with her feelings, and you are there for her, warmly, attentively, knocks down the wall between you and opens the way to forgiveness.

Critical Task #3: Apologize—genuinely, non-defensively, responsibly.

An apology is more than a simple "I'm sorry," though that's a fine way to begin. It's also a way of saying that you take responsibility for your actions, care deeply about the pain you caused, and intend never to repeat the transgression.

I'd like to think, or perhaps I'd like you to think, that there aren't many times when I need to ask others to forgive me. But let's be real. Here's one of them. After verbally assaulting my husband, I framed him as the problem, then struggled to take ownership of my own inappropriate rage and the mess I alone had created.

After my mother died, I moved my father from Florida to Connecticut so that he would be closer to the rest of the family. It was an exhausting project, filled with a million details—researching independent living facilities, transferring medical records, closing down his condominium, furnishing his new apartment. By the time I flew him back to Connecticut, I was totally fried. My husband, Michael, picked us up at the airport and brought us to Dad's new home. Finally, everything seemed to be in place. But just before we said good night, Michael uncorked a bottle of red wine for a welcome toast and splashed it across everything I had set up on the kitchen counters—the medication charts, the new food, the clean utensils. To be honest, I decompensated and went for the kill: "How could you be so stupid? It was so obvious that this would happen!" and on and on. Not my finest hour. Dad and Mike stared at me in silence, appalled.

Did I fall apart because of the stress of the move? I was so anxious about relocating Dad, still shocked at the loss of my mother, so bone-tired from the entire ordeal. Did I fall apart because I am who I am—a woman with a deep-seated need for everything to be perfect? Should I blame my early childhood experience as a caretaker, as an overly responsible person who always took on too much? Does it matter?

It does. As much as I wanted to make excuses for myself and blame Mike for my reaction, I knew this was cowardly and false. I finally mustered up enough inner strength to approach these two profoundly important men in my life. "I want to apologize for my behavior," I said sheepishly. "I know, Mike, you were just trying to be helpful and sweet. I acted terribly and I'm ashamed of myself. I'm sorry."

Lest I sound too mature, reasonable, and integrated, let me admit how hard it was for me to say these words. Certainly, my demonic behavior contradicted my "official" story of myself as a controlled, sensitive psychologist and forgiveness expert. But I knew in my heart that if I blundered recklessly and simply let myself off the hook, I didn't deserve forgiveness—from the people I hurt, or from myself.

Why Are Apologies So Important?

When you fail to apologize, you're likely to feel the way I felt about myself—crummy. You usually know when you've wronged someone and have to live with that knowledge. If you try to minimize or dismiss it, you seal in your guilt. Apologize, and you begin to re-create yourself, restore your self-respect, and repair the tear within. A reintegration takes place. You know you did wrong. You know you can do better.

Your apology conveys respect for the person you harmed—another precondition of forgiveness. You admit that she deserved better and that you crossed a line. This admission humbles you, elevates her, and restores a measure of equilibrium.

Your apology may help to reconnect the two of you. When you come clean, you not only disarm her and allow her to feel more kindly toward you; you clear your own conscience and are more likely to allow yourself to reattach to her. As Beverly Engel points out, "Knowing we have wronged someone may cause us to distance ourselves from the person, but once we have apologized we feel free to be vulnerable and intimate."[17]

What Makes for a Good Apology?

To make a good apology, I recommend the following seven guidelines:

Guideline 1: Take responsibility for the damage you caused.

Behind every injury is an injurer. For your apology to take hold, you must acknowledge your role: "I am the perpetrator. I did this to you." As Beverly Flanigan, author of *Forgiving the Unforgivable*, writes, "Someone is wrong. Someone must be identified. Then someone can be forgiven."[18]

At a memorial to 1,600 Jews massacred in Poland during World War Two, a monument was unveiled that read, "To the memory of Jews from Jedwabne and the surrounding area, men, women and children, inhabitants of this land, who were murdered and burned alive on this spot on July 10, 1941." Though Poland's president publicly asked for pardon in his own name and "in the name of those Polish people whose consciences are shocked by this crime," many Jewish leaders and sympathizers were angry that the inscription did not explicitly blame the Polish townspeople.[19] Nowhere did it say, "We did this."

As part of her healing process, the injured party needs to assign blame and to have you, the offender, accept culpability. An effective apology, therefore, is not just some vague reference to the fact that someone, somehow got hurt, but a pointed acknowledgment that "I wronged you, and for that I'm sorry."

Guideline 2: Make your apology personal.

The most effective apology is exquisitely personal. It's not just an admission that "I did something wrong." It's an admission that "I wronged *you*. I did this to *you*." What helps the hurt party heal and move the forgiveness process forward is not just that you care about violating your *own* standard of conduct but that you care about having violated *her*.

When Jane discovered that her husband had slept with her unmarried half-sister Ellen, Jane confronted her. "I think about it every day," Ellen admitted. "I don't like to—it doesn't fit my idea of myself. But I have to face what I did."

Jane listened to Ellen's confession but remained angry and unnerved. She soon realized why. "I don't care if Ellen feels bad about herself or believes she broke some personal code of honor," Jane told me. "So what if she let herself down? What I want to know is whether she is upset for *me*. Does she care what she did *to me*?"

Jane wrote Ellen a letter, asking her to address this issue. Ellen never replied, and Jane never forgave her.

A sixty-two-year-old patient, Roy, offers another good example of what an effective apology entails. When he confessed to his wife that he was a sex addict and had been seeing other women for more than fifteen years, he explained that he had been sexually abused as a child. "I've suffered, too," he told her.

His wife was spectacularly unmoved. "His apology has more to do with his pain than mine," she told me. "He hurts for himself, not for me."

There are times when you may not understand the deeply personal impact of your defense. To flesh this out, you could say to the hurt party something as simple as, "I'd like to understand how I may have reopened old wounds, and apologize to you. Can you help me?"

Jack, a forty-year-old electrician, tried to follow this advice when he told his wife that he had been cheating on her during her last month of pregnancy. First, he encouraged her to talk out her pain and took in everything she had to say. Then he apologized, mirroring back to her what she needed him to grasp: "I want to apologize for hurting you so terribly, and violating you in ways in which you were already vulnerable," he told her in my office. "I understand that when I cheated on you during your pregnancy, you felt trapped, with no one to turn to and nowhere to go, which was exactly how your parents made you feel when you were a kid and they abandoned you. I abandoned you in the same way. You thought you could count on me, but all I've done is reinforce your belief that no one is there for you."

Jack's willingness to get inside his wife's experience and see how his behavior added yet another layer of emotional scar tissue to her already damaged self opened her to the possibility of forgiveness. His personal apology was a beginning.

Guideline 3: Make your apology specific.

When you apologize, don't just say, "I'm sorry." You need to capture *exactly what you're sorry for*. You need to describe not just the broad brushstrokes of the injury but the fine details. You need to be boldly concrete, apologizing not only for hurting someone but for precisely *how* you hurt her. Only then will she trust that you appreciate the harm you caused her and will never cross that line again.

I suggest, particularly to those of you who have injured your life partner or someone with whom you have a meaningful past, that you try to list everything you have done to hurt her over the years— not just the single, obvious, mega-wound you just inflicted.

When Amy, a fifty-two-year-old hair stylist, apologized to her husband for being unfaithful, she did not simply say, "I'm sorry I had an affair." She tried to convey how her affair had devastated him and what exactly she was sorry for. She also thought beyond the affair to other ways in which she may have injured him. "There are times over the past thirty years when I've treated you in totally indefensible ways," she began. Then she listed the behaviors she was sorry for:

- I exposed you to the risk of sexually-transmitted diseases each time I slept with someone else.
- I kept secrets from you and relegated you to the role of an outsider who knew less about me than some stranger.
- I made you doubt yourself and question your place in the world.
- I tarnished many otherwise happy memories of our life together.
- I blamed you when I felt lonely, instead of addressing my own lifelong sense of loneliness.
- I shut you out when I was feeling angry and frustrated about our relationship, instead of talking to you directly about what was bothering me.
- I drank too much and working excessive hours, increasing the distance between us.
- I gave up on our relationship without letting you know, making it impossible for us to work things out together.

Amy's husband, Paul, knew that he wasn't totally innocent—he had abandoned her, too, in his own way. He responded by writing her his own apology. "I want to apologize for not being there for you over the years, and for all the frustration and pain I brought you. Specifically, I'm sorry for being so concerned about financial security that I ignored the quality of our life together. I was unavailable to you when your sister died. I packed my anger away and got back at you in passive-aggressive ways, which made it impossible for you to respond directly to my grievances."

Guideline 4: Make your apology deep.

If you want to be forgiven, you have to cough up the whole wretched truth of what you did. Don't be content with easy admissions;

keep scraping away to uncover deeper, darker truths. Let yourself burn with embarrassment, if that fits the bill. As Albert Ellis has been known to advise patients who are engaging in personal growth exercises, "If you're feeling uncomfortable, you're probably doing something right."

It may be helpful to write and rewrite your apology, each draft cutting closer to the unflattering truth. That's what a patient named John did. He began with a superficial note apologizing to his wife for hurting her feelings. Then he tried again. "Over the years, I've spoken to you with contempt," he began. "I've put you down to raise myself up. I've hidden how insecure and unworthy I felt, how afraid I was of losing you or getting close to you. I preyed on your kind soul. I pretended I was superior at your expense. My mother behaved exactly the same way toward my father and me. I hate this in myself."

Here are some other examples of effective apologies:

- A mother tells her daughter, "I never made you feel that you were OK, that you were great just the way you were. I was always trying to change you, to make you more feminine, more like your sister, to get you to live up to my image of the proper little girl. I don't know why I felt so anxious, why I doubted you. But this is my issue, not yours."

- A daughter tells her mother, "Growing up, I was tough on you and angry that you seemed so preoccupied. Now that I have my own child, I see how hard it is to manage a home and a job and still be tuned into your kids' feelings. With Dad drinking and providing no support, I don't know how you held it all together. I thought only about myself. It never occurred to me to think about you."

- One friend tells another: "I've said small, mean things to you, like, 'Not everyone is born with a million dollars in the bank.' I hate to admit this, but there are times when I feel jealous of you. Your life seems so easy compared with mine."

- A brother apologizes to his sister, "I let you take care of Dad and do nothing to help. I pretend I'm busy, but the truth is

I'm busy doing things for myself. You like to help others, so I let you. I milk this. I don't have to be you, but it's not fair for me to do so little."

Guideline 5: Make your apology heartfelt.

Sometimes people apologize well, but for selfish reasons—to rid themselves of guilt, to reduce conflict and make their lives easier, to show themselves off to God or friends as decent human beings. Need I say that your apology is likely to fall on deaf ears if your heart isn't in the right place? Anyone can be trained to utter polished words of remorse. The challenge is to experience and convey "a transformation of heart."[20] For you to be genuinely forgiven, your remorse must be real, profound, enduring.

My mentor Rabbi Israel Stein likes to remind his congregation during Yom Kippur, the High Holy Days of the Jewish people, that God is not impressed with our commitment to fasting. Fasting is by itself just rote behavior, he points out. But fasting done with heart has meaning and purpose. It agitates the soul. It inspires us to reach out to those whom we have wronged. During the services for the Days of Atonement, a ram's horn—a shofar—is blown in the synagogue to awaken the congregants from their slumber, to stir their hearts. "God," Rabbi Stein asserts, "is not interested in our rituals. He is interested in our humanity."

How do you convey a heartfelt apology? One way is through a tone of voice that is gentle, warm, and earnest. Another is through appropriate body language. When people apologize to each other in my office, I ask them to put down whatever they're holding, face each other, uncross their arms, and look into each other's eyes. If they're sitting, I suggest they both uncross their legs and lean toward each other. I then coach the offender to speak very slowly, letting the injured party feel the sincerity and absorb the truth of his words.

In *Sex, Love, and Violence: Strategies for Transformation,* family therapist Cloe Madanes requires anyone who has sexually abused his victim to express repentance on his knees before her.[21] Whether you prostrate yourself or not, genuine humility must lie at the core of your apology. Only when you strip away your sense of self-importance and shed your defensive tactics can you begin to convince the injured person that you're truly sorry.

Marie's father failed to do this. When she was thirty-five, she received a letter from him telling her that he was dying and that he wanted to apologize in person for his behavior over the years. "I want you to know I'm sorry for everything I did to hurt you," he wrote. "Now they've given me two months to live, and it would give me great peace of mind if you forgave me before I died."

Marie remembered that, when she was five, her mother had kicked her father out of the house for denying his alcohol problem and ignoring his family. "All those years he never sent cards, gifts, or child-support payments," Marie told me. "Now he wants me to save his soul."

The father's bland, blanket apology did nothing to earn him a place in his daughter's heart. She needed to hear him voice a profound sadness for the impact his behavior had had on her, but all she heard was his fear of hell.

How sad is this story? Who is to say that his contrition wasn't real—that with different words he might not have healed them both? But hearing nothing more than a perfunctory "I'm sorry" reinforced Marie's assumption that his apology was merely expedient—a way to win himself a place at God's table. She never spoke to him again.

Guideline 6. Make your apology clean.

The most effective apologies are pure, straightforward, and uncomplicated, with no *buts,* no fancy embellishments, or caveats.

Qualified apologies tend to backfire. When you try to pass off your misconduct as a mistake, an insignificant event, an understandable reaction to her misbehavior, the person you hurt is likely to feel even more battered and enraged than before. It's up to her to see the injury in a softer light, not you.

At times like these, it helps to remember that when you

acknowledge blame, the hurt person is more likely to acknowledge hers, too. That's what happened with Stan and Naomi.

After living with his wife's alcoholism for twenty-six years, Stan got involved with another woman. "I felt unloved and dismissed long enough," he told me. "Naomi's drinking makes her mean, and the way she carries on in public embarrasses me."

Naomi didn't blame Stan for causing her alcohol problem—she had drunk too much even in college—but he traveled a lot, entertaining Japanese clients in Tokyo strip bars, and her loneliness fed her addiction. She, too, felt unloved and abandoned.

When Stan came clean about his affair, the couple's relationship quickly unraveled. They tried to rebuild it. Privately, they knew they had wronged each other, but all they did was trade accusations. "I had an affair because you were off in a world of your own and refused to change," Stan told her. Naomi shot back, "I drink to drown out my loneliness because you're never there for me. You're not perfect either."

I suggested that they write apologies to each other at home simultaneously, then come to our next session prepared to read them. I encouraged them to overcome their "I need you to lick my wounds before I lick yours" approach to relationships and take turns acknowledging blame.

What they wrote served as a stepping-stone to forgiveness. Stan began, "I apologize for making you feel insecure and lonely, and for getting back at you by staying away. I'm sorry for managing my hurt by hurting you back rather than by doing something constructive like getting into therapy or Al-Anon."

Naomi wrote, "I'm sorry for making you feel so desperate that you had to turn to someone outside our marriage to be heard, rather than to me. I'm sorry for ignoring my drinking problem, and for compromising you publicly."

What this couple learned is that you can't accuse someone and apologize to him at the same time, just as you can't give and take with the same hand at the same time. One gesture cancels out the other. The two of you must put your recriminations aside and take turns, making full apologies and giving them a chance to sink in.

Guideline 7. Apologize repeatedly.

For "surface wounds," a single apology may be enough to win forgiveness. But for more serious injuries, you may need to apologize again and again, particularly if you hope to reconcile. As a patient of mine told her husband after she caught him secretly running up debts on their credit cards, "I don't want you to say you're sorry. I want you to be sorrowful with me. I want you to carry the sorrow the way I carry the sorrow, to walk the walk with me every day."

Don't wait for the perfect or right time to apologize. Make time. And don't wait until you've found the magic words; you can revise or add to them later.

An Apology Goes Beyond a Confession.

When you confess, you admit the wrong you did. When you apologize, you express remorse for the wrong you did. Each response has its value. A confession is a statement of fact: "As a priest I molested young boys." "As a father, I slapped my children with a belt that left welts on their bodies and souls." "As a wife, I pulled away from you sexually and made you feel inadequate." An apology, in contrast, is a feeling statement. It goes beyond the facts and reveals how you feel about them.

Confession has value because it shows that you have the insight and moral fiber to distinguish right from wrong. Apology goes further because it shows that you have the courage and humility to be judged by the person you wronged. "Confession lays bare your limitations," Beverly Flanigan points out. "Apology places those limitations in another's hands to be accepted or rejected."[22]

Sometimes the hurt party doesn't know you wronged her until you own up to it. This revelation gives her power and status. Suddenly she's as close to the truth as you are. As Frank Pittman once said, the issue "isn't whom you lie with. It's whom you lie to."[23] The person you're sharing secrets with is the one with whom you share a closer bond.

Both confession and apology can reduce shame, foster dialogue, and repair the connection between you. But only an apology, which shows regard for the hurt party's feelings, can earn forgiveness.

The limitations of confession alone, without apologies, are illustrated in this story of Connie and her fiancé, Martin. After an eight-month engagement, she asked him to attend "Pre-Cana" classes with her. These classes were organized by her church to help couples resolve conflict and find their way back to each other and to God. Martin hesitated. "I don't know," he said. "They ask lots of questions."

"What are you hiding from me?" Connie wanted to know.

Martin finally confessed that he had a history of genital warts. He had knowingly exposed her to this contagious disease, for which he was treating himself secretly with nitrogen hydroxide.

Though shocked, Connie was grateful to know the truth. But she needed to find out how he felt about what he had done and pressed him to talk about his feelings. Martin began to cry. "I was ashamed to tell you and afraid you wouldn't want to marry me if you knew the truth," he said. "I'm so sorry I kept such an important secret from you. I was incredibly selfish. I put you physically at risk. I crippled your ability to trust me in the future. You're probably wondering what else I'm keeping from you, who I am deep down inside, what our relationship is really about."

Martin's confession gave Connie information. His apology gave the relationship a chance to live.

Your Apology Needs to Go Beyond an Expression of Regret.

An expression of regret is *intrapersonal*—something you offer by and for yourself. It reveals how you feel about your behavior, not how you feel about the person you harmed. It says, "I'm sorry for what I did. It probably wasn't worth the consequences I suffered." It doesn't necessarily acknowledge that you care about her, or even that you believe what you did was wrong. It may be nothing more than an expression of displeasure that you stirred up trouble for yourself and made your life more complicated. An apology, in contrast, is *interpersonal*. It's all about your feelings toward the person you harmed. It conveys, sometimes explicitly, your promise never to injure her again.

In April 2001, an American reconnaissance plane flew into Chinese airspace and collided with a Chinese military jet. President Bush publicly expressed regret for the loss of a Chinese airman. Secretary of State Powell eventually used the word "sorry," but the word was translated into a Chinese term that carried no acknowledgment of guilt. These linguistic nuances illustrate the delicate art of forgiving. The Chinese held out until the American administration used a word implying that "the speaker acknowledges wrongdoing."[24]

An Apology Needs to Go Beyond "Icing on a Rancid Cake."

When you hurt someone, you may want to show remorse by doing nice things for her. But these loving behaviors, no matter how sincere, cannot substitute for a straightforward, heartfelt apology. As collateral gifts, they may convey an honest wish to make up, but they're not enough to earn forgiveness. I call these indirect offerings *icing on a rancid cake.*

The mother of one of my patients, David, tried to gain her son's forgiveness in the final days of her life. While selling her house the year before, she had accused him of stealing from her. Insulted and demeaned, he had hired an accountant and proved that she, in fact, owed him more than $100,000. Not only did she not apologize, she taunted him with her favorite line: "Muhammad never goes to the mountain; the mountain comes to Muhammad." A few months later, in a bid for his affection, she offered him her crystal glassware—"icing on a rancid cake."

"I think this is her idea of a peace offering," David told me, "but I turned her down. How could she question my integrity? I've been such a good son. I love her and want to have a relationship with her, but she makes it so hard."

A year later, as his mother lay in a hospice dying of lung cancer, David finally spoke up. "Before you die, I'd like you to do me a favor," he said. "I'd like you to apologize for saying I took your money." His mother took his hand and said, "I made a mistake, and I'm sorry for hurting your feelings. You've never given me any reason not to trust you. This suspicion thing comes with old age. You feel more vulnerable, more anxious. It's about me, not you. You've been a wonderful boy." She smiled and added, "Now will you take the crystal?"

Recently, I was sitting on a train beside a woman who was holding a bouquet of long-stem roses. Always ready to hear a good story, I said, "May I ask the occasion?" She answered with a wicked twinkle in her eye, "It's an 'I'm sorry.'"

"You must have done something really bad," I joked.

"Not me," she smiled. "Him."

I pointed at the flowers. "So does this do the trick?"

"No way!" she shot back.

"What does he need to do?" I asked. "Address the problem itself?"

"You'd better believe it," she said.

What these stories illustrate is a basic lesson about forgiveness: If you want to heal an injury you can't just have fun together or offer superficial gifts. You must directly address the pain you caused.

Examples of Bad Apologies

A bad apology is everything a good apology isn't. In a bad apology, you deny, discount, or dismiss the injury. You convey the attitude that you're terribly put out at having to make amends. You let the injured party know how ponderous and silly this process of earning forgiveness is. You apologize in ways that block healing and keep the injury alive.

Here are a few examples of bad apologies:

- The two-second apology: "Sorry."
- The sanitized apology: "I'm sorry for whatever I did wrong."
- The shirk responsibility apology: "I'm sorry *if* I hurt your feelings."
- The lack of ownership apology: "I'm sorry your feelings are hurt."
- The perfunctory apology: "As I've said before, I'm sorry."

- The vindictive apology: "I'll show you what it means to be sorry."
- The grudging apology: "I *said* I was sorry. What else do you want?"
- The expedient apology: "I know I'm in the doghouse unless I say I'm sorry, so here it is."
- The "yes . . . but," blame-deflecting apology: "I'm sorry I did X, but you're no Mother Teresa either."
- The "Oh, what the hell" apology: "Heh, I'm sorry, pal."
- The obsequious apology: "I'm so sorry, I'm so sorry, I'm so sorry (but don't ask me why)."
- The contemptuous apology: "I'm sorry for stepping on your big fat ego."
- The exaggerated, manipulative apology: "I hate myself for what I did. Can you ever, ever forgive me?"
- The guilt-inducing apology: "Do you really need me to apologize for *that*?"

An Example of a Good Apology

A middle-aged doctor named Alex had a sexual and emotional relationship with an out-of-state business associate during the sixteen years of his marriage. His wife, Kate, was raised by a sexually abusive, alcoholic father, and carried into her adult life a fear of anger and confrontation. Alex had a drinking problem, too; this and a condescending tone, made it impossible for Kate to enjoy sex with him. When she learned that he was leading a double life, he ended his affair. While in couple therapy, he wrote Kate the following letter, which captures many elements of a good apology:

I'm sorry, Kate. The list of apologies is long and hard to write. Starting backward, I am sorry to have brought you (us) to this point. . . . I hope I'll be able to express these thoughts in a way that will convey the sincerity of my remorse and my very real desire to rebuild our relationship. . . . I'm sorry to have spent so many years in an alcoholic fog, ignoring your loving warnings and turning my back on the presence of a demon, now obvious, that stalks our families. Alcoholism is never good, but in our case it was doubly bad because it recalled all the horror of that aspect of your childhood. And mine. It crippled my ability to face reality, it distorted my personality, and, most devastating, it erected a wall between us.

I'm sorry that I left you to bring up the children largely on your own. While I hid from my shortcomings in caves— work, alcohol, and someone other than you—you made your way along the difficult path of caring for the children without the comfort and help I should have provided. You managed masterfully, even preserving for me a loving place in their lives. How much better it would have been to have agonized over their troubles together. It would have done much for our relationship and for the children.

In our physical relationship, I also let you down in many ways. Rather than working at what neither of us much understood, I made it impossible. First by shattering the personal and emotional relationship that is essential for a happy sex life. It should have been an enhancement, an expansion of our commitment to one another. Instead, I withdrew the foundation. Then I added alcohol, bringing in fear, fear of the unknown past, and making you feel used and unloved. Finally, betraying our marital bond, I left you feeling cheated and deprecated rather than sacred. These things cannot be erased as if they never happened. The actions are irretrievable. The debt is enormous, and no doubt can never be fully made up. If I am able to regain your trust, I will try.

"You weren't even nice to me." I confess to being startled to hear you say this. I know now it is true, and I am ashamed. This disgraceful behavior I hope to replace with actions that will let you know that, though we are in many ways different, I respect, admire, love, and indeed cherish you.

The list could go on and on. The painful particulars could be spelled out. At least these things need saying. Saying is surely easier than doing, but it's a beginning.

Critical Task #4: Seek to understand your behavior and reveal the inglorious truth about yourself to the person you harmed.

When she asks you, "Why did you do it? Why did you hurt me so?" and you respond, "I don't know," she's likely to go ballistic. If you haven't a clue, why wouldn't you hurt her again? Why should she feel safe with you? Why should she forgive you?

Pete's habit of arranging to meet his wife at two and then showing up at four, without calling, may have developed because he had difficulty organizing his time, or because he believed that his time was more valuable than hers. For her to forgive him, he needs to dig deep inside himself and discover what his offense reveals about him and about his attitude toward her.

There's not much you can do to make good once you've violated someone. You can't redo your behavior. You can't wash away the pain or devastation you have caused. But you can spend time figuring out why you behaved the way you did and then trust the hurt party with your revelations.

If you tend not to confront yourself critically and hesitate to reveal your flawed self to others (this covers most of us), you may want to explore your issues with the help of a therapist. It's easy to come up with shallow, self-serving explanations, but this is empty, meaningless work, not the work of forgiveness. You must be willing to face harsh realities about yourself that on some level you know are true but fight hard not to own. You must also resist the unjustified urge to blame others—to cast them in the worst possible light and hold dear to your "official" story, which maintains your innocence.

Explore the Sources of Your Behavior.

Your offensive words or actions may be an automatic, well-worn response to anyone who seems to threaten you, and say more about you than they do about the person you harmed. You can read more about this and other key factors in Part Three, Acceptance.

Both of you should understand that this exercise in self-discovery, this turning inward, isn't meant to dismiss or diminish what you did.

You're just trying to shed light on your vulnerabilities so that you can behave in a more conscious and conscientious way in the future.

In confronting why you wronged another human being, I encourage you to ask yourself these hard questions:

- What allowed me to violate her rights—to devalue her and treat her without respect?
- What was I thinking? Was I thinking at all?
- How did I justify what I did? How did I give myself permission to act the way I did?
- What can I learn about myself from this? What was my behavior about? What am *I* about?

Why Is This Work Necessary?

You may ask yourself, "Why do I need to analyze my behavior and expose my dark inner core? Is it to disgrace myself in order to make her feel better? To castigate myself for my crime?"

It may help to reframe this task, seeing it, rather, as a way of unearthing your faults and creating a landscape where forgiveness can take place. Your willingness to dissect yourself publicly and lay claim to your issues is likely to help her trust you as someone who, of his own volition, wants to take control of his behavior.

"But will all this self-analysis authenticate my remorse, and convince her that I'm 'cured?'" you may ask. No, of course it won't. Insight alone won't make an unfaithful partner faithful, give an abusive parent more self-control, or make a coldhearted boss warmer. But without insight into the origin and meaning of your behavior—or, more to the point, *without your willingness to take an interest in these issues*—the hurt party has little reason to trust you again, and even less reason to forgive you.

One patient, Karen, found herself unable to forgive her unfaithful husband. "Why should I," she asked, "when he can't face why he strayed?" For two years Karen debated whether to recommit to him or file for divorce. Throughout this time, he refused to join her in therapy or discuss their relationship. "He tells me he can't look back, that something happened to him as a child, some form of abuse that would have catastrophic consequences if he uncovered it," she told me. "He tells me he'll never have another affair, because he's on medication for high blood pressure, which makes him impotent. And this is supposed to make me feel safe? I said to him, 'I need you to understand, and help me understand, why you cheated on me—to let me in on your secrets and work with me to make our marriage more solid and loving.' You know, it's not the affair that makes his behavior unforgivable. It's his unwillingness to talk about it or try to make sense of it. I'm left dangling. He's too busy protecting his feelings to tend to mine."

Injured parties like Karen need more than words of remorse. They need to be convinced that you've changed for good, particularly if they're thinking of reconciling. "He says he's sorry and won't do it again," Karen told me. "But how do I know he's sincere? How do I know he's changed for good? What if I open myself up to him and get slammed again?"

For you to answer "Because I won't" isn't going to spark much confidence. It's better to say, "Because I saw what my behavior did to us, and I don't want it ever to happen again." Best, though, is to say—and to demonstrate—"Because I have a depth of understanding about myself today that I didn't have before. I'm more conscious of where I'm coming from. I know my vulnerabilities, what sets me off, and how I tend to react. When I see what I don't like in myself, I don't look away or blame you, as I used to. I look more closely at myself."

Moving from Level 1 to Level 2 Explanations

In answering the question "Why did I do it?" your initial responses may be shallow or disingenuous. I call these Level 1 explanations. Level 2 explanations go deeper and are often upsetting in what they reveal about you. They require honesty, awareness, and humility.

Here are three Level 1 explanations. They move to Level 2 as you dig down into yourself and get closer to the truth.

Example 1: When Ron, a trial lawyer, ended his affair with a woman who worked in the courthouse, he agreed to tell his wife, Amelia, whenever he needed to go there. One day Amelia drove by the courthouse and saw his car in the lot. "Why did you break your promise?" she asked him that night. "Why would you want to destroy my trust in you again?"

Ron's Level 1 responses included: "I forgot to call you." "I didn't have time." "I was just going to run over and pick up some papers." "She doesn't work there on Tuesdays, so I didn't think it was important for you to know."

Ron agreed to work at being more honest with himself and with Amelia. Moving to Level 2, he admitted to her, "I realize it's important for you to know where I am. But there's something about being so accountable—something about knowing how important this is to you—that makes it hard for me to give you what you want. Calling you makes me feel like a prisoner who must meet the warden's demands. I'm still fighting my father's control, still defying his will, and you're caught in the middle."

Example 2: Stephen's teenage daughters confronted him about his explosive temper. He tried to explain. Operating on Level 1, he said, "The world is a tough place. I need to be tough. I need to teach you to be tough. When you provoke me, you push me over the edge."

His Level 2 response was more thoughtful. In a letter addressed to his kids, he wrote, "You ask, why do I act the way I do. I think I'm a product of my past. My father was a manic-depressive. He'd be silent for days, then blow up. And when he did, I felt obliterated. I couldn't speak up to him, but I swore I'd never let anyone else treat me like dirt. I know I get hot too fast. I take things too personally. My anger is a mask. It makes me feel tough and in control. It's like a shield I put up against the humiliation, the sense of helplessness, I'm feeling at the time. I never wanted to be like my father. Guess what? I am, and I hate it."

Example 3: A year after her daughter was born, Tory told her husband, Warren, that she wanted a divorce. At first she offered a Level 1 explanation for her coldness—"I'm just responding to the way you treat me."

As she reached into her past, Tory moved to Level 2: "I grew up with a father who kept a record of my behavior inside a locked kitchen cabinet. Every time he thought I was bad, he put down a

gold star. When I earned ten—and I never knew when that was—
he lashed me with a strap. Where was my mother? I learned that
relationships were dangerous and that if I was going to survive I'd
have to rely on myself. Did I expect to get married and have it easy?

"When it comes to us, I get angry when you don't look at me when
I talk to you, when you monopolize the conversation, when you don't
ask me what I think. I assume you don't respect me. I understand that's
your way—you can be self-absorbed and distracted. If I didn't overre-
act, I could point out your pattern, and you'd probably try harder.
You're flawed, but you're not evil. I've been cold from the get go
because I expected you to harm me. I never gave the marriage a chance.
I was out of here before I signed the papers."

Critical Task #5: Work hard to earn back trust.

Your words convey your intent; your behavior demonstrates your
capacity for change. To earn forgiveness, you need to back up your
words of remorse with acts of repentance. Just as critical as "I'm
sorry, I won't do it again" are your bold, concrete gestures, day after
day, which drive home the point that you mean what you say.

Concrete Acts of Atonement and the Restoration of Trust

Here are four ways to restore trust and demonstrate your desire
to produce lasting change.

1. Engage in low-cost and high-cost trust-building behaviors.

In my book on recovering from infidelity, *After the Affair,* I
developed the concept of low- and high-cost trust-building behaviors. The "cost" refers to the emotional, not necessarily the mone-
tary, expense, to the offender.

A low-cost, trust-building behavior is something you can do
regularly, with relative ease, to demonstrate the sincerity of your
penitence. A high-cost behavior requires much more of you. It often
involves a great sacrifice that makes you feel uncomfortable, defensive, or resistant. In choosing appropriate acts of atonement, you
have to give the hurt party what matters to *her,* what *she* needs to

trust you again. There's no formula, no prescription, for healing. Just be wary of an anemic response—too little, too late. You may be asked to provide a significant intervention—not a few drops of blood, but a transfusion. It's better to err on the side of generosity.

When it comes time to script your repentance, don't assume that the two of you are going to be on the same page. I encourage you, therefore, to pinpoint her needs either by asking her exactly what you can do to win back her trust or by making suggestions and asking her to rate their importance to her.

If you want to be forgiven for an affair, common low-cost, trust-building behaviors might be:

- changing your cell phone number so that your former lover doesn't know how to reach you;
- encouraging your partner to call you at any time;
- letting your partner know as soon as you run into or hear from the lover;
- giving your partner a copy of your monthly telephone and credit card bills;
- sending and reading E-mail only in your partner's presence; and
- telling your partner when you feel angry or annoyed at her rather than storing your feelings, as you may have done in the past.

High-cost behaviors might include:

- changing jobs, if you and the lover work in the same office;
- changing homes or communities, if you and the lover are neighbors;
- formally ending your relationship with the lover in your partner's presence; and
- putting a significant portion of your savings in your partner's name.

Here are high- and low-cost behaviors that can be used to redress other violations:

- exploring your early childhood wounds in therapy and writing the hurt party a letter revealing what you learn about yourself and your present behavior;
- acknowledging the truth of her accusations both to her and to those who matter to her (her spouse, her children);
- respecting her need to distance herself from you (not touching her when you greet each other, if that's her wish);
- not pressuring her to forgive you.

2. Fill out a Dysfunctional Thought Form (DTF).

Another way to convey remorse is to fill out a Dysfunctional Thought Form (DTF). This form, developed by Aaron Beck,[25] helps you talk back to the negative or distorted ideas that shaped the way you perceived, felt toward, and treated the person you hurt. Here's how to fill one out.

Dysfunctional Thought Form

1. Describe the situation— the facts	2. Describe how you feel	3. Record your automatic thoughts	4. Record your corrected ideas

In the first column, write down the objective facts—what happened, separate from any thoughts or feelings you have about it. In the second column, describe the various ways you feel: offended, humiliated, challenged, angry, anxious, frustrated, depressed, and so on. In the third column, write down your automatic thoughts—those that flow through your mind. Don't edit or embellish them; just record them. In the fourth column, try to talk back to these automatic thoughts, identifying errors in your thinking. Behind this exercise is the idea that your thoughts fuel your emotions but are often irrational or mistaken. When you correct your ideas, your emotional response changes, too, and becomes less reactive, more calibrated to the realities of the situation. For a more detailed description of how to challenge your maladaptive thoughts, I recommend *Mind Over Mood* by Dennis Greenberger and Christine Padesky, and *Feeling Good: The New Mood Therapy* by David Burns.

Let's look at Maria, a patient who used the DTF and this "cognitive restructuring exercise" to earn her husband's forgiveness.

Maria grew up in a large, vocal Italian family. "Everyone talked at once," she told me. "You learned to raise your voice to be heard. My mother had a temper from hell and fought with me and my sister all the time, but we'd fight back, and the air would clear. My husband, George, comes from a different planet. His family ignores conflict and tends to live in silence. When I get angry, I let loose. For me, anger is a release. It means nothing. For him, it's the end of the world. There's no question that he provokes me, but I stoke the fire. He's had it with me. We're maybe one argument away from splitting up."

Here's how Maria filled out the form.

Column 1: Describe the situation. We were having a party, so I asked him to hang four flowerpots outdoors while I ran errands. He was home with our two young children. When I returned three hours later, he hadn't followed through, and the computer was turned on.

Column 2: Describe how you feel. I'm furious at him. I want to decapitate him.

Column 3: Record your automatic thoughts. I ask him to do one damn thing for me, and he can't. Do I have to do everything myself? Of course he still finds time to play with the computer.

Column 4: Challenge your automatic thoughts. Ask yourself: Are my ideas accurate? Are they useful? Is my response typical of me? What could I do differently?

Are my ideas accurate? The truth is, George did a lot for the family today. He took the kids to the park and weeded the garden while they played in the yard. He didn't hang the plants, he told me later, because he didn't feel comfortable being on a ladder with power tools while the kids were running around him. He put the computer on for a minute while the kids were eating a snack.

Are my ideas useful? I jump to conclusions and polarize us—I'm perfect, he's a bum. I work hard, he's lazy. Then I speak to him with contempt, which makes him hate me and want to do even less.

Is my response typical of me? Yes. I need to calm down and watch my tone of voice. I grew up in a family very different from George's, where conflict was handled differently. What seems benign to me is lethal to him—and to us. I get revved up too fast and lash out.

What could I do differently? I could ask him what happened rather than assume the worst. I could ask him when he could get the work done. This is important to him. I have to make it important to me. Changing the way he wants me to change won't hurt me. In fact, I'd feel better about myself if I tried.

By getting at the ideas behind her behavior, critiquing them and providing new, more constructive responses, Maria demonstrated that she was serious about becoming a more responsive partner. What she said, in effect, was, "For you to forgive me, it's not enough for me to apologize or own up to my behavior. I need to change the way I treat you. I want to do this. I will work to make it happen."

3. Realization notes

Realization Notes are brief cards or E-mails you send to the hurt party to demonstrate that you're disturbed by your behavior and are trying to change. Filling them out allows you to go beyond general expressions of regret or promises of change and share specific insights into yourself that make your repentance more credible.

A patient, Victor, was a typical conflict avoider. When something bothered him, he either didn't process it consciously or he extinguished his feelings, telling himself that speaking up would do no good, that his wife would just feel criticized and retaliate. For years, he stored up his grievances, layer upon layer.

After fifteen years of marriage, Victor had an affair with a woman he met on the Internet. When his wife, Beth, found out—their college-age son had been secretly reading Victor's pornographic E-mails for months—Victor felt sick with shame and agreed to do a number of things to make his wife feel safe and cherished. One was to fill out Realization Notes.

First, Victor listened to what Beth most needed him to do to restore trust. She told him, "I want to know when you're unhappy. You're always very nice to me, very giving, very involved. But I don't know what goes on inside you. How can I tell when something I do pushes you away? I need you to come to me, to tell *me*—not someone else. Not some stranger. Not even some therapist."

So Victor began to work on this—to take an interest in his feelings and write about them in a journal every day, fighting back his natural inclination to stifle conflict. When something bothered him, he wrote out a Realization Note and gave it to Beth.

One day he brought home flowers from the supermarket. "The flowers there really aren't very fresh," Beth reminded him. "And, for future reference, we need two bunches to fill the vase."

Victor paused to register what he felt. In the past he would have held onto his anger until he had calmed down enough to bury it. This time, he wrote Beth a card that said, "It's hard for me to admit this—I'm so used to letting conflict go. Your comment made me feel kicked in the butt. Say what you want about the flowers, but I need to hear that you appreciate my efforts. I need to be able to please you."

Beth prickled when she read the card. But she also saw it as an act of contrition and intimacy. "It's better than having you bottle up your feelings and express them in bed with someone else," she told him.

4. Plan a recommitment ceremony.

It's important to take the initiative here and plan the details in a way that says, "This is something I believe in and choose to do." You can conduct the ceremony in front of your children, relatives, or close friends, but not necessarily in a public forum.

You may begin by reading out loud what you promise to do for the person you hurt, taking responsibility for the future of the relationship and the reestablishment of a secure, caring bond. You may say, for example, "I promise to rededicate myself to making you feel safe and cherished. I promise to give up alcohol and attend AA meetings at least six times a week. I promise not to bury my feelings but to talk to you when I'm feeling hurt or annoyed." The other partner then makes promises of her own.

All these exercises are designed to help you make the hurt party feel safe, valued, and cared for, and deepen the forgiveness process. Time alone won't warm the space between you.

Critical Task #6: Forgive yourself for injuring another person

When you hurt someone, you debase yourself. When you work to earn that person's forgiveness, you not only honor her, you bring honor to yourself. A "spiritual convalescence"[26] takes place when you meet your obligation to confront and correct the damage you caused another human being.

What Do You Need to Forgive Yourself For?

Here are some behaviors for which you may want to forgive yourself:

- You overreacted to someone and responded in hurtful or vindictive ways.
- You treated someone unjustly because you were treated unjustly. You subjected her to the same abuse you experienced as a child.
- You humiliated another person to prop up your own shaky self-esteem.
- You treated someone with contempt for not living up to your impossible standards.
- You acted poorly toward someone because you couldn't face your own guilt and complicity.

- You failed to get your addiction under control, then compromised the safety and well-being of those around you.
- You deliberately broke promises or broke the law.

For these and other ways in which you harmed others and compromised yourself, I encourage you to apologize, seek repairs, and earn Genuine Self-Forgiveness.

What Does It Take to Forgive Yourself?

There's a good deal of controversy over what's required of you, the offender, to forgive yourself. Is Self-Forgiveness a free, unconditional gift to yourself, or is it a prize you need to work hard to earn? Is it a healing balm for your guilt that inspires you to do better, or is it a convenient anesthetic that dulls your awareness of the pain you caused and lessens your responsibility for it? How much of the process goes on in your own head, and how much goes on in interaction with the person you violated? What I would argue, contrary to popular belief, is that Self-Forgiveness can and must be earned, and that as you perform meaningful acts of repair, you heal yourself.

You can approach Self-Forgiveness in four ways.

Approach 1: You refuse to forgive yourself.

Some of you won't forgive yourselves for what you did, no matter how remorseful or repentant you are, no matter whether the person you hurt forgives you or not. This response is unhealthy, heightening your depression, anxiety, and low self-esteem.[27] When you relentlessly, oppressively incriminate yourself, there's no room for atonement or redemption, and there's no penance demanding enough to release you from your guilt. As Harriet Lerner points out, "How can we apologize for something we are, rather than something we did?"[28]

A thirty-five-year-old lawyer, Jon, is a case in point. After sleeping with his wife's sister, he felt so wretched and impaired that he couldn't work to renew his marriage. A crushed soul, he believed he deserved to be punished forever and moved out of the house. He and his wife stayed in therapy, though, where he continued to embrace his share of blame. Over time, his wife invited him to return home and work on starting a family, but he refused. "I don't think I'd be a good enough father," he told me. "I don't think the kid would love me, or that I'd love him enough." Jon's inability to see himself in a merciful, benevolent light—as a person worthy of loving and being loved—blocked him from doing the work necessary to seek his wife's forgiveness. Eventually, she gave up on him and filed for divorce. She arranged for artificial insemination and had her child without him. Jon dropped out of therapy. Today he lives alone, dominated by shame and a sense of worthlessness.

Approach 2: You forgive yourself too easily (Cheap Self-Forgiveness).

You may have grown up believing that whenever you hurt someone, that person has a moral obligation to forgive you, and you, in turn, have the right to forgive yourself—to treat yourself with the same compassion and generosity of spirit she extends to you. The emphasis is on making you, the offender, feel better rather than on making you be better. And so, with no compunction to work for forgiveness, you gift yourself an easy, mindless substitute.

Forgiving yourself too quickly, without understanding your behavior or making amends directly to the person you injured, is a shallow and expedient way to release yourself from suffering. This unearned Self-Forgiveness represents "the new opiate that not only blinds [you] to [your] faults, but makes those faults all the more likely to occur without guilt."[29] Relieved of a moral conscience, you choose a superficial sense of well-being over self-awareness or personal growth.

Some of us feel so good when we forgive ourselves that we want to sin again just so that we can be forgiven again—particularly when our forgiveness demands so little of us. Some people, according to Marshal Frady, sin repeatedly in order to experience "the soul-regenerating wonder of forgiveness and redemption."[30] In his biography of Martin Luther King, Jr., Frady honors Dr. King's immense social achievements but posits a spiraling need to engage in "indulgences" and "sexual corsairing" in order to experience the subsequent spiritual cleansing that comes with contrition. "It may not be too fanciful to suggest," Frady asserts, that King "was driven to crucify himself over and over again on a cross of guilt with his secret licentiousness in order to renew his soul with the experience of yet another resurrection into grace and restoration to his high calling."[31]

You may believe that Self-Forgiveness motivates you to confront and correct the wrong you did. But often the reverse is true. As Solomon Schimmel points out in his brilliant book *Wounds Not Healed By Time,* "There is greater moral danger than moral promise when self-forgiveness is encouraged in someone who has a weak conscience, with low levels of guilt and shame after having transgressed. Such a person needs more guilt and shame, not less."[32] In other words, Cheap Self-Forgiveness may release you from the need to confront and relieve the suffering you caused.

I once attended a Sunday morning service led by an Episcopalian minister. Inviting the congregation to rise, he asked each of us to think about someone we had harmed and then to recite the Lord's Prayer. As we sat down, smiling warmly to ourselves and each other, I thought to myself, "Easy enough!" On some level, I felt cleansed. But on another, I felt dishonest, and asked myself, "Why doesn't the minister tell us, 'Now, when you leave this sanctuary, go to the person you wronged and apologize'?" I felt let off the hook and questioned whether my forgiving myself in this quick-fix way would inspire me to undertake the hard work of repair.

Approach 3: You forgive yourself after taking responsibility for your actions, but without making amends to the person you harmed.

When you follow this model, developed by forgiveness expert Robert Enright, you confront and criticize yourself for wronging another person, and replace "self-resentment" with "compassion, generosity, and love" toward yourself.[33] However, you feel no obligation to extend yourself to the hurt party or make reparations. This, I contend, leaves out a critical element of Self-Forgiveness and makes it cheap.

Approach 4: You forgive yourself, but only after taking responsibility for your actions and making amends.

When you apologize directly to the person you hurt, your Self-Forgiveness is likely to feel more deserved and therefore more genuine. You're also more likely to learn and grow from the experience, and reduce the chance that you'll repeat the offense.

What happens, however, when the person you hurt is dead or otherwise unavailable? If Genuine Self-Forgiveness must be earned, where does that leave you? Can you still forgive yourself? I would say yes, there's much you can still do to acknowledge your violation, demonstrate contrition to the world and to yourself, and make yourself feel whole. These indirect acts of repair won't rehabilitate the relationship, but they may help you rehabilitate yourself. However, when you can't make good directly to the person you harmed, your Self-Forgiveness is unlikely to feel entirely satisfying, cleansing, or complete.

Gandhi once taught a man how to forgive himself, even though his victim was dead. The man, a Hindu fanatic, had smashed the head of a Muslim child against a wall in retaliation for the murder of his own son, and he was smitten with grief. "I know a way out of hell," Gandhi said. "Find a child. A child whose mother and father have been killed . . . and raise him as your own. Only be sure that he is a Muslim and that you raise him as one."[34] Adopting the boy would have been a relatively easy pay-back. Raising him as a Muslim, however, would have forced the Hindu to acknowledge, day after day, that no group of people, no set of beliefs, is inherently superior to another—a realization that "would redeem him and allow him to experience himself as human again."[35]

Should the person you harmed be unavailable to you, you can follow Gandhi's advice: humble yourself and pay penance daily, in a way that relates directly to your offense. This may help you restore your shattered sense of decency and self-respect—a crucial step toward Self-Forgiveness. You can also feel sorrow for yourself as the victim of conditions that triggered the worst in you—another component of Self-Forgiveness.

Another question arises: What happens when the person you hurt is available but refuses to forgive you, no matter how earnestly you try to make repairs? Can you still forgive yourself? Here again I would say "yes . . . but"—and for the same reasons. *Yes,* you can still reach out unilaterally and make reparations that are humbling, self-challenging, and directly related to the suffering you caused. *But* your Self-Forgiveness is likely to feel more tentative, less solid, when the hurt party won't honor your efforts.

A Model for Earning Self-Forgiveness

I propose the following five-stage model for earning Self-Forgiveness:

Stage 1: Self-confrontation. You confront the wrong you did and the harm you caused. You strip away all self-righteous rationalizations, all self-serving justifications and excuses, and try to pry open the truth. It may help to ask the injured person to fill in the blanks and tell you exactly how your behavior scarred her.

Stage 2: Self-appraisal. You sharply criticize your words and actions, knowing that they violated another person and failed to represent you at your best. But you also put what you did in perspective, acknowledging that you're more than your transgressions, and identifying those aspects of yourself that you value. As you earn forgiveness, you remind yourself that your efforts to make amends are also part of who you are and what you're capable of.

Stage 3: Self-compassion. You probe the reasons for your behavior, uncovering all the factors—the stresses, personality traits, biological influences, formative life experiences—that add up to the person you are today. This self-scrutiny is meant not to excuse what you did but to help you feel compassion for yourself and open the door to change.

Stage 4: Self-transformation. You do what you can to make good—directly to the person you harmed, when possible. Your tasks include confronting your resistance to earning forgiveness; paying attention to the pain you caused; apologizing genuinely, non-defensively, and responsibly; unveiling the truth of your behavior (what it says about you); and working to earn back trust.

Stage 5: Self-integration. You accept that you can never make right what you did wrong, but you let your acts of repentance and repair transform the way you feel, know, and treat yourself. You don't necessarily replace feelings of self-hate with self-love, but you give yourself permission—and cause—to feel less estranged from yourself, more integrated, more whole. You continue to accept culpability for your misdeeds, but you give up the need to continually punish and despise yourself for them. You strive to create a new life narrative that incorporates your transgression, but in a way that adds meaning and purpose to your life. As you release those you hurt from their pain, you release yourself from your pain.

In Conclusion

As I wrote in *After the Affair,* "Self-forgiveness doesn't relieve you of responsibility for your words or actions, but it may release you from self-contempt and from a 'crippling sense of badness' that makes you believe, 'I can't do better.' With Self-Forgiveness, you bring a gentle compassion to your understanding of who you are and why you acted the way you did, and reclaim what you most value in yourself."[36]

I would add that Self-Forgiveness is not just about feeling acquitted or absolved—it is certainly not just about feeling better. Principally, it is about trying to earn redemption from those you damaged and working to make *them* feel better. The two goals are intertwined, since the work you do to heal them helps you heal yourself. I would argue, therefore, against the concept of Self-Forgiveness as a private offering to yourself, an internal reckoning with what you did wrong. I encourage you to see it, rather, as a process that begins when you admit your complicity and make amends directly to the person you harmed. As you seek to earn her forgiveness, you're likely to experience your own in a way that is bolder, more substantial, and more instructive than when it is gifted only by yourself, to yourself.

WHAT YOU, THE HURT PARTY, MUST DO TO GRANT FORGIVENESS

Yes, the offender must work hard to earn forgiveness—to prove the sincerity of his remorse, to right his wrong, to salve your wound. But forgiveness is a two-person project. There can be no healing if he reaches out to you and you cut off his hand.

Three Critical Tasks for Granting Forgiveness

I'm not saying that you must or should forgive him. But if you're going to consider this option, here's what you must do.

Critical Task #1: Look at your mistaken assumptions about forgiveness and see how they stop you from granting it.

Critical Task #2: Complete all ten steps of Acceptance—not alone, but with the offender's help.

Critical Task #3: Create opportunities for the offender to make good and help you heal.

Let's examine each of these critical tasks.

Critical Task #1: Look at your mistaken assumptions about forgiveness and see how they stop you from granting it.

Here are several erroneous assumptions you may have made about forgiveness. Each may sabotage your willingness to forgive.

Mistaken Assumption: I can't enter into the process of forgiving until I feel perfectly safe, comfortable, and ready.

No matter how penitent the offender is, you may never feel quite ready to forgive him. If you wait until you are, however, you're likely to wait out your life, or the life of the relationship. Therefore, even if you have reservations, you might consider giving him a tentative green light to prove himself. This means letting him know that if he works to make amends, you'll work to open yourself up to him and not play out your doubts and anxieties with each interaction. Remain negative and dismissive, and he'll eventually give up on you or react in kind—and then what have you gained?

Mistaken Assumption: Forgiveness is a unilateral pardon; I shouldn't ask for anything in return.

"Forgiveness can't be earned," argues Karlotta Shanahan, M.A., LCMHC, in a thoughtful letter she wrote to me after one of my infidelity workshops. "I agree that the unfaithful or offending partner needs to work to regain trust and to demonstrate his desire to restore the relationship, and that he needs to be willing to hold the pain for the hurt partner, but those behaviors cannot earn forgiveness. He can earn trust, and he can earn healing. But forgiveness [occurs] when the partner who has been hurt says, 'I give up my right to hurt you for hurting me.'"

This traditional belief—that forgiveness is unconditional—has been championed in the psychological literature by Robert Enright and the International Forgiveness Institute. Enright draws on the work of Kohlberg[37] to map out stages of forgiveness that reflect our moral development. The "lowest" end of the hierarchy is what he refers to as "revengeful forgiveness": "I can forgive someone who wrongs me only if I can punish him or her to a similar degree to my own pain." The next stage is "restitutional forgiveness": "If I get back what was taken away from me, then I can forgive." The "highest" stage is "forgiveness as love": "I forgive unconditionally because it promotes a true sense of love. Because I must truly care for each person, a hurtful act on his or her part does not alter that sense of love."[38]

My concern with this assumption—that if you are a morally and psychologically developed human being, you'll gift forgiveness unconditionally—is that it closes the door on forgiveness for many of us. "Why look only to me to forgive an unrepentant offender?" you wonder. "Why not urge *him* to relieve the suffering he caused *me* and help *me* forgive *him*?" For many of you, granting forgiveness unilaterally seems divine—but not for you.

Beverly Flanigan, clinical professor at the University of Wisconsin School of Social Work, captures the difference between a one-sided pardon and the interactive quality of Genuine Forgiveness when she asserts, "Forgiveness takes work. Pardoning is conferred. The forgiver frees herself of hatred, but does not free the injurer of responsibility."[39] I would add that a pardon is a gift that asks nothing of the offender. Forgiveness, in contrast, comes with a price and must be earned.

Mistaken Assumption: Forgiveness happens immediately.

Forgiveness is often thought of as an instant transformation, something that happens all at once. This idea has been reinforced by the work of Frederick DiBlasio, professor of social work at the University of Maryland. He recommends a single cathartic "forgiveness session" lasting up to six hours during which the victim and perpetrator come together under his guidance to redress the injury.

This approach has much to recommend it. You discuss the injury together—the facts, the attendant feelings, the consequences. The offender flushes out secrets from his past and commits himself to concrete acts of atonement. The danger is that you may end up feeling pressured to forgive and reconcile before both of you have fully appreciated the damage that was done. The offender's efforts to earn your forgiveness may then amount to nothing more than a quick fix.

At what point does forgiveness really take place? For most of us, it's a gradual process that unfolds in stages as the offender apologizes and delivers on his promise never to harm you again. It may take time for your emotions to catch up to your decision to forgive, and for you to believe that his efforts are trustworthy.

Some of you may grant forgiveness almost immediately if the offender steps forward with sincere, substantive acts of repentance. Others may grant it suddenly, but not until years later. It took one patient, Annie, fifteen minutes to forgive her former mother-in-law Linda for an injury that had happened nineteen years earlier.

"When Tom divorced me and went off with the baby-sitter, his mother, Linda, cut me off," Annie told me. "She never called. She never reached out to me or acknowledged me again. We had been very close. Overnight it was like I had never existed. I thought there must be something wrong with me."

Almost two decades later, when Linda's husband died, Annie decided to pay her a condolence call. "Linda greeted me with a big hug," Annie recalled. "She asked me about my career and my husband. Then she took me aside and whispered that there was something she wanted to say. With tears in her eyes, she said, 'You know I always loved you. When Tom left you, he was so angry. He said terrible things about you—that you were trying to steal the family business, that you were trying to take custody of the kids. He couldn't tolerate my having a relationship with you. I felt torn. But he was my son. He seemed so fragile, so I stood by him and left you out in the cold. Now I'm in the cold, and I know how lonely that can feel. I'm sorry for any hurt I caused you.'

"Since the divorce, Linda has always been decent to my kids," Annie conceded, "taking them on trips, supporting their education. I learned to accept her. But it's only now, hearing her admit how bad she feels for hurting me, that I can think of forgiving her. It took her nineteen years, but that doesn't make her apology any less significant or powerful."

Mistaken Assumption: Forgiveness is perfect and complete.

You may also refuse to forgive if you assume that forgiveness must be 100 percent. Treating it as an all-or-nothing proposition, you may feel forced into a corner and conclude, "I'm far from yes, so I must say no." Such rigid, categorical thinking doesn't allow for a response that's in between, but "in between" is where most of us reside.

You may forgive 5 percent when he first apologizes and 65 percent as he demonstrates his remorse. But 35 percent may always remain unforgivable. That may be fine. Who's to say how much forgiveness is sufficient? Whatever the percentage, I encourage you to consider a model that allows for *partial* forgiveness, for forgiving *enough*.

You may fall head over heels in love with someone, only to discover months later that you were basking in the glow of romantic love and didn't really know what mature love was. The same may be true of forgiving. You may believe one day that you've forgiven someone, and then, as he generates more goodwill and continues to restore your faith in him, come to forgive him more deeply than you ever thought possible. Conversely, if he injures you again or breaks his promise, you may withdraw your forgiveness and end up back at square one, or worse.

Forgiveness is not a science but a highly subjective process. Some of you may not care much for verbal apologies—if the offender has said "I'm sorry" once too often, hearing it again may do nothing for you; only concrete acts will convince you of his remorse. Others may insist on words of contrition—the more, the better.

When the offender gives you some of what you need but not all, your forgiveness is also likely to be partial. That was Peggy's experience. When her husband, Mark, had a sexual rendezvous with an old high school sweetheart, he apologized to her dozens of times. "He's become accountable to a fault," she told me. "He comes home earlier from the office. When I call him, he seems genuinely happy to hear from me. He makes us breakfast on weekends and arranges for us to play tennis. Our sex life is good, and he leaves loving notes for me in the refrigerator. He hates talking about painful things, but we have a good marriage and I believe his heart is in the right place. I want to forgive him if I can."

According to Peggy's scorecard, Mark had completed three of the four tasks for earning forgiveness: He had listened openly to her pain, had apologized to her in a meaningful way, and had worked hard to make her feel safe and cherished. What he hadn't done was peer into himself to try to understand and communicate why he had betrayed her. "Whenever I mention the affair," she told me, "he snaps at me, 'Do we have to talk about this again?' I need to know *why* it happened. I ask him, 'Did you feel I had no time for you when I was taking my mother for chemotherapy? Why did you start to use Viagra—were you worried about your sexual performance, your health, getting old?' But he won't talk about it. And frankly, that scares me. If he won't get to the root of the problem, how can I trust that it won't happen again?"

Peggy did her best to focus on all that Mark was doing to repair his damage, but she resented the way he closed up on her. She chose to forgive him, not completely but partially—enough for them to have a fulfilling, authentic, intimate life together.

Mistaken Assumption: When I forgive, I relinquish all negative feelings toward the offender.

It is commonly assumed that when you forgive, your negative feelings are completely replaced by positive ones. The problem with this expectation is that it's so categorical, that it puts forgiveness out of reach and leaves you with no alternative but to not forgive at all.

When you grant Genuine Forgiveness, you make room for anger and recognize it as normal and adaptive. You don't replace it with compassion or love and simply wipe the slate clean. This sort of magical reversal is not what happens to real people who have suffered real emotional injuries.

Even years from now, when you think about how you've been hurt or when something calls up the memory of your suffering, your old pain may resurface, grab hold of you, and drag you down. To expect otherwise is to deny the power of the human brain to conjure up traumatic moments and force you to re-experience them with the same clarity of detail, the same visceral intensity, as when they first occurred.

The theologian Lewis Smedes wrote that when you forgive someone you stop hating him, or that you stop hating him but continue to hate the offense.[40] I agree with Smedes up to a point, but I would add this: Even if you forgive an offender, even if you're committed to a life of equanimity, there may be times when you experience spasms of hate and cannot separate what he did to you from who he is. You are still human, and to think your response can be divided into neat boxes is unrealistic. Accepting this will broaden your understanding of what it means to forgive and make room for negative spikes in emotion that are bound to arise.

What happens when you genuinely forgive is not that you necessarily empty yourself of all hostile feelings, but that you allow other emotions to co-exist with them—more tender or positive emotions, such as sadness and grief. Along with your anger comes a richer, more balanced, more complex reaction—encompassing both what the offender did wrong and what he did right, both the damage he inflicted on you and his efforts to make good.

Be prepared: Forgiving won't wash away the injury; you may be left with a residue of bad feelings and an overwhelming sense of loss. This is what my patient Wendy experienced. Although she forgave her husband, Russell, for his affair, she continued to struggle with bitterness and sorrow. "I know he's trying hard to make me feel valued and safe," she assured me, "but I've lost the idealized image I had of him—forever. My feelings continue to oscillate between empathy and an unbearable sense of betrayal."

The exact moment when Russell revealed his affair remains indelibly etched in Wendy's mind. As the anniversary of that terrible time approached, she was surprised by the intensity of her grief. "Russell wants us to spend the day together and create new, positive memories," she told me. "I'm grateful, but it's all so bittersweet. He's reaching out to me, and that feels great. But it also feels sad, because the more he does, the more I remember how much he hurt me. I keep asking myself, 'Will we ever share moments of pure joy again?'"

Two years after Russell revealed his affair, Wendy sent me this note: "The affair still hurts very much, although the therapy helps. So does reading and the passing of time. We live with it and do the best we can, and we both love each other."

It could be said that Wendy hasn't forgiven Russell yet because her positive feelings toward him are at times tainted with negative ones. It could also be said that she has partially forgiven him and may forgive him more over time. I would argue that the final chapter isn't written yet.

When you forgive, you don't flip a switch. Wendy lost her belief in perfect love, in the specialness of her marriage, and it's natural for her to grieve over these losses and blame Russell for them, no matter how much he does to make amends. But the grief and resentment she feels don't have to cancel out her gratitude to him for his genuine acts of contrition, or pre-empt her feelings of forgiveness.

Mistaken Assumption: When I forgive, I admit that my anger toward the offender was exaggerated or unjustified.

People often tell me, "When I think of forgiving, it's as though I'm trivializing the offense. And I'll be damned if I'll do that."

But when you forgive you don't say, "What you did wasn't that bad." You stand by your recognition that the offender crossed the line. And he stands with you, convincing you that he knows what he did was "that bad." Unless he consciously acknowledges his violation, he has no claim to your forgiveness. Unless *you* consciously acknowledge it, there's nothing for you to forgive.

When Dave, a middle-aged accountant, apologized to his thirty-year-old daughter Jenny for his chronic drinking problem, she accepted his apology and agreed to forgive him. Dave's estranged wife, Sandy, was less charitable. "I feel betrayed," she told me. "What right does Jenny have to write off all those years? He's gotten off cheap. He doesn't deserve it."

But Dave offered his daughter more than cheap apologies. He flew halfway across the country to explain in person how ashamed he was of his behavior. "My addiction must have frightened and embarrassed you for years," he told her. He promised to stop drinking, and to give reality to his promise he committed himself to a rehabilitation program. Jenny, in turn, gave up her need to keep her distance—her customary way of punishing him—and allowed herself to feel compassion, respect, even love for him. She continued to condemn his former behavior but released him from its effects, so long as he held himself accountable for them.

This interpersonal exchange is at the core of Genuine Forgiveness. Jenny gave up her need to indict her father because he convinced her that he understood how horribly he had wronged her and took valiant steps to change. He became the judge of his own behavior. She could give up the job.

Mistaken Assumption: When I forgive, I empower the offender and make myself weak and vulnerable.

If you deny your pain in order to make peace, you're likely to share Nietzsche's conviction that forgiving is for weaklings.[41] But Genuine Forgiveness takes strength and resolve. Standing up for yourself, you insist that you've been wronged and require an accounting in the "ledger of justice."[42] You don't give up your position of power; you give up your preoccupation with power. You don't dismiss your need for restitution; you let him work with you to achieve restitution.

Mistaken Assumption: Forgiveness means reconciliation.

If you link forgiveness with reconciliation, you may be reluctant to offer either. But these are separate processes and should be considered separately.

When you choose to forgive but not reconcile, you allow the offender to make amends for past wrongdoing but refuse to give him another chance to hurt you. No matter how guilty he feels, you close the door on all future interaction.

After a significant violation, you may want to end the relationship before you consider any type of reconciliation. If your spouse was unfaithful, for example, you may decide it's best to get divorced and secure a fair settlement and custody arrangement before asking yourself, "What next?" When the dust settles and you're no longer under pressure to show goodwill, you may feel safer spending time together, seeing what he's capable of, and working to reinvent the relationship. Sometimes an old relationship has to die before a new one can be born.

In reality, however, forgiveness and reconciliation often lead to each other, whatever the sequence. If the offender is emotionally and physically available to you—if he listens empathically to your pain and works hard to correct his behavior—you may be more willing to welcome him back into your life.

Of course, there are many degrees of reconciliation, as there are many degrees of separation. Choosing to relate to him doesn't mean that you share a friendship, enjoy a supportive connection, or feel deep love for each other. These warmer feelings may evolve, but only over time as he demonstrates his trustworthiness.

Critical Task #2: Complete all ten steps of acceptance—not alone, but with the offender's help.

Do Genuine Forgiveness and Acceptance call for the same response? To a great extent, they do. With both, you work hard to give up your hatred, your hurt, your obsessive need for revenge. With both, you try to see the offender and the offense clearly and accept an appropriate share of blame. With both, you define a relationship that protects and promotes your best interests.

Only with Genuine Forgiveness, however, does the offender walk with you and lend a helping hand. His active participation has profound implications, allowing for a depth of cleansing both inside you and between you that can't be achieved through Acceptance alone.

Let's look at some of the ways in which he can help you feel better about yourself, and him.

Step 1: The offender helps you honor the full sweep of your emotions.

You don't need him to acknowledge your feelings in order to make them legitimate. But when he does acknowledge them, he helps you restore the center of gravity within yourself—a necessary step toward healing.

My patient Vivian experienced the impact of having the offender first dismiss her feelings and then validate them. When she told her mother at age eighteen that her father, a respected physician, had anally raped her throughout her childhood, her mother responded flatly, "Shut up. You're a troublemaker." Vivian felt annihilated. "I began to wonder what was real and what was not," she told me.

Five years later, after her father had died and she had given birth to her first child, Vivian received a letter from her mother asking to be part of her life again. In a series of conversations, the mother managed to hear Vivian's story and acknowledge the truth. "When you were in elementary school," her mother admitted, "you'd often be sent home suffering from diarrhea. You were chronically anxious and sick. Looking back now, I can see your terror, your numbness, your humiliation. What happened to you was evil."

What you may find, as Vivian did, is that when the offender steps into your world and sits with you in your damaged emotional space, he helps to provide a stable holding ground—a relatively safe place where even your worst feelings can be voiced and heard. No longer do you scream into a void. When you express pain, he listens and mirrors it. "I hurt," you say. "You hurt," he reflects back. "My feelings matter," you assert. "Yes, your feelings matter," he replies. This verbal pas de deux is likely to calm you and help you attend to your muddled emotions. How much harder it would be to identify and sort through them if you proclaimed, "My feelings matter," and he responded, "Like hell they do"; or if you said, "I've been wronged," and he retorted, "You're crazy."

The offender can help you wade through the chaos, overcome the sense of powerlessness and meaninglessness created by his violation, and give birth to a new narrative in which you feel more grounded, more in control, more whole. With Genuine Forgiveness, he becomes the reader of your story, immersing himself in your experience, page by page, word by word.

Together, you take a stand "against the erasure of your experience."[43] No longer do you need to cut yourself off from your feelings, or be flooded by them. No longer do they represent a destructive force that alienates you from yourself and from him. They become, instead, an invaluable source of enlightenment and reconnection. As he bears witness to your trauma, trying on your suffering as though it were his own, he helps you integrate all that you feel, including, perhaps, some new, warmer feelings toward him.

Step 2: The offender helps you give up your need for revenge, but not your need for a just resolution.

When he listens compassionately to your distress and takes responsibility for violating you, he helps restore your sense of dignity and justice.

He may also reduce your need to punish and humiliate him, and make it easier for you to forgive him. In the end, your vindication comes not from inflicting pain on him, but from his efforts to lift the burden of shame from your shoulders and place it where it belongs.[44] As Rabbi Harold Kushner points out in *Living a Life That Matters,* our "thirst for revenge is really a need to reclaim power, to shed the role of victim and substitute action for helplessness."[45] You may have less need for retribution if the offender steps forward and accounts for his wrong.

Step 3: The offender helps you stop obsessing about the injury and reengage with life.

When he deliberately recalls how he hurt you and atones for it, he allows you to relax, clear your head, and fill your life with more inspiring and stimulating diversions.

A psychologist, Anne, drove this point home for me. During one of my infidelity workshops, she described how she had been scarred by her own therapist. "When I discovered that my husband was cheating on me, we got into counseling to try to find a way back to each other," she volunteered. "I couldn't stop thinking about what he had done to me, and how I had missed the boat in my own house while I was out rescuing other people's lives. He had ended the affair and was ready to move on. So was our therapist. The only one stuck in the past was me. I felt both of them getting increasingly annoyed at me. Believe me, if I could have done better, I would have. It was not fun being inside my head, and I knew I wasn't being constructive. I even took Paxil to try to control my raging thoughts. Feeling their pressure and contempt, I felt worse and worse about myself and the world. Eventually I dropped out of therapy, and my husband filed for divorce. Looking back, I think I was traumatized twice—first by my husband's affair and then by my therapist, who made me feel I was both a bad wife and a bad patient."

I asked Anne whether she had had any further contact with the therapist. She said no. I suggested that she might write her a letter explaining why she had dropped out of therapy. Anne agreed. In a phone consultation several weeks later, we drafted a letter together—one that invited the therapist to respond openly and non-defensively.

Anne mailed the letter and to her surprise received a quick response, which she shared with me. "Anne, I feel bad that you dropped out of therapy for something I failed to give you or help you with," the therapist wrote. "I was acutely aware of how much you were suffering, and I did feel terrible that nothing I was doing was making you feel better. I probably took this personally and felt inadequate. Instead of sharing my self-doubts with you, I somehow conveyed to you that you were bad for not recovering sooner. Infidelity is a severe trauma, and the last thing you needed was a therapist who tried to rush you to give up your pain. If you ever want to talk more about this, I'd be happy to meet with you again—at my expense. I wish you the best—Dr. X."

You, like Anne, may find that when the offender reacts to your pain with patience and compassion, not with judgment or disdain, he helps you feel more normal, less shattered and alone. As he listens empathically, with no personal agenda, and accepts that your recovery won't necessarily follow a straight upward line—that there will be false starts and regressions along the way—he sends a signal that he's not just invested in his own egocentric need to get you off his back but wants to be there for you in your suffering, however long it takes. His willingness to take up your protest may release you from your obsessions and open your mind to forgiveness.

Step 4: The offender helps protect you from further abuse.

Here's how one father created a safe haven for his daughter, giving her the confidence to invite him back into her world.

When Debbie was a child, her father, Dave, drank heavily and sexually molested her. She remembers watching television with him on the living room couch, too afraid to move, while he insinuated his arm around her shoulder and fondled her breasts.

A decade later, when she gave birth to her first child, she began to recall these repressed traumatic memories. She invited her father to join her in therapy, where he neither confirmed nor denied her

accusations. "I don't remember what I did," he told her. "I was drinking too heavily at the time."

In the years that followed, Dave made genuine efforts to control
his destructive impulses, to honor his daughter's rules for safety, and
to prove his trustworthiness and love. He committed himself to an
AA program and gave up alcohol. Respecting her need to be in control of her world, he agreed not to intrude on her space uninvited:
He would never call her at home or pick up the phone in his own
house when caller ID displayed Debbie's number. He would never
touch her in any way, even when they greeted each other in public.
He would never ask to baby-sit for her children or be alone with
them. At one family gathering, he acknowledged privately that he
must have done something terrible to her. She gradually forgave
him, but she maintained her boundaries.

Another ten years passed. Although Debbie was now divorced,
she felt more self-assured and anchored, and she began to allow her
father into her life. He selflessly offered help. When she moved into
a new house, for example, he vacuumed the floors before the movers
arrived. Later that year he planted a garden in her yard. When his
mother died, Debbie joined him at an out-of-town wake. He continued to keep a respectful distance but was warm and appropriate
when she walked by. He never approached her for comfort or consolation, never asked her to take care of him.

It took many years and many corrective interactions, but
together Debbie and her father restored her sense of safety. As he
continued to prove his dependability, Debbie slowly, painstakingly
opened the door to him. His efforts mended the tear inside her and
between them. No longer was he merely the source of her trauma;
he was part of the cure.

*Step 5: The offender helps you frame his behavior in terms of his
own personal struggles.*

When someone violates you, you may feel permanently altered,
not at all the person you were before. At such times, you feel not
poisoned by the trauma but *poisonous*.[46] You absorb a sense of inner

badness and feel flushed with shame. As the offender reverses this process, acknowledging that his behavior is a reflection on him, not you, he helps you drain away the poison and reinhabit your valued self. With his support, you overcome your estrangement from your "good self"—and perhaps from his "good self."

It's important to distinguish between humiliation and shame. Humiliation is a condition imposed on you by the offender. Shame, in contrast, refers to your inner experience of yourself as unworthy. When someone injures you, humiliation and shame can become blurred. You confuse his hurtful, demeaning behavior with your private sense of who you are.

With Acceptance, you sort this out alone. With Genuine Forgiveness, the offender assists you, not by saying "shame on you," but by saying "shame on me"—not "You are dirt" but "I treated you like dirt"; not "You deserved what I did to you" but "My issues got in the way."

Arnold, a forty-six-year-old gay man, arranged to meet someone he had communicated with in an Internet chat room. "I drove ninety minutes to a designated spot—the parking lot of a local CVS," he told me. "The guy—Ted—was twenty minutes late, even though he lived only five minutes away. When he arrived, he just sat in his car. I got out of mine and walked over to him. He took one look at me and said, 'I pass.' Then he rolled up his window and drove off."

Tears welled up in Arnold's eyes. "I was devastated," he said. "Where did this guy get the right to treat another human being so inhumanely?"

Pastoral counselor John Patton writes that an individual who, like Arnold, reacts to violation with shame recognizes the offender not "as a center of independent initiative" who "happens to be at cross-purposes" with you, but as "an offending part of the shamed person's self."[47] In other words, Arnold took Ted's behavior on the most personal level, becoming the vile creature Ted rejected, an object of hate and derision.

Eight months later Arnold received an E-mail from Ted, saying, "I want to apologize for how I acted when we met. I'm sure my behavior felt cruel and insensitive. I want you to know that I take complete responsibility for this—there was nothing you did, nothing about you, that made me act the way I did. I had just come out and, frankly, when faced with the reality of actually getting together with someone who was available to me, I freaked. I hope you'll find more stable characters on your future Internet dates. I'm very sorry."

For Arnold, as for you, the offender can help strip away the intensely personal nature of his affront and free you from an obsessive, self-immolating sense of blame and defectiveness. In the process, he may become less hateful and more forgivable.

What happened to Karen and her boyfriend, Forrest, is another case in point. She was ready to leave him after learning of his affair, but she put her decision on hold when he committed himself to a year of therapy to address a deeply entrenched pattern of infidelity. "If he figures out what's going on inside him, maybe he'll change," she told me.

Forrest came into my office confused and distraught. "I don't know what I'm doing," he confessed. "I got divorced five years ago when my wife found out I was cheating on her, and now I'm dating Karen, who I'm crazy about, while seeing someone else who means nothing to me. Why would I deliberately create such a mess for myself? Why can't I learn?"

Forrest's quest for self-awareness led him back to his childhood. As we talked, he revealed a history of abandonment and abuse. "When I was six, a camp counselor used to sit me on his lap and run his hands over me," he said. "I came home that summer and found out my parents had separated—without telling me. A few years later, my older brother did things to me physically that I'm still not ready to talk about."

Forrest began to understand how, for him, relationships were never protected zones, but minefields, where he felt at constant risk of being abandoned or exploited. He had learned over the years to pre-empt the inevitable by abandoning others first, fleeing from affair to affair. In the chemical throes of romance, he could feel not only loved but powerful and free. Yet his sexual exploits only exacerbated his feelings of loneliness, isolation, and shame.

Forrest shared his insights with Karen and helped her understand his pattern of betrayal. "I realize he's been running away from
relationships his whole life, and that his behavior is not about me,"
Karen told me. "What I care about—what keeps me in the ring with
him and makes me feel there's hope—is that he seems to realize this,
too. I don't know if I trust him enough to marry him, but his curios-
ity about himself, his willingness to subject himself to painful self-
scrutiny, makes it easier for me to forgive him."

When you, like Arnold and Karen, stop seeing the offender
solely in terms of your own injury and develop insights into his, you
get to the heart of his motivation. When he points the way, you'll
find it easier to feel compassion for him, and for yourself.

Step 6: The offender helps you reconcile with him.

When you genuinely forgive the offender, you let his acts of
restitution strengthen your attachment to him. Mercy and humility
may feed your desire to stay connected, but the offender's contrition
seals the bond. You don't let him back into your life because such
magnanimity makes you feel like a decent person; he earns his way
back by proving his decency as a human being.

Reconciliation is not a yes-or-no decision; it offers you a range
of options with varying degrees of involvement, intimacy, and trust.
You may, for example, forgive a remorseful partner, divorce him, and
continue to interact for the sake of the kids. You may also stay intimately attached to him and work to reintegrate your lives as he
proves his trustworthiness.

That's what one patient, Michelle, did when she chose to
remain with her husband, Henry, and give him a chance to make
good, long before she felt any love for him.

Henry, a successful, fifty-year-old architect, decided that for
religious and family reasons, he would give up his lover and work on
his marriage. He consulted a therapist who told him, "If you're going
back to your wife, you must be scrupulously honest and tell her
everything."

Henry went home and told Michelle that he had been involved

with a business associate for two years but had decided to end the relationship because this was the right thing to do. "I'm very angry that I have to give up this woman—she's my best friend—and I'm not sexually attracted to you anymore," he told his wife. "But I'm willing to see what we can work out together."

Michelle looked at him as if to say, "Are you out of your mind?" But because she wanted to hold the family together, had spent thirty-two years sharing critical life experiences with him, and understood that she had helped to create the void between them, she made a conscious decision to join him in couple therapy and try to rebuild the marriage.

For two years, with Michelle's encouragement, Henry worked hard to reconnect with her. But during all those months his terrible words—"This woman is my best friend; I'm not sexually attracted to you"—rang in her ears.

One day he told her, "Let me start again. I want to apologize for what I said when I recommitted to you. I was vicious. Frankly, I wanted to hurt you. I blamed you for my unhappiness and couldn't face my own guilt for destroying our family. But I know something today I didn't know then—and that is, I do love you. I know absolutely that this is where I want to be, and I'm grateful to you for letting me back into your life."

Michelle turned to him and said, "I'm sorry, that's not good enough. What you said to me two years ago is unforgivable."

My response to Michelle was this: "Henry's harsh words must have sickened you. But they may have been the best he was capable of at the time, given his ambivalence about coming back. Most people have an idealistic view of reconciliation. They imagine their partner flying back to them on the wings of love. But often, particularly after a devastating offense like an affair, love comes only at the end of a long, difficult journey. The work begins when the offender gives up the lover and renews his commitment to you, his life partner. Then you open the door to the possibility of forgiving him and allow him to make meaningful repairs. Treating each other with tenderness and respect, together you foster intimacy and trust. Finally, perhaps, feelings of love reemerge. People don't want to hear this. It's counterintuitive and unromantic. It requires you to act loving before you feel loving. Realistically, though, love usually comes last, not first, and only after hard work."

"Pop culture gives us a cheap brand of love," I added—"the quick pitter patter of the heart, the flood of emotion that washes over us and seems so effortless. Mature love, in contrast, requires fearless perseverance. It asks Henry to admit his culpability and atone for failing someone he cares so deeply about. And it asks you, Michelle, to manage your disillusionment and not let it negate Henry's very real efforts to earn forgiveness and make a life with you."

Step 7: The offender helps you forgive yourself for your own failings.

You don't need his input to forgive yourself, but it can smooth the way.

My friend Donna told me about an incident going back to her dating years. "I met a guy I thought I was crazy about and invited him to an art exhibit at a downtown gallery," she reminisced. "He said he'd check his schedule and get right back to me, but I didn't hear from him until the day before the show. His message was succinct. 'Sorry, Donna, I can't make it.' I never heard from him again. It wasn't the worst thing that's ever happened to me, but it came at a very vulnerable time in my life and it reinforced my already insecure feelings about myself and my hopelessness about ever finding a loving partner. Twenty years later—guess what?—I ran into him in a bookstore. We exchanged the usual pleasantries. Then he said, 'I want to apologize for acting like an idiot back then. I had picked up the idea that if I treated a woman well, she'd treat me like shit; and that if I treated her like shit, she'd treat me well. I had a lot to learn. You were smart to dump me.'

"The truth is, though, I hadn't dumped him. He had dumped me. But by that time in my life, I didn't need his confession to boost my self-esteem. I was happily married and feeling OK about myself. I had moved on. When he apologized, I quickly forgave him. But I realized suddenly that he wasn't the only person who needed forgiving. I had become my own worst enemy when I let his rejection destroy my self-confidence and darken my life. So I took his cue, apologized to myself, and accepted my own forgiveness."

Many of my patients have told me stories of how someone who hurt them helped heal them. Stuart and Jane are typical. Though they were still in college, he insisted on getting married when he got her pregnant—"It's the right thing to do," he told her. But he felt trapped and resentful from the minute they exchanged vows.

Jane experienced his silent rage, his continuous infidelities, as confirmation of what she had learned about herself from her remote, hypercritical parents—that she was not attractive or good enough for anyone to love her. Three years and two children later, she and Stuart got divorced.

By the time their eldest daughter, Nancy, became engaged, Stuart had developed a more honest view of his role in the relationship. Realizing that he and Jane would be interacting at the wedding, he hoped it wasn't too late, even now, to apologize.

He sent her this letter:

> Dear Jane,
>
> Now that Nancy is about to get married, I'd like to share some thoughts I've had about our marriage and our life together. I want to apologize for making you feel you were the reason I wasn't happy or faithful. No one could have satisfied me. You had the bad luck to be married to someone who didn't have a clue who he was or what it meant to be in a relationship. Blaming you gave me the excuse I needed to run around and not be there for anyone but myself. I'm very sorry. You got a bad deal. None of it was your fault. The problem was me. As for the kids, I want you to know you've always been a great mother.
>
> *Stuart*
>
> P.S. I look forward to seeing you at the wedding. Will you save me a dance?

Jane was grateful for his letter. She wrote back:

Dear Stuart,

For years I assumed you left because of me. I blamed myself. Your thoughtful words helped me forgive you, but more important, they helped me forgive me. I, too, look forward to celebrating our daughter's wedding together. Thank you.

Jane

The fact that Stuart had treated Jane in a conciliatory, considerate way over the years certainly made it easier for her to accept him. But when he took ownership of the harm he had done, he released her from her excessive self-blame, her unbearable self-doubts—and helped her forgive herself, and him.

Critical Task #3: Create opportunities for the offender to make good and help you heal.

To cut a path to Genuine Forgiveness, you need to create opportunities for the offender to hear your pain, care about your feelings, and compensate for the harm he did. If you treat him as evil incarnate and blast him with your silence or rage, you can be sure that nothing corrective will take place.

There can be no Genuine Forgiveness either if, for the sake of an easy peace, you dismiss or deny your injury and treat him as though he had never hurt you. Ask nothing of him, or of yourself, and why should he feel any compulsion to make amends? He may not even know he hurt you. When nothing is faced or resolved, the best you can offer him is a cheap substitute for forgiveness.

Genuine Forgiveness requires reciprocity. You must decide whether to open the door and let him in; he must decide whether to cross the threshold and reach out to you. Either of you can take the first step. He can come forward and ask to be forgiven, or you can let him know what you need from him in order to heal. In an ideal world you'd probably want him to take the first step, but in an ideal world he wouldn't have hurt you.

If he says "no" to the work of forgiveness, you don't have to forgive him—you can accept him instead. But if he wants to make amends, why stand in his way? Why not let him help you heal your past, even if you don't want him in your future? Why deny yourself the health, the possibilities, that may spring from his desire to make good? You can choose to move forward slowly, but why block progress altogether?

In her work with couples who have suffered "attachment wounds," Susan Johnson tries to help both partners become more responsive to each other and "foster positive cycles of comfort and care."[48] This delicate give-and-take is exactly what happens with Genuine Forgiveness. While the offender works hard to bind your wounds, you allow him to comfort and care for you. Each of you helps the other to put his best self forward—the self most likely to elicit a healing response.

How exactly can you encourage the offender to reach out and earn your forgiveness? Here are several ways:

Open Yourself Up and Share Your Pain with Him.

You shouldn't assume that he knows you're hurting, or that if he did know, he wouldn't care. Tell him, and give him a chance to make amends. When you spill out your angst directly to him, and he listens attentively and caringly, the two of you engage in an act of healing.

When twenty-year-old Lydia came to my office, she was developing anorexia and drinking heavily. Her father's affair had scarred her, but what cut her even more deeply was what she saw as his attachment to his girlfriend's daughter, Mary. "He never loved me as much as he loves her," Lydia told me.

I listened with fascination because Lydia's story had nothing to do with her father's version of reality. I had seen him in therapy over the past five months while he struggled to extricate himself from his affair, and not once did he express any affection for Mary—he never even mentioned her.

I brought Lydia and her father together in my office and encouraged her to pour out her feelings—her sadness, her anxiety, her jealousy. Afraid of further alienating him, she was reluctant to speak her mind. She was also afraid to have her worst fear confirmed—that she really didn't matter to him. Eventually, though, she opened up. "When I had my wisdom teeth removed," she told him, "you never came to the hospital to visit me; you went to Mary's graduation instead. When I was home on vacation, you took her and her mother on a trip to Spain."

Her father listened closely. I had coached him to mirror what Lydia needed him to understand, so he pulled his chair close to hers, looked her in the eyes, and said, "I understand that you believe I had a closer relationship with someone else's daughter than I have with you—that I did things with her and for her that make you feel I don't love you as much, or that I don't love you at all. You feel replaced."

Lydia nodded.

"May I respond to that?"

Lydia nodded again.

"Lydia, you're my only daughter, and you're the one I love. As you know, I got involved with someone I shouldn't have and lost myself and hurt you and your mother terribly—I'm more sorry for this than I can ever say. But I didn't have a close relationship with her daughter. I spent time with her because I spent time with her mother. Mary never meant to me what you mean to me. She was part of the package I bought into. I can see why you'd think differently. I'm sorry for not being there for you when you were sick. I'm sorry for abandoning you and making you feel unwanted. I want us to get to know each other again."

Lydia hung on her father's words. It was he who invited her back into his life, but it was she who started the healing process by sharing her inner turmoil. Her silence would have incubated her pain and made forgiveness impossible.

Speak from the Soft Underbelly of Your Pain.

You may believe that unless you rage at the offender, he won't understand the severity of his violation. You may also think, as many mental health professionals have, that you need to explode in order to discharge toxic emotions from your system. This "cathartic model" is false and destructive, however. We now understand that when we release rage—particularly when we do so repeatedly—we do not deplete our supply; we may, in fact, increase it. As we express rage, it continues to foment inside us.

How you convey your outrage or shame is likely to affect the way the offender responds to you. John Gottman, one of the nation's leading marital researchers, has observed in his "love lab" that the way a person sends a message shapes the way it comes back. "Discussions invariably end on the same note as they begin," he reports.[49] He therefore recommends a "soft start-up," in which you hold back your harsh words of criticism or contempt and invite the offender in. If you share not the hate but the hurt—what I call the "soft underbelly of your pain"—you're likely to evoke a less defensive, more supportive response.

That's what my patient, Marcy, learned to do with her husband, Jeff. Often in the past, when she returned from a business trip, she would find that something had gone wrong at home that Jeff had failed to fix. Her standard response was to attack his competence. "I don't know how I get involved with such helpless men," she would blurt out. "You're just like my first husband. You use people. You want a free ride. You want me to do all the work and pay the bills, too."

It was only when Marcy stopped shredding his manhood and began sharing her more vulnerable inner core that he was able to address her pain and respond as a loving partner. She learned to convey to him, "I'm feeling overwhelmed and taken for granted. When you wait for me to get home to fix the phone or garage door, I feel like a workhorse. My whole life I've taken care of people. I'm asking that when there's a problem, you try to solve it, whatever it is. It doesn't matter if you succeed. It only matters that you try. Then I'll feel you're in this marriage with me. I need your help."

Marcy changed the tone of her message in two ways. First, she went from expressing hard emotions such as hatred, bitterness, and contempt to expressing softer emotions such as sadness, loneliness, insecurity, anxiety, and shame. Second, she went from talking to him in a finger-pointing, "you're no good" kind of way, to talking about herself—her hurt, her fatigue, her despair.

When you express only hard emotions in a raw, accusatory manner, you're likely to win a Pyrrhic victory, crushing your opponent but losing the game. The person who hurt you may get your point but want no part of you. You may succeed in making him feel rotten about himself, but you won't get a shred of compassion in return. Buffeted by your intense hostility, he's likely to respond by emotionally distancing himself, counterattacking, or feeling just plain paralyzed—all death knells to forgiveness.

It's natural to feel angry and guarded toward someone who has injured you, but if you want him to redress your wound, I advise you: Don't make it easy for him *not* to earn forgiveness. Don't give him an excuse *not* to come forward. Don't reinforce his idea that nothing he does will make a dent in your feelings. As one apologetic offender told his wife, "If you act like a tiger, how can I embrace you?"

When you express soft emotions, you create a climate in which he's more likely to feel your pain and respond in a comforting, empathic manner. This doesn't mean that you should swallow or sugarcoat your anger. It means that you should try to go beyond anger, convey the depth of your hurt and fear, and speak from the heart.

Your goal should be to elicit not just his empathy but his compassion. How do they differ? When he empathizes with you, he stops judging your behavior from his own myopic point of view and tries to understand what happened through your eyes.[50] Telling him your side of the story helps him do this. When he shows compassion, he feels sympathy and wants to reach out and alleviate your suffering. He's more likely to do this when you share not just the details of your story but also your pain.

Some of you may be incapable of such a nuanced response, at least initially. You may need first to pour out your grief. Emily, a very proper sixty-eight-year-old Episcopalian—a normally soft-spoken and emotionally reserved woman—is a case in point. One day she

found a box of papers in her basement that turned out to be trust
fund agreements for two children she knew nothing about. After
some probing, she discovered that her husband had had an affair
seventeen years before and had fathered two children whom he had
been supporting ever since. The affair had ended more than a
decade ago, but he continued to send the woman money for the
children.

When the couple met in my office, Emily screamed obscenities
at her husband until she became hoarse. As they left, she paused,
then turned back to me with tears in her eyes. "I'm so ashamed of
myself," she said. "I used words today I didn't even know I knew. I'm
so sorry."

I responded by trying to normalize her feelings and reduce her
sense of shame so that she could begin a constructive dialogue with
her spouse. He wanted desperately to win her forgiveness.

"Sometimes screaming out loud is the only available and
authentic human response," I told her. "To be true to yourself, you
may need to release the venom trapped inside you. Just keep in mind
that while this is a normal, healthy response to a significant injury—
the place where most of us begin—you can't stay locked in your rage
forever if you hope someday to forgive or to heal. Over time, you'll
have a better chance of being heard when you can convey the hurt
underlying your hostility."

Help Him Locate Your Pain, and Tell Him Exactly What You Need in Order to Heal.

For the offender to earn your forgiveness, you may need to tell
him precisely how you're hurting and what you need if you are to
recover. When you help him *locate your pain* and tell him how to
treat it, you create an opportunity for him to apply a specific salve to
a specific wound that is hurting and needs attention.

Here's an example. Nineteen years after an ugly, brutal, two-
year-long divorce, complete with battles over finances and child custody, Ruth and Eliot spent a weekend together celebrating their
son's college graduation. As they walked together across campus,

Eliot apologized for making her life miserable. Ruth was deeply touched but felt he had failed to address the most devastating part of his betrayal. She considered letting the moment pass—she didn't want to spoil the occasion, and he had shown more regard for her feelings than ever before—but she knew that to fully forgive him, she needed him to address a pivotal issue.

Ruth collected her courage. "I appreciate your apology," she said. "It means a great deal to me. But there's something you did that was much worse than cheating on me or divorcing me, and I'd like us to talk about that."

"Shoot," he said.

"It seems to me you deliberately tried to turn the kids against me. You wanted them to love you and hate me. You told them things about me that were vicious and untrue."

Eliot didn't hesitate. "You're absolutely right," he said. "I did do that. And I did it consciously and calculatingly. I want you to know I'm ashamed of my behavior. I hurt you and the boys selfishly, recklessly."

Ruth continued to locate her pain and encourage him to address it. "It would help me to know why you did what you did," she said.

Eliot paused before answering. "Truthfully, I never thought about it until just now," he said. "Apologizing and admitting I'm wrong, you know, aren't my strong suits. But I think I did it because I felt guilty, and hating you kept me from feeling bad about myself. I know I felt insecure, and in some small-minded, immature way I believed that if the kids loved you, they'd turn against me. And I was terrified of losing their love. I want you to know," he added, "they never fell for my manipulation. They're too smart, they love you too much, and you're too good a mother."

Eliot then took another step to address the wound that had cut Ruth so deeply. He walked into the restaurant where the boys were waiting, and said, "I just apologized to your mother for treating her in ways she didn't deserve." And he repeated to them what he had told Ruth, and apologized again to her—and to them.

This story illustrates the exquisitely collaborative process of forgiveness—how you, the hurt party, can help the offender earn forgiveness and how he can help you grant forgiveness. Eliot was genuinely sorry for his behavior, and he apologized. But he couldn't read Ruth's mind or know what lay buried in her heart. Only she knew that there was unfinished business. Only she could bring it to his attention and ask him to attend to it. Only then could he produce the exact words and actions that would heal her.

In my work with infidelity, when a hurt partner tells her spouse what he needs to do to earn back trust, the spouse sometimes feels coerced, bristles, and says no. Other times, however, the spouse embraces the challenge. "I'd like to repair the damage I've done, but I honestly don't know what to do or where to begin," he says. "Tell me. I want to know. I want to follow through."

When you reveal what you need from the person who hurt you, you take a calculated risk. On one hand, you may learn that he doesn't give a damn about you or what you want. On the other hand, you may give him a long-awaited opportunity to reach out to you. That's what happened when my patient Cheryl confronted her mother.

Throughout Cheryl's childhood, her mother was addicted to pot and cocaine. "By the time you came around, I was heavily into drugs," her mother acknowledged. "You didn't get much nurturing from me."

Cheryl was grateful for this confession, but it wasn't enough. "It wasn't really much of an apology," she told me. "I still don't know how she feels about what she did. Does she have any remorse? If she does, I'd like to hear about it."

I encouraged Cheryl to go back and ask for more. She agreed. "I've always wondered how you felt about your addiction, and if you're sorry for what you did to me," she told her mother. "I don't want you to lie or make something up, but if you feel bad, it would help to know."

"I feel worse than you can imagine," her mother replied. "I wasn't as good a mother as you deserved, as I hoped to be, and I feel terrible for all the anxiety I put you through—for forcing you to take care of me instead of being a carefree kid. I'm sorry for all the times you came home from school and instead of having me around to ask you about your day or help you with your homework, you found me zonked out in the bedroom with the shades down. I'm sorry for the time I took an overdose and you had to call the ambulance to rescue me. How scary that must have been. I could go on, and I will if you'd like."

It comforted Cheryl to hear this. It also taught her that when you tell someone what you need from him, you clear the way back to your heart. And so I advise you: Don't set up *invisible hoops* for the offender to jump through. Be concrete. Tell him, "This is what will help me mend and let my anger go. This will allow me to get closer to you, perhaps forgive you."

Specific behaviors you may want to request include:

- "I need you to *ask* me to forgive you."
- "I need you to go to your family and tell them that you lied about me."
- "I need you to let me talk out everything you've done to hurt me, and for you to listen without getting angry."
- "I need you to repeat what I've told you, so I feel that you 'get it.'"

When you tell him, "I need nothing from you," you cut yourself off from him and give him no chance to make meaningful repairs. What you are saying, in effect, is, "I need nothing, because I'm committed to hating you and keeping you out in the cold." In contrast, when you map out what you need, you give him direction and create a path to forgiveness.

As Gaston Bachelard writes:

What is the source of our first suffering?
It lies in the fact that we hesitated to speak.
It was born in the moment
When we accumulated silent things within us.[51]

Allow Him to Make Reparations.

When a person injures you, he's in your debt. To pay it off, he needs to make regular, reliable payments. When you refuse to let this happen, you put Genuine Forgiveness out of reach.

That's what a patient named Mark did. When his father died, Mark wanted to move in with his mother for a few days to keep her company, and to bring his older son with him. But his wife, Marge, who was eight months pregnant, said no, she couldn't manage alone with their two-year-old son, and she insisted that Mark stay home. He agreed, kept silent, then got even with her by sleeping with a neighbor's wife. Even though he cheated on Marge, he considered himself the hurt party.

After Marge found out about his affair, she and Mark came to my office to work on forgiving each other. Mark started off by saying he was the one who had been unfaithful and Marge had done nothing equal to his transgression. "I feel uncomfortable, like a baby, asking you to listen to my issues," he told her. "Let's focus on yours first." This sounded reasonable, so we proceeded, not knowing Mark's hidden agenda.

Marge poured out her pain. Mark listened and then wrote her an apology, capturing all the ways in which his affair had ravaged her life.

The couple scheduled an appointment the following week, when Mark would detail *his* grievances and Marge would write him an apology. But two hours before the session, Mark canceled it. He scheduled a new time, but then arrived alone and said that he had forgotten to tell Marge. "What's going on?" I asked him. Finally, he confronted the truth: He didn't *want* Marge to address his anger. He didn't want to give up his grudge. He didn't want to heal. "If I tell her how much she hurt me, I know she'll listen and apologize for not supporting me, and then I'll have to forgive her," he explained. "You know," he said, smiling, "I'm Sicilian. Sicilians never forgive."

What Mark's humor tried to hide was a troubled childhood. He had been born late in his parents' lives and was often treated as a nuisance, an unwelcome guest. Marge's lack of support felt oddly comfortable to him. He was determined to play the aggrieved victim and cast Marge as the withholding wife—roles that were all too familiar for him. Allowing Marge to reach out to him would have forced him to rewrite his life story—an option that was more difficult, more threatening, than remaining dysfunctional and distressed.

For Mark, as for you, apologies are sometimes hard to accept—harder than the injury itself. When you allow the offender to apologize, you may be forced to cast him in a different light—to see him as a mixture of good and bad, as, God forbid, a fellow human being, vulnerable and worthy of forgiveness.

The brutality of a compassionate apology is evident in my work with infidelity. My patient Jen is typical. When she sent a letter to her partner's former lover, Lauren, the woman responded with a sincere display of remorse. "I want to apologize for the hurt I've caused you," she wrote. "I think about it every day. I'd like not to face the fact that I did this to you, because it doesn't fit my idea of myself, but I did do it, and I live with that reality every day. I'm about to get married myself soon, and I pray that someone doesn't do to me what I did to you. If there were something I could do to take away your pain, I would do it. I don't expect you to forgive me, but I want you to know how deeply sorry I am."

How awful it was for Jen to learn that Lauren was capable of guilt and compassion! How unsettling it was to find herself liking this "beast" and understanding why her husband had been attracted to her. Hostility or silence would have been easier to swallow. "Lauren's apology felt like new skin over a wound," Jen told me, "but I wanted to tear it off and let the blood flow free again."

Let Him Know What He's Doing Right.

The offender is unlikely to reach out to you if you fail to notice or approve his efforts. I advise you to encourage him whenever he:

- bears witness to your pain and listens with an open heart;
- apologizes generously, genuinely, and responsibly;
- reflects on the origin and meaning of his behavior; and
- works to rebuild trust.

A school administrator named Ellen failed to nourish her husband's efforts, with predictable results. After she and her husband, Nick, had been in therapy for three months, I suggested that they review the lists of changes they had asked of each other, and discuss their progress. One of Ellen's key requests was that he stop deriding her, and making her the butt of jokes, particularly in public. He had tried hard to change, but Ellen was not impressed.

Nick was discouraged. "Exactly when did I last put you down?" he challenged her.

Ellen merely shrugged. The next time we were alone, I asked her what she was thinking. Was Nick exaggerating his good behavior? Had she not noticed any changes? Was she afraid to admit any?

"I don't want to let him off the hook too easily," she admitted. "I'm afraid if I tell him I'm pleased with his efforts, he'll revert to his old ways."

I encouraged Ellen to talk out her fears with Nick rather than act them out. I suggested that she support his efforts by telling him, "I'm afraid to show gratitude because I'm afraid you'll stop trying. What you're doing is helpful. It lets me feel closer to you. I hope you'll continue." Letting Nick know what he was doing right—patting the bunny, as they say in sophisticated psychological circles— was more likely to elicit the response she wanted than criticizing him for what he was doing wrong.

I have found, particularly in intimate relationships, that the offender's greatest fear is that you'll never forgive him—that no matter how hard he tries to win back your affection or respect, you'll always despise and punish him. It's hard for him to keep producing positive, trust-building behaviors when he believes you'll make your time together a living hell. And so I counsel you again: don't be afraid to massage his efforts. You're likely to be the beneficiary. If you're not, you can always stop.

Apologize for Your Contribution to the Injury.

You may be completely innocent, and the person you call the offender completely guilty. Usually, though, there are two biased versions of the truth. If you hope to move the forgiveness process along, you need to take full responsibility for whatever you did wrong, no matter how minor, and apologize without qualifications.

In cases of infidelity, I often say to the unfaithful partner, "If you've had an affair, take 100 percent responsibility for it. No one causes you to be unfaithful, just as no one causes you to develop an eating disorder or an alcohol addiction. That's how you managed or mismanaged whatever you were struggling with at the time." But I also say to the hurt party, "You, too. Take responsibility for what you did wrong—for contributing, perhaps, to your partner's grievances, and making room for a third person to come between you."

If you feel that someone wronged you more than you wronged him, you'll probably want him to apologize first. That's fair and understandable. But you should assure him that you'll take a turn—and then keep your promise.

Recently, I was asked to consult with a colleague's patient, Sharon, who couldn't bring herself to forgive her husband for his affair. "I'm stuck," she told me. "He's doing everything under the sun to get me to forgive him and love him again—and I'd like to. But my obsessions and my rage seem to get worse over time, not better."

"Sharon, this is a one-time consultation, so let me be direct," I told her after hearing her story. "You tell me you were emotionally deprived as a child. Your mother never made you feel loved or good enough, your father never stood up for you, never came to your defense. You did your best to win their approval, but they weren't impressed. You've made what the world would consider a success of your life, graduating with honors from an Ivy League school and getting advanced degrees in psychology and finance. You've got wealth, prestige, and a beautiful family. You've worked your whole life to shine brighter than anyone else, and you believe you've done everything right. But then one day you find out that this intellectual husband of yours is having an affair with a young, uneducated baby-sitter—and what happens? Your 'official story' is torn to shreds, and you feel disgraced and wronged.

"You say, 'This shouldn't have happened.' But it did. And you're trying to understand why. There are many answers. Some have to do with your husband's personal issues. He's always been so responsible, so determined to do things right—the affair may have accessed what was missing in his life. Some have to do with opportunity and romantic chemistry—she came on to him, and he was swept up in an obsession he didn't understand and couldn't control. The hard answers, though, have to do with you. By your own admission, you were immersed in your career and children, at his expense. When he called you at work, you hung up as quickly as you could. When he approached you for sex, you often turned the other way. When his brother had a serious car accident, you were too busy to visit him in the hospital. Before his affair, you saw the two of you as a happy, picture-perfect couple. You see him now as yet another person who treated you shabbily, who did this terrible thing to you that you didn't deserve and won't ever forgive him for. Your anger frames and preserves this picture. But if you're going to move on—if you're going to forgive him and let him back into your life—you're going to have to face the truth. And the truth is that you've been an accomplice to the crime; you're culpable, too. That level of self-awareness is going to hurt, but it may also help you heal."

Sharon listened thoughtfully and said, "It's hard for me to hear what you're saying, but I think you're on to something. What are you recommending?"

I answered, "It's been fourteen months since your husband gave up his affair and dedicated himself to repairing the marriage. If you really love him and want to forgive him, I suggest that you write him an apology describing all the ways you've wronged him over the years, all the ways you've pushed him away and blamed him for the breakdown of the marriage."

"You're kidding," Sharon said.

"You don't have to, of course," I went on. "You can continue to be aggrieved and righteous. But if you want to cleanse yourself of those feelings and forgive him, you have to rewrite your story, stop proclaiming your innocence, humble yourself, and accept some of the blame. When you acknowledge to him, 'Look, I'm not perfect. I know I did things to offend you, too,' you accomplish two goals. First, you see your injury more clearly and discover that you may have less to forgive than you thought. You may even find that you're the one who needs to be forgiven. Second, you give him no excuse to be defensive. On the contrary, you demonstrate that you have enough character to admit doing wrong and inspire him to do the same."

A week later, I received a letter from Sharon. "I want to thank you for our session," she said. "You were provocative but helpful. I took your advice and owned up to my share of the problem. It was the hardest thing I've ever had to do, but it needed to be done."

What Sharon came to realize is that Genuine Forgiveness happens not between two competitive, insecure, retaliatory individuals, but between those who have the steady courage and self-possession to confront their culpability in each other's presence.

From Not Forgiving to Genuine Forgiveness: A Case Study

Genuinely Forgiving someone doesn't necessarily mean that from now on you radiate only goodwill toward him. It does mean that you allow his reparative efforts to soften the way you feel about and perceive him. You release him from your hatred not just because a life of hate is a prison sentence you refuse to condemn yourself to, but because he has earned a more positive response.

When Mary first visited me, she was a depressed twenty-seven-year-old who abused alcohol and was sexually promiscuous. As she told me her life story, it became clear that the way her parents treated her throughout her youth was now her way of knowing and treating herself.

Mary was four when her alcoholic father left home. She heard from him rarely—a birthday card, a phone call. When she was nine, her mother remarried a man whose idea of play was trying to stick his fingers into Mary's vagina while she struggled to hold her legs tightly together. Her mother never tried to protect her. Even after her mother's second marriage ended in divorce, she continued to deny that Mary had been violated.

At sixteen, Mary left home and got involved in a series of abusive romantic relationships. Eventually she moved in with Eddie, a relatively stable, responsible young man who claimed to love her. When he proposed marriage, she panicked and came into therapy. We used her life story as a window into why she feared intimacy and a committed relationship. It became clear that a relationship to her was a place of harm, where she could expect to be exploited or deserted.

Mary divulged to me a pivotal incident between her and her natural father. "Three years ago, I located him in Austin and arranged to meet him and his latest girlfriend—Rhonda—and introduce them to Eddie," she told me. "The meeting was a colossal failure. My father hardly asked me a single personal question. When he got up to go to the men's room I asked Rhonda how she and my father had met. 'At a bar,' she told me. 'I asked him what his astrological sign was and he said, "Vasectomy, because I never wanted to have children."' I felt stunned and sick. I couldn't get out of there fast enough. When my father came back to the table, I told him I wasn't feeling well, grabbed Eddie, and took off. All my life I believed I meant nothing to him. This was the ultimate proof."

For the next few years Mary worked to stabilize herself. She got into college, where she proved her competence. She gave up drugs, alcohol, and random sex and began to separate how she felt about herself from the way those who had abused and abandoned her had made her feel. She refused to bury herself in bitterness.

When she thought of her father, however, she still ached over the loss of him. I suggested the following intervention. As Mary's therapist, I would E-mail him and try to gain more insight into his behavior. I would share the information with Mary only if I thought it was constructive. My first goal was to get the facts straight, to show him the "soft underbelly" of Mary's pain, and test his capacity to demonstrate concern.

Here's what I said:

Dear Mr. Samuels,

I'm writing on behalf of your daughter Mary. I'm a clinical psychologist who's been working with her in therapy.

The idea of writing an E-mail to you is completely my own; Mary was anxious about it, but I thought it might be useful.

I won't go into a lengthy discussion about what's happening to Mary, except to say that you, her natural father, are a very important person to her. I don't know if you realize how important.

A lot has taken place, but now she's a young woman who's about to get married. There are two ways you can help her. One is to let her know why you've stayed away from her. What I'm asking for, if I could be so presumptuous, are your honest thoughts on this. What does it say about you? What does it say about your feelings for her? Mary has taken your absence on the most personal level—she believes that she is not lovable—and it would be wonderful if you could help her think differently about her value as a human being.

The other way you might help is to stay in touch with her—not just a single contact, and not necessarily every week or month, but regularly. I told Mary I'd be contacting you, but I wouldn't necessarily reveal what you told me. If you E-mail or phone me, you can tell me if you'd like me to share with her what you have to say.

I wish you well and hope you will take up this healing journey with your daughter. It would be more than any therapist could possibly do for her.

Regards, Dr. Spring

Mr. Samuels E-mailed back, "I'm more than happy to help Mary in any way possible. A day has not passed in almost twenty years that I haven't thought of her. I always assumed she wanted to keep me at a distance. I know her mother did. When they moved to another state, no one told me or gave me the new address. I think it would be very helpful if we spoke. E-mail me back with a good time to call you. I have no problem with your sharing anything we discuss with Mary, if you see fit."

In a phone call with him, I asked about his vasectomy comment.

"What I said was that I never wanted any *more* children," he told me.

I suggested that he write Mary a letter (sent to me, which I would screen before showing it to her), acknowledging how his comment must have sounded to her and apologizing for it. I added, "You can also explain what you meant, if you'd like. I think it would be good for her to have it in writing so she can read it over and over again. Your apology, I believe, is as important as your explanation, however."

He wrote:

Dear Mary,

I'm sorry for whatever I said that hurt you. I don't remember the exact words—it was years ago—but I know in my heart that what I meant to say was that "I never wanted *more* children." That was the real reason I got a vasectomy. After you moved to Philadelphia, I fell apart. I missed you very much. Your mother didn't make it easy for me to see you, and I didn't feel good enough about myself to insist. It was at this point that I had the vasectomy. I was marrying Jane [his second wife, whom he later divorced], who didn't want children because she had diabetes and was afraid of passing it on. I didn't want children either, because I had a wonderful daughter and I didn't want to go through the horror of losing another child to divorce. What you heard in that restaurant was a perversion of anything I ever believed or said. I love you and am thankful every day of my life that you were born.

Love, Dad

Mary took all this in and began to correspond and meet with her father. They talked and talked. Slowly, as he proved his trustworthiness and demonstrated that he wasn't going to disappear again, she let him back into her life. As of today, she's still unsure how much of a relationship she wants with him and wonders who will walk her down the aisle on her wedding day. But she feels more resolved about the past. "I've forgiven him somewhat—enough—for what he's done, even though I still hurt when I think about it," she told me recently. "I feel better about myself and can see him as a decent, complicated dad who's had his share of problems—his alcohol addiction, his financial pressures, his injured pride at being replaced by another father. But what lets me forgive him is the work he's done since all this has come out in the open. He's convinced me that he's genuinely sorry, that he's angry at himself for his behavior, and that I mean something to him."

And so the delicate healing journey continues. Mary's father jump-started it by stepping forward and encouraging Mary to talk out her pain, then listening to her with a loving heart. Mary opened the door and invited him in to know her. She took the risk of telling him exactly how he had hurt her, and she allowed his behavior to redeem him in her eyes and earn him a place in her life.

This father-daughter story illustrates the arduous, interactive, and deeply corrective work of Genuine Forgiveness. Through the offender's acts of contrition, he proves to you that he is not all evil, that he is more than the sum of his offenses. Through your efforts to let him heal you, you prove to him that you're not all condemning, that you're more than his judge. Together you detoxify the injury and relegate it to the periphery of your relationship. It becomes a chapter in your life, certainly not the best, but perhaps not the last or most central.

I recently attended a conference at Harvard Medical School on the topic of forgiveness—the first of its kind. I went with a mixture of anxiety and excitement, wondering how my ideas would hold up against what is currently accepted, and what I would learn about this complex, mysterious, universal topic.

What I discovered was that the work of forgiveness continues to be seen as something initiated and completed by the hurt party alone—in her head, in her heart, through her belief in a higher being, through her empathy and benevolence, through her need to relieve her suffering. Nothing is asked of the offender himself. This threw me, particularly in light of growing evidence that humans heal in connection with a caring other. In restoring our bodies and souls, the power of being listened to with respect and compassion, of being part of a caring bond, is undisputed.

Herbert Benson, founder of Harvard's Mind/Body Institute, presented a fascinating study demonstrating that hospitalized patients who were treated empathically tended to recover sooner than those who were treated more perfunctorily. When anesthesiologists spent time the night before surgery talking to their patients—answering their questions, attending to their anxieties—the patients reported less pain, needed less pain medication during their hospital stay, and left the hospital 2.7 days sooner than patients whose doctors provided just brief factual information about the upcoming procedure.[52]

The results of this study shouldn't surprise us. Care matters. Kindness is conducive to good health. When someone takes interest in our pain, it helps us mend.

Armed with these conclusions, we need to ask ourselves certain questions. In recovering from a violation, why must we go it alone? Wouldn't it make sense for the offender to spend as much time earning our forgiveness as we spend struggling to grant it? Since research shows that we're more likely to forgive those we feel close to, and since we're more likely to feel close to those who reach out to help us heal,[53] shouldn't we ask the offender to participate in the forgiveness process?

Clearly, a radical revision is in order. The time has come to formulate two concepts of forgiveness—one when the offender works to right his wrong, and the other when he does not. We must also learn to integrate what is often seen as "Christian" forgiveness, emphasizing empathy, humility, gratitude, and mercy, with what is often seen as "Jewish" forgiveness, emphasizing justice, repentance, and atonement.

Regardless of our religious or secular beliefs, we are reminded by Harry Stack Sullivan that "we are all more simply human than otherwise." As human beings, we need to find ways to stop inflicting pain on ourselves and on each other.

Appendix

HOW THE OFFENDER'S CHILDHOOD WOUNDS SHAPED THE WAY HE TREATED YOU

*I*n trying to understand the offender's behavior apart from anything you said or did, it helps to look into his past and speculate about his critical early life experiences.

Dr Jeffrey Young identifies five "core emotional needs"[1] everyone must satisfy in order to develop into a healthy, well-adjusted individual. When these needs are frustrated, he points out, we develop a warped view of ourselves, of the world, and of others. The person who hurt you is likely to carry his share dysfunctional thoughts and feelings into adult life, and into his relationship with you.

I invite you to look at the following list of core emotional needs and ask yourself, "Which of them do I think the offender was deprived of?" Even if you know little or nothing about him, it may be helpful to consider his unmet emotional needs, if only to remind yourself that he has now, and always has had, a life independent of your own.

The five core emotional needs are:

1. Secure attachments to others
2. Autonomy, competence, and a sense of identity
3. Freedom to express valid needs and emotions
4. Spontaneity and play
5. Realistic limits and self-control

Someone who is deprived of any of these core needs is likely to react in one of three ways: *surrender, avoidance,* or *overcompensation.* These coping styles usually start out as healthy strategies that help the offender survive and adapt to toxic childhood situations. By the time you cross paths, however, these strategies may have become maladaptive and destructive.

Let's take the example of a boy whose father abandoned his family for another woman.

If the boy adopts the coping pattern called *surrender,* he may grow up seeking out people who allow him to feel just as alone and unwanted as he felt when his father deserted him. He may find himself attracted to someone who isn't there for him, thus reopening familiar childhood wounds.

If he adopts the coping pattern called *avoidance,* he may stay away from people who trigger disturbing memories or feelings from his early years. He may avoid relationships altogether.

If he adopts the third coping pattern, *overcompensation,* he may behave in ways that allow him to do battle against the painful thoughts and feelings he experienced as a child. For example, to overcome a sense of helplessness and the expectation of loss, he may take control of his life, preempt your abandoning him by abandoning you first, and throw himself into a series of affairs designed to reduce his dependence on anyone.

People who surrender to their painful experiences are less likely to hurt you than those who practice avoidance. Those who practice avoidance are less likely to hurt you than those who overcompensate.

Let's look at each of the five core needs and try to determine which of them the person who hurt you was deprived of, how he coped with his deprivation, and how his coping strategy may have hurt you. What matters is not that you distinguish every coping pattern but that you recognize how the offender's behavior may predate you, and learn not take it too personally.

CORE EMOTIONAL NEED #1: SECURE ATTACHMENTS TO OTHERS

We all seek a sense of connection and the feelings that come with it—stability, safety, acceptance, nurturance, empathy, respect. If the offender was stunted by any of the following traumatic experiences, particularly in his early years, he is less likely to form satisfying, enduring attachments as an adult:

- Abandonment
- Mistrust and abuse
- Emotional deprivation
- A sense of personal defectiveness (disapproval, censure, and reproach)
- Social exclusion

Abandonment

If the person who hurt you was abandoned, physically or emotionally, by a parent, he is likely to treat you in one of the three ways we discussed above. First, he may surrender to his expectation of abandonment. This could take the form of clinging to you with possessive jealousy if he feels insecure about your love, or fleeing to a more depriving, abusive relationship if he feels that your love is too safe or too sure. Second, he may avoid the pain of rejection by refusing to get close to anyone, including you, no matter how caring and committed you are. Third, he may overcompensate by detaching from you and denying his need for connection, or by abusing you in the same way in which he himself was abused.

Matt and Judy, a couple in their mid-thirties, were both abandoned as children, but they resorted to different coping strategies as adults. Matt fought his unmet need for connection by overcompensating—making his wife feel as irrelevant and unwanted as he had felt as a child. Judy responded by surrendering—tolerating a partner who made her feel as irrelevant and unwanted as she had experienced herself as a child. While he disavowed any need for a family, she desperately sought one.

When I met Judy, she was pregnant for the first time and had just had an ultrasound test. The fetus was doing well, but Judy was in tears. "I got Matt to come with me to the radiologist's office," she said, "but he was so bored, he couldn't keep his eyes open. Then he started flirting with the technician. Maybe he'll add her to his list of conquests."

Judy tied herself in knots, wondering, "What's wrong with me? Why am I not good enough for him?" She found some answers when she looked into his past.

"Matt's father was an alcoholic," she told me. "His mother walked out on him a month after he was born and then drank herself into a clinical depression. Matt can't do enough to push me away, but he's not as cold as he pretends to be. He's just terrified of believing in us, in life, in the idea that two people can love each other and be loyal and supportive. I understand his tortured past and feel really sorry for him. But my understanding goes only so far—I'm not his therapist, I'm his wife—and I'm not going to let him destroy the way I feel about myself anymore. I'm going to have the baby and get on with my life. Our early wounds may be similar, but we've ended up in different places."

In the end, Judy came to accept Matt for who he was and what he had done to her through no fault of her own. She also decided to terminate the marriage, six months after the baby was born. Acceptance, she saw, did not require reconciliation.

Mistrust and Abuse

If the offender suffered physical or verbal abuse, he may come to believe that a relationship is a dangerous, unpredictable place where personal boundaries are violated, and grow up treating everyone, including you, with mistrust. Surrendering to childhood patterns, he may find himself drawn to bullies who allow him to experience himself in ways that are seductively familiar. Or, seeking to avoid further abuse, he may stand guard over himself and refuse to let you get too close. He may also hide from the damage that was done to him. This was what the mother of my patient Sharon did.

Sharon grew up being sexually abused by her half-brother, and hating her mother for not protecting her. When Sharon came to see me, she had just learned that her mother had been sexually abused herself as a child, and that her failure to rescue Sharon was part of a deeply entrenched defense, based on denial and repression.

"I can never forgive my mother for ignoring what was going on," Sharon told me. "But I can finally understand and accept her silence as her way of coping with her own childhood trauma. As for me, I'm still trying to overcome the feeling that I'm unlovable and not worth being cared for."

Another person may overcompensate for his own early experience of mistrust and abuse by identifying with the person who mistreated him and treating you in equally hurtful ways. Sickened by other people's vulnerability, which mimics his own, he may prey on someone like you who needs his love or approval. The injuries he suffered as a child may trigger a destructive sense of entitlement that in his eyes gives him permission to inflict similar damage on you.

A forty-two-year-old patient, Peter, fit this model until he looked back over his life and realized the harm he was doing to himself and to his teenage kids. As a child, he had been victimized by a father with an explosive temper. As a parent, he repeated the pattern, walling himself off in impenetrable silence and then suddenly blowing up at his sons in restaurants and other public places.

"When they refused to spend Thanksgiving with me," he told me, "I finally woke up and realized what a bully I was—intimidating them, disgracing them, just as my father had done to me, and his step-father had done to him. It was horrible but fascinating to see how everything was connected. When my father felt threatened, he thought he could come crashing down on me with that disgusting tone of voice of his, and that I'd still respect him and want to be friends. I'm doing the same shit with my kids. Of course they don't want to get near me."

Seeing these intergenerational patterns helped Peter challenge the idea that his father had singled him out for abuse because he deserved it. Reminding himself that his father was a victim, too, pummeled in his youth by his step-father, made Peter feel less emotionally battered and more able to accept his father for who he was— a man with faults, responding to his own frightening childhood experiences. Armed with these insights, Peter worked to embrace his kids and let his father back into his life—not fully, but in a limited way that worked for him. Peter learned that he didn't have to repeat unhealthy patterns. "The violence stops here, with me," he told me. "I'm not going to pass it down to another generation."

Emotional Deprivation

If the person who hurt you grew up without nurturance (warmth and attention), without empathy (understanding and sharing of feelings), or without protection (direction and guidance), he may carry into adult life a sense of loneliness and disconnection. Not made to feel special as a child, not valued for himself but treated simply as an object to glorify a narcissistic parent, he may feel cheated of love and expect you to fill in the blanks of his childhood.

As an adult, this person may cope in various ways. Surrendering to the past, he may seek out a partner who is as cold and aloof as his parents were, a strategy that allows him to feel just as unloved as they made him feel. Seeking to avoid the trauma of the past, he may withdraw from you rather than risk being hurt again. Or overcompensating, he could veer in one of at least three directions. First, he could become self-indulgent, spending exorbitantly on material possessions to make up for the human connection he never received. Second, he could become what Young and Klosko refer to as an "entitled dependent"[2]—someone who feels deprived and therefore entitled to have you take care of him. Whenever he perceives you as not there for him, he's likely to feel mortally let down and turn on you. Third, he could compulsively seek your love and attention to compensate for the emotional deprivation he endured as a child. Nothing you do is likely to be enough.

Rick discovered this neediness in his wife Jan when he peeked through the open basement door late one night and found her glued to the computer—in a black teddy. "I could only guess who she was writing to," he told me. "I said nothing, but my confidence went down the drain. I wondered what this guy gave her that I didn't. I always thought we got on well together sexually—now I couldn't even get an erection. This sounds funny, but I almost bought myself some Viagra. I wondered, 'How could I have screwed up the most important relationship in my life?' I confronted her finally, and she told me about her ritual—bathing with oils, putting on sexy lingerie, and pouring her heart out to this guy, someone who called himself a priest. She found the whole thing incredibly arousing."

This revelation threw their marriage into crisis, but it also forced Rick and Jan to talk honestly for the first time in years. Jan admitted how empty and lonely she felt. Rick listened and confronted his own complicity. "I know I'm partially to blame," he told me. "I'm off in my own world sometimes, too. She needs more from me—more attention, affection, and understanding—and I'm willing to work on that. But I also know she's felt alone her whole life, with a workaholic father who was never home and a manic-depressive mother who blamed the kids for making her life unbearable."

Rick realized that he alone hadn't created Jan's neediness, that it was triggered at least in part by her unnurturing parents. This relieved him from some of the burden of blame and allowed him to feel adequate again as a husband. It also helped him accept Jan's longing for connection, while rejecting its inappropriate expression in on-line chat rooms. "I'm not your mother or your father," he told her. "And I'm not a bad husband. When you're lonely, I'd like you to come to me, not to some stranger on the Internet. Give me a chance to be there for you."

Rick also understood what Jan was never able to grasp—that if their relationship was going to survive, she would need to tolerate a degree of loneliness that no one could ever fill. After catching her in several cyberspace affairs, he accepted her behavior with equanimity, and left.

A Sense of Personal Defectiveness

The person who hurt you may have been damaged by parents who were exceedingly critical or demeaning and made him feel unvalued and unlovable. As a child, he may have been compared unfavorably with a sibling, or he may have had a neurological problem such as ADD or dyslexia that made him feel incompetent. As an adult, he may continue to feel shame about who he is and be afraid of exposing his inferiority. He may perceive his flaws as internal ("I'm boring; I'm stupid") or external ("I'm not much to look at; I'm socially inept"). If he could articulate his feelings, he might tell you, "I'm an imposter. If you really knew me, you couldn't possibly like me."

A person who grew up in such damning circumstances may treat you in a number of dysfunctional ways. He may surrender to criticism that reinforces his negative view of himself, as my patient Lois did. "My parents used to refer to my brother as the one with all the brains," she lamented. "Compared with him, I always felt stupid. The truth is, I did better in college than he did because I killed myself to get good grades, while he skipped classes and got messed up with drugs. But to this day, my parents talk about his intelligence and my 'sense of style,' as if I'm a less capable human being. The sad thing is, on some level I still believe them."

People like Lois who succumb to feelings of unworthiness are unlikely to say or do anything to harm you, but their insecurity may wear you down. Those who resort to avoidance tactics, suppressing their genuine thoughts and feelings in order to hide from your critical eye, are also unlikely to hurt you. But you'll need to watch out for someone who overcompensates for feelings of defectiveness by projecting his fragility and insecurities onto you. This person is likely to lord over you, trying to make *you* feel stupid, incapable, never good enough. Acting in arrogant and superior ways, he may assume an air of perfection, shielding himself behind a hard, crusty exterior that prevents you or anyone else from knowing him.

Brad's mother knew him too well to expect much from him, least of all empathy. Brad bludgeoned everyone, including her, with his belief that he was smarter, cleverer, more successful than just about anyone else in the world. What he didn't realize was that he was profoundly disliked. His mother still accepted him, however, because she understood where his self-esteem problems were coming from. "His father's a self-made man and pretty grandiose himself," she told me. "Brad was our first born, the one who inherited his father's booming business and his grandfather's pitted skin. His younger brother looked like Mr. Universe—athletic, muscular, handsome. Brad couldn't help comparing himself with the other two men in the family and coming up short. He still has a chip on his shoulder. No matter what he accomplishes on his own, he never feels like a winner. So when he's mean to me, or condescending, I try to remember how much sadness there's been in his life, and let him be."

Social Exclusion

A person who is snubbed or ostracized as a child because of his economic status or race may grow up feeling anxious and inferior in social situations. As an adult, his response to you may vary. Someone who surrenders to memories of rejection may believe he's indeed inferior and behave toward you in a submissive or obsequious manner. Someone who tries to avoid rejection may distance himself from social situations altogether. Others overcompensate—trying to be so beyond reproach, so flawless in everything they do, that no one could possibly find fault with them. Or they may do everything they can to draw attention to themselves, then fight their anticipated rejection with rejection, and ridicule others the way they were ridiculed themselves.

One patient, Carol, had to deal with this pattern in her husband, John. It wasn't easy for her to suffer his abuse.

John's father had walked away from him when he was two. His mother remarried a pedigreed Bostonian named Randall. John wanted desperately to fit in, but his half-brothers treated him like a pariah. He took up lacrosse, though he hated it, to ingratiate himself with his stepfather, who had been a lacrosse star at Princeton. His classmates poked fun mercilessly at his last name—Balls. John wanted desperately to adopt his stepfather's name, but when he got up the courage to ask, Randall said, "I'll think about it," and didn't mention it again for seven years. When he finally extended the offer, John said, "Thanks, but no thanks."

"It was typical of him, saying no to something that meant so much to him," his pregnant wife, Carol, told me. "He's been doing that all his life. His family shunned him. Now he ignores me. They made him feel like a second-class citizen. Now he treats me with contempt. The one time he spoke to me at a party last night, he called me Orca the whale—in front of my whole family."

I asked Carol why she stays with him. "Because there are times when he owns up to his issues and reaches out to me," she said. "He'll tell me, 'My whole life I've wanted to be accepted. Sometimes I do things that are stupid and immature just to get attention, even if it's negative attention. Sometimes I put you down when we're out with friends because I'm feeling insecure. I try to be funny, thinking people will like me, but then I go over the top and say obnoxious things, and people don't like me more; they like me less. I don't know how to be myself around others. But I'm trying. Please give me a chance.'"

Living with John was like living in a combat zone. What made it easier for Carol to accept him, and preserve her dignity and self-respect, was knowing that he had brought his prepackaged, damaged self into the relationship, and that his issues did not begin, or end, with her. That *he*, too, understood this opened the door to forgiveness.

CORE EMOTIONAL NEED #2: AUTONOMY, COMPETENCE, AND A SENSE OF IDENTITY

As children, we all need to be encouraged to explore, to learn from our mistakes, to develop a clear sense of ourselves independent of our parents or caretakers. If the person who hurt you was overprotected or made to feel inadequate, he may have grown up doubting his ability to survive on his own and make a success of his life. Carving out a future in such an uncertain world may seem fraught with danger and likely to end in disappointment.

A person with these doubts and fears is likely to relate to you in one of the three ways we discussed above. First, he could surrender to the way he experienced himself in the past and rely on you for everything. Second, he could try to avoid these childhood feelings by refusing to face new challenges. Anything—planning a vacation, getting a leaky faucet fixed—may seem too much. Third, he could overcompensate by disavowing his early feelings of dependence and becoming "counterdependent."[3] Trying to appear less weak or frightened than he felt as a child, he may never ask for anything and treat you as superfluous.

CORE EMOTIONAL NEED #3: THE FREEDOM TO EXPRESS VALID NEEDS AND EMOTIONS

We tend to flourish in an environment in which we're free to express our legitimate needs and emotions. The offender who was reared by authoritarian or needy parents may learn at an early age to stifle self-expression and be overly responsible.

People who surrender to or avoid these familiar patterns are unlikely to do anything that requires your forgiveness—in fact, their modus operandi is to behave in ways that increase the chances that you'll appreciate them or at least get along with them. Never knowing what they really think or feel—they themselves may not know either—you are more likely to find them annoying or boring than troublesome. You may detect a basic inauthenticity in your relationship and may find it hard either to like or to dislike them. You may not realize that although they project an air of selflessness and sacrifice, deep inside they resent you for making them feel as marginalized, as subjugated, as they experienced themselves as children—a response you never intended.

The third way in which an offender may cope with childhood patterns of repression is to overcompensate. If he was muffled as a child—coerced into being someone other than himself, someone his parents needed him to be—he may as an adult fight back in maladaptive ways, with you as the victim. To extricate himself from the role of the good, compliant child, he may do something totally out of character, totally selfish and reckless, such as having an affair or trashing you.

CORE EMOTIONAL NEED #4:
SPONTANEITY AND PLAY

We all need times when we can give in to the moment, go with our natural inclinations, and have fun. If the offender grew up in a home that imposed strict rules, valued impulse control, and conveyed a need for perfection, he may never have learned to value "nonproductive" activities that promote happiness, creativity, and intimacy—like sex or socializing with friends.

A person who surrenders to his parents' unrelenting standards may not hurt you—after all, his compulsive behavior punishes him as much as it punishes you, and his criticism is likely to be directed mostly at himself. But life with him is likely to be tense and dry.

Another person, growing up in the same punishing environment, may overcompensate by becoming punitive himself, constantly criticizing you for not living up to his impossibly high standards, and making you feel inadequate for being your own unique, imperfect self—in other words, for not being him. Believing it's his job to teach you a lesson and shape you into a "better" human being, he may try to recreate you in his image, leaving you feeling devalued and oppressed.

CORE EMOTIONAL NEED #5:
REALISTIC LIMITS AND SELF-CONTROL

If the offender's parents taught him to be responsible, respectful, and empathic, he is likely to grow up learning to balance his personal rights against his obligations to others. But if he was spoiled by indulgent parents—if no one set appropriate limits on his behavior or taught him the importance of reciprocity—he may grow up thinking that he is privileged and above the dictates of common decency. He may act superior, not because he is, but because he needs to feel powerful and exert control over you. A stranger to the word "no," he's likely to have an inflated sense of entitlement and an exaggerated sense of his importance to you and to the world.

As we have seen, people respond to the same damaging influences in various ways. If the person who hurt you grew up without self-control or realistic limits, he may surrender to feelings of grandiosity and behave toward you with the same disrespect that he displayed toward others as a child. Unable to control his actions or emotions, he may expect you to wait on him and lash out at you when you threaten to puncture his inflated sense of self.

Another person may cope through avoidance, perhaps drifting from one job or one relationship to another, or succumbing to immediate gratification through sex, alcohol, or illicit drugs.

A third person may overcompensate, becoming excessively responsible or disciplined, always forfeiting his own agenda to tend to yours. This person is obviously not likely to hurt you, unless he resents his subordination and makes you pay for it.

Two sisters, Becky and Laura, coped with their parents' fractious divorce in dramatically contrasting ways. Pampered and unconstrained, Becky manipulated her parents, knowing that she could get away with anything. As an adult, she surrendered to these same egocentric impulses. Laura, in contrast, overcompensated, putting her needs aside and taking care of everyone but herself.

Thirty years later, Laura, the older sister by four years, came into therapy. "My sister has used me all my life," she told me. "I'd like to see what I can do to make peace—if not with her, then with myself."

Laura told her story. "When our parents split up, we got shuttled from Mom's house to Dad's every few days. Becky was good at playing the child-of-divorced-parents game. She'd make up excuses for staying home from school, and Mom, who was petrified that we'd love Dad more, would let her. Becky would forget her lunch or track shoes, and Mom would dash off to school with them, like she had nothing else to do. Dad's the opposite. He's an expert at not feeling guilty about anything. He'd leave us home with cash and baby-sitters. Becky would invite her friends over and trash the house, and the poor baby-sitter, who was frightened to death she'd lose her job, would clean it all up. It didn't take long to figure out that if we did something wrong in Mom's house, Mom was too needy or depressed to punish us, and that if we did something wrong in Dad's house, by the time he found out—well, we'd be back home with Mom."

Laura brought the story up to the present. "Becky still has no trouble hitting that 'me' button," Laura told me. "To this day, I've never met anyone so totally self-absorbed. Her motto is, 'What can I do for myself today?' She's great to have fun with, but I don't think anyone really matters to her—except herself. When I tell her it hurts that she never calls on my birthday, that she gets in touch only when she needs something—like my clothes or my apartment so she can shack up with her boyfriend—she just gets defensive and tells me I shouldn't call her on *her* birthday either. It's so maddening. She doesn't understand that I'd like us to be closer, but I need to feel I matter to her first."

To break down the barriers between them, Laura combed through their lives, trying to understand the factors that had shaped them—their age difference, their personalities, the impact of the divorce. What she came to realize was that "Becky was Becky" and would probably always put herself first. Laura could accept this or not, but it wasn't going to change her sister. It could, however, change Laura.

"I'll never be as close to Becky as I'd like," Laura told me, "but she's my sister, my only sibling, and I'd rather have some relationship with her than none at all. When she's thoughtless and demanding, I remind myself, 'It's not like she's out to get me; she's the same way with everyone, and has been from Day One'—and I try to let it go. I'm still unhappy with the way she treats me, but I don't let it crush me anymore."

It's hard *not* to feel crushed when someone expands to fill the space you're in and leaves no room for you. But if you can step out of the picture and see the degree to which the offender's behavior is a statement about him, not you, you will be better equipped to stay centered, maintain your self-respect, and rise above the violation.

$\mathcal{N}otes$

ACKNOWLEDGMENTS

1. Safer (1999), p. 166.

INTRODUCTION: IS FORGIVENESS GOOD FOR YOU?

1. My gratitude to Rabbi Israel Stein for telling me this story; it can also be found in Kushner (1997), p. 108.
2. Smedes (1996), p. 91.
3. A. Beck (1999), p. 8.
4. Schnur (2001), p. 18.
5. Enright and the Human Development Study Group (1996); p. 108.
6. Smedes (1996), p. 45.
7. Patton (2000), p. 294.
8. Herman (1997).

PART ONE: CHEAP FORGIVENESS

1. Emmons (2000), p. 159. See also Roberts (1995).
2. Horney, in Paris (2000), p. 266.
3. Gilligan and Brown (1992).
4. Wetzler (1992), p. 34.

5. Wetzler, p. 95.
6. Young, Klosko, and Weishaar (2003), p. 248.
7. Karen (2001).
8. Woodman (1992), in Gordon, Baucom, and Snyder (2000), p. 212.
9. Katz, Street, and Arias (1995); in Gordon, Baucom, and Snyder (2000), p. 224.
10. Thoresen, Harris, and Luskin (2000), pp. 258–259.
11. Temoshok and Dreher (1992), pp. 38–39.
12. In Temoshok and Dreher (1992), p. 24
13. Lerner (2001), p. xii.
14. Ibid.
15. Bass and Davis (1994), p. 479.
16. Young, Klosko, and Weisharr (2003), p. 247.
17. Jack (1999), p. 282.

PART TWO: REFUSING TO FORGIVE

1. Horney, in Paris (2000), p. 257.
2. Ibid., p. 265.
3. A. Beck (1999), p. 37.
4. Witvliet, Ludwig, and Vander Laan (2001), p. 122.
5. A. Beck (1999), p. 33.
6. McCullough, Bellah, Kilpatrick, and Johnson (2001), p. 601.
7. Young, Klosko, and Weisharr (2003), p. 17.
8. A. Beck (1999), p. 7.
9. American Psychiatric Association (2000), p. 294.
10. Emmons (2000), pp. 164–165.
11. Ibid., p. 163.
12. Thoresen, Harris, and Luskin (2000), p. 263.
13. Fromm (1963).
14. Horney, in Paris (2000), p. 263.
15. Karen (2001), p. 35.
16. Ibid., p. 279.
17. Horney, in Paris (2000), p. 261.
18. Kasen (2001), p. 35

19. Maslow (1968).

20. Thoresen, Harris, and Luskin (2000), p. 257.

21. Witvliet, Ludwig, and Vander Laan (2001), p. 122.

22. Horney, in Paris (2000), p. 267.

PART THREE: ACCEPTANCE

1. Herman (1992), p. 192.

2. Baldwin, in Engel (2001), p. 87.

3. Efran, Lukens, and Lukens (1990), pp. 164–165.

4. Solomon and Higgins (2000), pp. 191–192.

5. Beck, Rush, Shaw, and Emery (1979), pp. 163–165.

6. Personal interview, December 2002.

7. Kabat-Zinn (1994), p. 140.

8. Sanford (1986).

9. Olio (1992), p. 78; in Patton (2000), p. 290.

10. McGoldrick and Carter (2001), p. 285.

11. Hargrave (1994), p. 30.

12. Steinem, *New York Times*.

13. Young and Klosko (1993).

14. Karen (2001), p. 99.

15. Ibid., p. 66.

16. Ibid., p. 264.

17. Horney, in Paris (2000), p. 273.

18. A. Beck, Rush, Shaw, and Emery (1979), pp. 254–255.

19. Ellis and Grieger (1977), p. ix; Ellis and Harper (1975), pp. 202–203.

20. Luskin (2002), p. 46.

21. J. Beck (1995), p. 119.

22. A. Beck (1976), pp. 29–38.

23. Klein, quoted in Karen (2001), p. 71.

24. Abrahms (Spring) and Spring (1989).

25. Scarf (1986), p. 93.

26. Spring (1997), p. 136.

27. Bowen (1978).

28. McGoldrick and Carter (2001), p. 289.

29. Lerner (1985).

30. Karen (2001), p. 184.

31. Spring (1997), pp. 242–243.

PART FOUR: GENUINE FORGIVENESS

1. Hargrave (1994), p. 15.

What You, the Offender, Must Do to Earn Genuine Forgiveness

2. *Mahzor for Rosh Hashanah and Yom Kippur* (1972), p. 129.

3. Matthew 5:44.

4. Enright and Reed (2002), p. 2.

5. Smedes (1984), p. 133.

6. Smedes (1996), p. 59.

7. Yancey (1997), p. 210.

8. Ibid., p. 25.

9. Ibid., p. 26.

10. Matthew 5:23–24.

11. *Mahzor for Rosh Hashanah and Yom Kippur* (1972), pp. 438–439.

12. Tangney, Wagner, Hill-Barlow, Marschall, and Gramzow (1996), in Exline and Baumeister (2000), pp. 142–143.

13. Exline and Baumeister, p. 143.

14. The psychologist Roy Baumeister refers to this as the "magnitude gap"; in Exline and Baumeister, p. 140.

15. Shafir (2003), p. 89, citing the communications model of Dr. Albert Mehrabian, author of *Silent Messages*.

16. Jordan (2001).

17. Engel (2002), p. 42.

18. Flanigan (1992), p. 107.

19. *New York Times International* (2001), pp. 1, 4.

20. Flanigan (1996).

21. Madanes (1990), p. 54.

22. Flanigan (1996), p. 155.

23. Pittman (1989), p. 53.

24. *New York Times* (April 2001).

25. Beck, Rush, Shaw, and Emery (1979), pp. 163–65.

26. Rabbi Israel Stein, personal communication.

27. Mauger, Perry, Freedman, Grove, McBride, and McKinney (1992).

28. Lerner (2001), p. 198.

29. Enright (1996) poses and then disputes this assumption, in Schimmel (2002) , p. 124.

30. Frady (2002), reviewed by Scott Malcomson (2002), p. 10.

31. Ibid.

32. Schimmel (2002), pp. 124–25.

33. Enright (1996), p. 116.

34. From the film *Gandhi,* cited in Karen (2001), p. 223.

35. Ibid.

36. Spring (1997), p. 244.

What You, the Hurt Party, Must Do to Grant Genuine Forgiveness

37. Kohlberg (1976).

38. Enright and the Human Development Study Group (1991), p. 138.

39. Flanigan (1996), p. 76.

40. Smedes (1996), p. 167.

41. Nietzsche (1887).

42. Boszormenyi-Nagy (1987), in Patton (2000), p. 287.

43. Schnur (2001), p. 18.

44. Herman (2000) in *American Prospect,* cited in Kushner (2001), p. 74.

45. Kushner (2001), pp. 79–80.

46. Johnson (2002), p. 121.

47. Patton (2000), p. 288.

48. Johnson, Makinen, and Millikin (2001), p. 147.

49. Gottman and Silver (1999), p. 161.

50. Malcolm and Greenberg (2000), p. 180.

51. Bachelard, quoted in Metzger (1992).

52. Egbert, Battit, Welch, and Bartlett (1964), in Benson (1966), p. 36.

53. People are more likely to forgive an offender who offers a sincere apology and tries to make up for the harm he caused (Exline and Baumeis-

ter, 2000, p. 137). They're also more likely to forgive if they feel empathy for him and are in a committed relationship with him (McCullough, Rachal, Sandage, Worthington, Brown, and Hight, 1998).

APPENDIX

1. Young, Klosko, and Weishaar (2003), p. 9. I am indebted to Dr. Jeffrey Young for allowing me to apply his schema therapy model to the forgiveness process, and for his invaluable assistance with this manuscript.
2. Young and Klosko (1993), pp. 161–62.
3. Ibid., p. 163.

Bibliography

Abrahms, Janis (Spring), and Spring, Michael. (1989). The flip-flop factor. *ICTN* 5(10), 1, 7–8.

Ahrons, Constance. (1998). *The Good Divorce: Keeping Your Family Together When Your Marriage Comes Apart.* New York: HarperCollins.

American Psychiatric Association. (2000). *Quick Reference to the Diagnostic Criteria from DSM-IV-TR.* Washington, DC: American Psychiatric Association.

Bachelard, Gaston. (1992). In Deena Metzger (Ed.), *Writing for Your Life: A Guide and Companion to the Inner Worlds.* New York: Harper San Francisco.

Bass, Ellen, and Davis, Laura. (1994). *The Courage to Heal: A Guide for Women Survivors of Child Sexual Abuse.* New York: HarperPerennial.

Baumeister, Roy F. (1997). *Evil: Inside Human Violence and Cruelty.* New York: Freeman.

Beck, Aaron T. (1976). *Cognitive Therapy and the Emotional Disorders.* New York: International Universities Press.

Beck, Aaron T. (1999). *Prisoners of Hate: The Cognitive Basis of Anger, Hostility, and Violence.* New York: Perennial.

Beck, Aaron T., Rush, A. John, Shaw, Brian F., and Emery, Gary. (1979). *Cognitive Therapy of Depression.* New York: Guilford.

Beck, Judith S. (1995). *Cognitive Therapy: Basics and Beyond.* New York: Guilford.

Benson, Herbert. (1975). *The Relaxation Response.* New York: William Morrow.

Benson, Herbert. (1966). *Timeless Healing: The Power of Biology and Belief.*
New York: Simon and Schuster/Fireside.

Benton, Sue, and Denbaum, Drew. (2001). *Chi Fitness: A Workout for Body, Mind, and Spirit.* New York: Cliff Street.

Boszormenyi-Nagy, Ivan. (1987). *Foundations of Contextual Therapy: Collected Papers of Ivan Boszormenyi-Nagy, M.D.* New York: Brunner/Mazel.

Boszormenyi-Nagy, Ivan, and Krasner, Barbara R. (1986). *Between Give and Take: A Clinical Guide to Contextual Therapy.* New York: Brunner/Mazel.

Bowen, Murray. (1978). On the differentiation of a self. In *Family Therapy in Clinical Practice* (pp. 467–528). New York: Aronson.

Brown, Lyn M., and Gilligan, Carol. (1992). *Meeting at the Crossroads: The Landmark Book about the Turning Points in Girls' and Women's Lives.* New York: Ballantine.

Burns, D. D. (1999). *Feeling Good: The New Mood Therapy.* New York: Avon.

Casarjian, Robin. (1992). *Forgiveness: A Bold Choice for a Peaceful Heart.* New York: Bantam.

DiBlasio, Frederick A. (2000, summer). Decision-based forgiveness treatment in cases of marital infidelity. *Psychotherapy* 37(2), 149–158.

Efran, Jay S., Lukens, M. D., and Lukens, R. J. (1990). *Language, Structure, and Change: Frameworks of meaning in psychotherapy.* New York: Norton.

Egbert, L. D., Battit, G. E., Welch, C. E., and Bartlett, M. K. (1964). Reduction of postoperative pain by encouragement and instruction of patients. *New England Journal of Medicine* 270, 825–827.

Ellis, Albert, and Grieger, Russell. (1977). *RET: Handbook of Rational-Emotive Therapy.* New York: Springer.

Ellis, Albert, and Harper, Robert A. (1975). *A New Guide to Rational Living.* New York: Wilshire.

Emmons, Robert A. (2000). Personality and forgiveness. In M. E. McCullough, K. I. Pargament, and C. E. Thoresen (Eds.), *Forgiveness: Theory, Research, and Practice* (pp. 156–175). New York: Guilford.

Engel, Beverly. (2001). *The Power of Apology: Healing Steps to Transform All Your Relationships.* New York: Wiley.

Engel, Beverly (2002, July/August). Making amends. *Psychology Today,* 40, 42.

Enright, Robert D., and the Human Development Study Group. (1996, January). Counseling within the forgiveness triad: On forgiving, receiving forgiveness, and self- forgiveness. *Counseling and Values* 40, 107–126.

Enright, Robert D., and the Human Development Study Group. (1991). The moral development of forgiveness. In W. Kurtines and J. Gewirtz (Eds.), *Handbook of Moral Behavior and Development,* 1 (pp. 123–152). Hillsdale, NJ: Erlbaum.

Enright, Robert D., and Reed, Gayle. (May 18, 2002). A Process Model of Forgiving. *www.forgiveness-institute.org.*

Enright, Robert D., Rique, Julio, and Coyle, Catherine T. (2000, September). *The Enright Forgiveness Inventory User's Manual.* Madison, WI: International Forgiveness Institute.

Estes, Clarissa Pinkola. (1992). *Women Who Run with the Wolves: Myths and Stories of the Wild Woman Archetype.* New York: Ballantine.

Exline, Julie J., and Baumeister, Roy F. (2000). Expressing forgiveness and repentance. In M. E. McCullough, K. I. Pargament, and C. E. Thoresen (Eds.), *Forgiveness: Theory, Research, and Practice* (pp. 133–155). New York: Guilford.

Fenton, J. C. (1963). *The Gospel of St. Matthew: The Pelican New Testament Commentaries.* New York: Penguin.

Fisher, Ian. (2001, July 1). "At site of massacre, Polish leader asks Jews for forgiveness." *New York Times International,* 1, 4.

Flanigan, Beverly. (1992). *Forgiving the Unforgivable: Overcoming the Bitter Legacy of Intimate Wounds.* New York: Macmillan.

Flanigan, Beverly. (1996). *Forgiving Yourself: A Step-by-Step Guide to Making Peace with Your Mistakes and Getting On with Your Life.* New York: Macmillan.

Frady, Marshall. (2002). *Martin Luther King, Jr.* New York: Lipper/Viking.

Frankl, Viktor E. (1997). *Man's Search for Meaning.* New York: Washington Square.

Friedman, M., and Rosenman, R. H. (1974). *Type A Behavior and Your Heart.* New York: Ballantine.

Fromm, Erich. (1963). *The Art of Loving.* New York: Bantam.

Gilligan, Carol, and Brown, Lyn M. (1992). *Meeting at the Crossroads: Women's Psychology and Girls' Development.* Cambridge: Harvard University Press.

Gordon, Kristina C., Baucom, Donald H., and Snyder, Douglas K. (2000). The use of forgiveness in marital therapy. In M. E. McCullough, K. I. Pargament, and C. E. Thoresen (Eds.), *Forgiveness: Theory, Research, and Practice* (pp. 203–227). New York: Guilford.

Gottman, John. (1994). *Why Marriages Succeed or Fail.* New York: Simon and Schuster.

Gottman, John M., and Nan Silver. (1999). *The Seven Principles for Making Marriage Work.* New York: Crown/Three Rivers.

Greenberg, Leslie S., Watson, J.C., and Lietær, G. (1998). *Handbook of Experiential Psychotherapy.* New York: Guilford.

Greenberger, Dennis, and Padesky, Christine A. (1995). *Mind Over Mood: Change How You Feel by Changing the Way You Think.* New York: Guilford.

Guilmartin, Nance. (2002). *Healing Conversations: What to Say When You Don't Know What to Say.* New York: Wiley/Jossey-Bass.

Hargrave, Terry D. (1994). *Families and Forgiveness: Healing Wounds in the Intergenerational Family.* New York: Brunner Mazel.

Harvey, Michael. (1996). An ecological view of psychological trauma and trauma recovery. *Journal of Traumatic Stress* 9, 3–23.

Herman, Judith. (January 31, 2000). Just dignity. *American Prospect,* 11 (9).

———. (1997). *Trauma and Recovery: The Aftermath of Violence—from Domestic Abuse to Political Terror.* New York: Basic Books.

Jack, Dana C. (1999). *Behind the Mask: Destruction and Creativity in Women's Aggression.* Cambridge: Harvard University Press.

Johnson, Susan M. (2002). *Emotionally Focused Couple Therapy with Trauma Survivors: Strengthening Attachment Bonds.* New York: Guilford.

Johnson, Susan M., Makinen, Judy A., and Millikin, John W. (2001, April). Attachment injuries in couple relationships: A new perspective on impasses in couples therapy. *Journal of Marital and Family Therapy* 27(2), 145–155.

Jordan, Judith. (2001). Keynote presentation at the Love and Intimacy Conference, Los Angeles, CA.

Kabat-Zinn, Jon (1994). *Wherever You Go There You Are: Mindfulness Meditation in Everyday Life.* New York: Hyperion.

Karen, Robert. (2001). *The Forgiving Self: The Road from Resentment to Connection.* New York: Doubleday.

Katz, J., Street, A., and Arias, I. (1995, November). Forgive and forget: Women's responses to dating violence. Poster presented at the Annual Conference of the Association for the Advancement of Behavior Therapy, Washington, D.C.

Katz, J., Street, A., and Arias, I. (1997). Individual differences in self-appraisals and responses to dating violence scenarios. *Violence and Victims* 12, 265–276.

Kohlberg, L. (1976). Moral stages and moralization: The cognitive-developmental approach. In T. Lickona (Ed.), *Moral Development and Behavior: Theory, Research, and Social Issues* (pp. 31–53). New York: Holt, Rinehart, and Winston.

Kohut, H. (1972). Thoughts on narcissism and narcissistic rage. In P. H. Ornstein (Ed.), *The search for the self: Selected writings of Heinz Kohut* (Vol. 2, pp. 615–658). New York: International Universities Press.

Kushner, Harold S. (2001). *Living a Life that Matters: Resolving the Conflict between Conscience and Success.* New York: Knopf.

Kushner, Harold S. (1997). *How Good Do We Have to Be? A New Understanding of Guilt and Forgiveness.* New York: Little, Brown.

Lerner, Harriet. (1985). *The Dance of Anger: A Woman's Guide to Changing the Patterns of Intimate Relationships.* New York: HarperCollins.

Lerner, Harriet. (2001). *The Dance of Connection: How to Talk to Someone When You're Mad, Hurt, Scared, Frustrated, Insulted, Betrayed, or Desperate.* New York: HarperCollins.

Lewis, Helen Block (ed.). (1987). *The Role of Shame in Symptom Formation.* Hillsdale, NJ: Erlbaum.

Love, Pat. (2001). *The Truth about Love: The Highs, the Lows, and How You Can Make It Last Forever.* New York: Fireside.

Luskin, Fred. (2002). *Forgive for Good: A PROVEN Prescription for Health and Happiness*. New York: Harper San Francisco.

Madanes, Cloe. (1990). *Sex, Love, and Violence: Strategies for Transformation*. New York: Norton.

Mahzor for Rosh Hashanah and Yom Kippur. (1972). Rabbi Jules Harlow (Ed.). New York: Rabbinical Assembly.

Malcolm, Wanda M., and Greenberg, Leslie S. (2000). Forgiveness as a process of change in individual psychotherapy. In M. E. McCullough, K. I. Pargament, and C. E. Thoresen (Eds.), *Forgiveness: Theory, Research, and Practice* (pp. 179–202). New York: Guilford.

Malcomson, Scott. (2002). Martin Luther King, Jr., reviewed in *The New York Times Book Review*. King for Beginners, p. 10.

Maslow, Abraham H. (1968). *Toward a Psychology of Being*. New York: Van Nostrand Reinhold.

Mauger, P. A., Perry, J. E., Freedman, T., Grove, D. C., McBride, A. G., and McKinney, K. E. (1992). The measurement of forgiveness: Preliminary research. *Journal of Psychology and Christianity* 11, 170–180.

May, Rollo. (1981). Freedom and Destiny. New York: Norton.

McCullough, Michael E., Bellah, C. G., Kilpatrick, Shelley D., and Johnson, Judith L. (2001, May). Vengefulness: Relationships with forgiveness, rumination, well-being, and the big five. *PSPB* 27(5), 601–610.

McCullough, Michael E., and Hoyt, William T. (2002, November). Trangression-related motivational dispositions: Personality substrates of forgiveness and their links to the big five. *Personality and Social Psychology Bulletin* 28, 1556–1573.

McCullough, Michael E., Hoyt, William T., and Rachal, K. C. (2000). What we know (and need to know) about assessing forgiveness constructs. In M. E. McCullough, K. I. Pargament, and C. E. Thoresen (Eds.), *Forgiveness: Theory, Research, and Practice* (pp. 65–88). New York: Guilford.

McCullough, M. E., Pargament, Kenneth I., and Thoresen, Carl E. (2000). *Forgiveness: Theory, Research, and Practice*. New York: Guilford.

McCullough, Michael E., Rachal, K. C., Sandage, S. J., Worthington, E. L., Jr., Brown, S. W., and Hight, T. L. (1998). Interpersonal forgiving in close relationships. II: Theoretical elaboration and measurement. *Journal of Personality and Social Psychology* 75, 1586–1603.

McCullough, Michael E., Sandage, Steven, J., and Worthington, Everett L., Jr. (1997). *To Forgive Is Human: How to Put Your Past in the Past.* Downers Grove: InterVarsity.

McCullough, Michael E., and Worthington, Everett L., Jr. (1999). Religion and the forgiving personality. *Journal of Personality* 67, 1141–1164.

McFarlane, A. C., and van der Kolk, B. A. (1996). Trauma and its challenge to society. In B. A. van der Kolk, A. C. McFarlane, and L. Weisaeth (Eds.), *Traumatic Stress: The Effects of Overwhelming Experience on Mind, Body, and Society* (pp. 24–45), New York: Guilford.

McGoldrick, Monica, and Carter, Betty. (2001). Advances in coaching: Family therapy with one person. *Journal of Marital and Family Therapy,* 27(3), 281–300.

McWilliams, N., and Lependorf, S. (199). Narcissistic pathology of everyday life: The denial of remorse and gratitude. *Contemporary Psychoanalysis* 26, 430–451.

Mehrabian, Albert. (1981). *Silent Messages: Implicit Communication of Emotions and Attitudes.* Stamford, CT: Wadsworth.

Metzger, Deena. (1992). *Writing for Your Life: A Guide and Companion to the Inner World.* San Francisco: Harper San Francisco.

Nietzsche, F. W. (1887). *The Genealogy of Morals.* P. Watson (Trans.). London: S.P.C.K.

Olio, Karen. (1992). Recovery from sexual abuse: Is forgiveness mandatory? *Voices* 28, 73–74.

Paris, Bernard J. (Ed). (2000). *The Unknown Karen Horney: Essays on Gender, Culture, and Psychoanalysis.* New Haven: Yale University Press.

Patton, John. (2000). Forgiveness in pastoral care and counseling. In M. E. McCullough, K. I. Pargament, and C. E. Thoresen (Eds.), *Forgiveness: Theory, Research, and Practice* (pp. 281–295). New York: Guilford.

Pittman, Frank. (1989). *Private Lies: Infidelity and the Betrayal of Intimacy.* New York: Norton.

Protinsky, H., Sparks, J., and Flemke, K. (2001, April). Using eye movement desensitization and reprocessing to enhance treatment of couples. *Journal of Marital and Family Therapy* 27(2), 157–164.

Puchalski, Christine M. (2002, September 17). Forgiveness: Spiritual and Medical Implications. *Yale Journal for Humanities in Medicine,*

www.info.med.yale.edu/intmed/hummed/yjhm/spirit/forgiveness/cpu
chalski.htm.

Roberts, R. C. (1995). Forgivingness. *American Philosophical Quarterly* 32, 289–306.

Rosenthal, Norman E. (2002). *The Emotional Revolution: How the New Science of Feelings Can Transform Your Life.* New York: Citadel.

Safer, Jeanne. (1999). *Forgiving and Not Forgiving: A New Approach to Resolving Intimate Betrayal.* New York: Avon.

Sanford, D. E. (1986). *I Can't Talk about It: A Child's Book about Sexual Abuse.* Portland, OR: Multnomah.

Scarf, Maggie. (1986, November). Intimate partners. *Atlantic Monthly*, 49–54, 91–93.

Scarf, Maggie. (1987). *Intimate Partners: Patterns in Love and Marriage.* New York: Random House.

Shafir, Rebecca Z. (2003). *The Zen of Listening: Mindful Communication in the Age of Distraction.* Wheaton: Quest.

Schimmel, Solomon. (2002). *Wounds Not Healed by Time: The Power of Repentance and Forgiveness.* New York: Oxford.

Schnur, Susan. (2001). Beyond forgiveness: Women, can we emancipate ourselves from a model meant for men? *Lilith* 26 (3), 16–19, 45.

Sheinberg, Marcia, and Fraenkel, Peter. (2001). *The Relational Trauma of Incest: A Family-Based Approach to Treatment.* New York: Guilford.

Simon, Sidney B., and Simon, Suzanne. (1990). *Forgiveness: How to Make Peace with Your Past and Get On with Your Life.* New York: Warner.

Smedes, Lewis B. (1996). *The Art of Forgiving: When You Need to Forgive and Don't Know How.* New York: Ballantine.

Smedes, Lewis B. (1984). *Forgive and Forget: Healing the Hurts We Don't Deserve.* San Francisco: Harper and Row.

Solano, L.; Costa, M.; Temoshok, L.; Salvati, S.; Coda, R.; Aiuti, F.; Di Sora, F.; D'Offizi, G.; Figa-Talamanca, L.; Mezzaroma, I.; Montella, F.; and Bertini, M. (2002). An emotionally inexpressive (Type C) coping style influences HIV disease progression at six and twelve month follow-ups. *Psychology and Health* 17(5); pp. 651–655.

Solomon, Robert C., and Higgins, Kathleen M. (2000). *What Nietzsche Really Said.* New York: Schocken.

Spring, Janis A. (1997). *After the Affair: Healing the Pain and Rebuilding Trust When a Partner Has Been Unfaithful.* New York: HarperCollins.

Tangney, June P., Wagner, P. E., Hill-Barlow, D., Marschall, D. E., and Gramzow, R. (1996). Relation of shame and guilt to constructive versus destructive responses to anger across the life-span. *Journal of Personality and Social Psychology* 70, 797–809.

Temochok, Lydia, and Dreher, Henry. (1992). *The Type C Connection: The Behavioral Links to Cancer and Your Health.* New York: Random House.

Thoresen, Carl E., Harris, Alex H. S., and Luskin, Frederic. (2000). Forgiveness and Health: An Unanswered Question. In M. E. McCullough, K. I. Pargament, and C. E. Thoresen (Eds.), *Forgiveness: Theory, Research, and Practice* (pp. 254–280). New York: Guilford.

Tsang, Jo-Ann A., McCullough, Michael E., and Hoyt, William T. (in press). Psychometric and Rationalization Accounts for the Religion-Forgiveness Discrepancy. *Journal of Social Issues.*

Van der Kolk, B. A., Van der Hart, O., and Marmar, C. R. (1996). Dissociation and information processing in posttraumatic stress disorder. In B. A. van der Kolk, A. C. McFarlane, and L. Weisaeth (Eds.), *Traumatic Stress: The Effects of Overwhelming Experience on Mind, Body, and Society* (pp. 303–327). New York: Guilford.

Wetzler, Scott. (1992). *Living with the Passive-Aggressive Man.* New York: Fireside.

Wiesenthal, Simon. (1997). *The Sunflower: On the Possibilities and Limits of Forgiveness.* New York: Schocken.

Wilburn, Gary A. (2002, July 28). Wild Justice: The Seductive Pleasure of Getting Even. sermon given to First Presbyterian Church of New Canaan.

Williams, Redford, and Williams, Virginia. (1993). *Anger Kills: Seventeen Strategies for Controlling the Hostility That Can Harm Your Health.* New York: Times Books.

Witvliet, Charlotte v. (2001, October). Forgiveness and health: Review and reflections on a matter of faith, feelings, and physiology, *Journal of Psychology and Theology* 29 (3), 212–224.

Witvliet, Charlotte v., Ludwig, Thomas E., and Vander Laan, Kelly L. (2001, March). Granting forgiveness or harboring grudges: Implications for emotion, physiology, and health. *Psychological Science* 12(2), 117–123.

Woodman, T. A. (1992). The role of forgiveness in marriage and marital adjustment. *Dissertation Abstracts International,* 53 (4-B), 2079. (University Microfilms No. DA9225999.)

Worthington, Everett L., Jr. (Ed.). (1998). *Dimensions of Forgiveness: Psychological Research and Theological Perspectives.* Radnor, PA: Templeton Foundation.

Yancey, Philip. (1997). *What's So Amazing about Grace?* Grand Rapids: Zondervan.

Young, Jeffrey E., and Klosko, Janet S. (1993). *Reinventing Your Life: How to Break Free from Negative Life Patterns.* New York: Dutton.

Young, Jeffrey E., Klosko, Janet S., and Weishaar, Marjorie E. (2003). *Schema Therapy: A Practitioner's Guide.* New York: Guilford.

Index